# SOCIAL WORK

# WORK

## INNOVATIONS
## AND
## INSIGHTS

# SOCIAL WORK

## INNOVATIONS AND INSIGHTS

EDITED BY

**MANOHAR PAWAR**
**WENDY BOWLES**
**&**
**KAREN BELL**

Australian Scholarly

First published 2018 by
Australian Scholarly Publishing Pty Ltd

7 Lt Lothian St Nth, North Melbourne, Vic 3051

Tel: 03 9329 6963 / Fax: 03 9329 5452
enquiry@scholarly.info / www.scholarly.info

ISBN 978-1-925801-28-6

*Cover design:* Wayne Saunders

# Contents

# Acknowledgements

This book is one of the outcomes of a symposium celebrating 25 years of social work at Charles Sturt University (CSU), *Social Work Education – Innovations and Insights*, from which it takes its title. During the 25 years the social work program has grown steadily, thanks to the strong support of its staff, students and graduates, and the many practitioners, field educators and employers who have supervised and mentored students in field education placements. Having so many travel to attend the symposium in Wagga Wagga NSW testifies to the commitment to regional education that our program inspires. We wish to acknowledge and thank the widespread family of students, graduates, practitioners, academics, managers, Board of Studies members and CSU staff who nourish and champion the program and without whom there would be no social work at the university.

During the Symposium we were honoured to hear keynote addresses from some of the people and organisations who have helped to shape CSU social work over the years:

- Emeritus Professor Ross Chambers (previously Head of School, Dean Faculty of Arts and Deputy Vice Chancellor (Academic) who championed the introduction of social work at CSU and supported it throughout his long career at CSU;

- Professor Margaret Alston, the first CSU social work academic to be appointed Professor, one of the founding academics in the program, recently retired Professor of Social Work at Monash university;

- Associate Professor Sue Green, leading social work academic and Kalari woman of the Wiradjuri nation, graduate of CSU's Graduate Certificate in Indigenous Language, Culture and Heritage;

- Dr Christine Craik, Vice President of the Australian Association of Social Workers (AASW), currently President of AASW.

- Industry partners and practice leaders

- Ms Philomena Saw (Department of Human Services); and

- Mrs Alison McDonald (ACT Health).

## Remembering CSU staff who have passed away

Sadly some colleagues with whom we have worked during the last 25 years have passed on. The 25th Anniversary celebrations included a memorial table of flowers with place cards in their honour. We remember with thanks their many contributions:

**Dr Claire Bundey** for her advocacy, establishment work, leadership and ongoing teaching and support for many years. Claire passed away in 2013. Wendy Bowles was invited to pay tribute to Claire's contribution to CSU social work at Claire's memorial service at UNSW which was attended by several CSU staff. A tribute from Professor Ross Chambers was read at the service.

**Ms Val Clark** whose leadership and personal style contributed to the collegiality that persists to this day. Val remained a good friend to CSU even after she joined Newcastle University, travelling to Wagga Wagga to continue to teach into residential schools and supporting CSU social work students during their field education placements in the Newcastle area. Val passed away in 2015.

**Ms Lila Kirilik** whose untimely death in 2002 represented a significant loss to students and members of the academic and social service community.

The high regard with which she was held lay in her focus on social justice in education for social service practice. Two scholarships and a graduation prize in her name are just some of her legacies.

**Dr Robyn Mason** who inspired us for the brief time she taught at CSU before accepting an appointment to establish the first MSW (qualifying) at Monash University. Robyn passed away in 2016.

**Mr John McClinton** is remembered for his teaching and the work he did with CSU briefly as part of a joint appointment with NSW Department of Community Services and CSU. John passed away in 2012.

## Pre-Millennial staff

Those foundational staff who attended the 25th Anniversary celebrations were presented with 'Pre-Millennial' Awards by Emeritus Professor Ross Chambers: Adjunct Associate Professor Bill Anscombe, Professor Wendy Bowles, Emeritus Professor Ross Chambers, Professor Manohar Pawar, Associate Professor Karen Bell, and Professor Margaret Alston.

Thanks to Dr John Healy with his band 'the Plough' who provided traditional folk music throughout the dinner: John Healy, Francis Duffy, Sharm Halloran and Daniel Duffy.

During the symposium over 25 papers were presented by a range of graduates, field educators, practitioners, CSU staff and researchers. Many of those presentations have been written into chapters for this book – testament in itself to the commitment CSU social work is privileged to enjoy. We thank all contributors for attending a series of research and reflective workshops, reviewing their chapters several times in light of reviewers' comments and suggestions and cooperating with us to complete this book. Finally, we sincerely appreciate Faculty of Arts, now Faculty of Arts and Education's, compact grant for conducting this research. We would also like to thank Australian Scholarly Publishing and their editorial and production team for publishing this book. On behalf of the staff at

CSU, we acknowledge and thank all those who have helped to nurture our program from its tentative beginning as a small seedling into the flourishing tree it has become today, with roots nourished in Wiradjuri country and branches reaching for the sky.

# ONE

# The Vision of Social Work at Charles Sturt University: Reminiscences of Founders and Innovations

*Manohar Pawar, Wendy Bowles and Karen Bell*

This chapter has two aims: to introduce the Charles Sturt University (CSU) social work program in its historical context and to introduce the book. First we discuss the rationale for the book, noting some of the innovative aspects of the program. Then we outline the story of the social work program and finally we introduce the chapters.

As CSU's social work program approached its 25th anniversary, staff members decided to mark this achievement with silver jubilee celebrations acknowledging students, practitioners and educators. Together these people have created a widespread family that continues to nourish the program and contribute to the social work project in Australia and overseas.

Thousands of students across Australia, including regional, rural and remote areas, have completed social work qualifications at CSU. Our graduates significantly contribute to the well-being of society by working in government and non-government organisations and in a range of contexts such as rural and urban communities, schools, hospitals, cross-cultural settings, family and child welfare, Indigenous communities, mental health, palliative care, income support, ageing and disability, and many non-traditional settings. The quality of CSU's social work alumni reflects the education they have received from CSU staff and community, who, over the period, have demonstrated remarkable innovations in learning and teaching, field education and practice, international social work, research and scholarship.

None of this would have been possible without the dedicated contributions of the practitioners who have taught into our programs, supervised students during placements, enrolled in higher education with us and partnered with academics in research. Over a period of 25 years, a lot of learning, teaching, practice and research has occurred. This book documents some aspects of this sustained engagement in celebration of the first 25 years of social work at CSU.

## Innovation and CSU's Social Work Program

The main objective of this edited book is to critically reflect on our education, practice and research; and to share some of the insights and innovations emerging from the community of practice that is social work at CSU. For the purpose of this book, innovation is defined and understood in a flexible manner. Innovation does not have to be something that is entirely new; extensive research undertaken by Grimm, Fox, Baines, & Albertson (2013) shows that the concept of social innovation is ambiguous and vague and can be understood differently from different disciplinary perspectives (e.g., Pol & Ville, 2009). It has been defined as goal-focused (Phills, Deiglmeier, & Miller, 2008; Young Foundation, 2007), process-focused (Mumford, 2002; Howaldt & Schwarz, 2010), and as dual focused on both goal and process (European Commission, 2010; Murray, Caulier-Grice, & Mulgan, 2010). For example, with a focus on the goal, Phills et al. (2008) define social innovation as – a novel solution to a social problem that is more effective, efficient, sustainable or just than existing solutions and for which the value created accrues primarily to society as a whole rather than private individuals. With a focus on process, Howaldt and Schwarz (2010) state that social innovation is a new combination and/or new configuration of social practices, with the goal of better satisfying or answering needs and problems than is possible on the basis of established practices. Here the word practice seems to suggest the focus on the process. Capturing both the goal and the process, Murray et al. (2010) state that social innovations are those innovations that are social in both their means and their ends. According to Grimm et al. (2013), in the field of social policy, social innovation generally describes new forms of governance and hierarchies. New user-provider relationships such as public consultation and participation in decision-making processes are also central to social innovation debates in public administration. These broad definitions of social innovation suggest that the concept is not limited to new policy but also includes, often in an incremental way, amending and changing an existing policy, resisting and opposing certain policies, questioning and changing organizational policies and practices, or lobbying to change policy decisions that significantly contribute to enhancing the wellbeing of people and communities (Pawar, 2014). The same may be applied to CSU's social work education, practice and research.

The CSU social work program is innovative in every aspect of the concept just outlined. Offering social work education through off-campus/distance mode in the early 1990s (now online) was a novel solution to address inequities in access to higher education opportunities in social work. In pioneering the delivery of distance education in social work, CSU's original program offered an alternative to traditional modes of higher education. At that time, existing options were based on full time, metropolitan on-campus tertiary education options, which were accessible for some but for not for others. For people living outside major cities, only those with the resources to relocate to metropolitan areas and study fulltime were able to access social work education. Essentially access to higher education was limited to city-based elites.

In contrast, social work via distance education offered access to professional entry and postgraduate social work education to people in non-metropolitan areas and to those who wished to study part time. According to keynote speaker Emeritus Professor Ross Chambers, accomplishing this at that time was both unconventional and innovative. Many academics and professional bodies had reservations about offering social work education through distance mode. Convincing them to do it was a challenge, though with the values inherent in social work – human dignity, human rights and social justice – it would seem self-evident that education should be accessible and affordable to all. Since its inception in 1991, CSU's social work program has reached thousands of non-traditional learners in rural and remote areas. In addition to this, as Professor Chambers stated in his keynote address, at the institutional level at the time, all undergraduate programs at CSU were of three years' duration – configuring a four-year undergraduate social work program was both challenging and innovative in the organisational context.

The CSU social work program demonstrated a new configuration of social work education practices with the aim of better meeting the needs of prospective students and the social work profession overall. For example, qualified social workers were in short supply in regional, rural and remote areas and rural social work was not highly visible in traditional social work curricula. CSU founding academics Richard Roberts and Wendy Bowles were leaders in the development of new social work curriculum to address the needs of distance education students, meet accreditation standards and to prepare graduates for professional practice in non-metropolitan communities. In particular the design of residential schools/intensive teaching sessions to develop interpersonal communication skills and field education programs to develop practice knowledge and skills amply demonstrate CSU's innovations in social work education which have stood the test of time.

Another early innovation was the establishment of joint appointments – positions shared between CSU and employing organisations such as Department of Community Services and New South Wales Health. These positions gave CSU direct links into contemporary practice with opportunities for research partnerships and field education placements. Although there are no current joint appointments operating, CSU staff continue their engagement with the social work industry through various board memberships, AASW roles, and social work networks.

In terms of governance and hierarchies, CSU's social work program is both innovative and non-conformist, compared to similar programs elsewhere. Although the social work team is led by social work staff, it is not organised as a stand-alone school of social work. Rather, it has always been located within the School of Humanities and Social Sciences, which most of the time is headed by non-social work staff. Despite it being a relatively large discipline group within the school, and despite having the size and capacity to operate as independent school or department, so far it has not. In the meantime many social work programs in Australia have been reconfigured and merged with odd or unorthodox disciplines in natural and medical sciences, whereas the CSU social work program retains its identity within the social sciences.

Using advocacy principles the social work team has tried its best to ensure that students have access to appropriate learning technologies within CSU. For example, when online delivery was first being implemented, the team advocated for students to have the option of continuing to receive print material, particularly for those located in remote areas with unreliable access to broadband internet. The current online mode of delivery poses ongoing challenges to some students for whom ready access to high speed digital technology remains an issue.

At the team level, the social work discipline has consciously cultivated a culture of non-hierarchical leadership, collaboration, cooperation, consensus building and cohesive team work. This culture has significantly contributed to maintaining high standards in education, practice and research and growing student numbers. Today, CSU's social work program is the largest in terms of student numbers. It is spread over multiple campuses in regional New South Wales: Dubbo, Port Macquarie, Albury, Bathurst and Wagga Wagga. While Wagga Wagga continues to be the hub for social work, there are ongoing social work staff based in all of these locations. On-campus delivery is offered at the Wagga Wagga, Dubbo and Port Macquarie campuses, encouraging people to remain in their home locations or to re-settle in regional areas, and to seek employment there following graduation. The 27 ongoing social work staff are supported by a raft of casual (termed 'sessional') staff and adjunct academics who teach into the field education program, at residential schools and coordinate on campus and online subjects.

It is not only CSU staff who claim that we offer a high quality and innovative program. The most recent external AASW Accreditation Panel (2015), following a thorough review of the programs – including course and subject documentation and meetings with current students, graduates, employers, field educators, members of the CSU Social Work Board of Studies, CSU Senior Management and staff – concluded their review with the following commendations (AASW, 2015: 7–8):

- Commendation 1. The program is to be congratulated on its uniformly high reputation in the field and with its students.

- Commendation 2. The collegiality of the program team was impressive and a credit to the leadership of senior colleagues. This collegiality has been achieved in the context of high workload and a very high number of sessional staff.

- Commendation 3. Program staff are to be congratulated on the clarity and transparency of field education processes, the training and support for field educators and the introduction of Professional Practice Assessment strand ... to replace RPL.

- Commendation 4. The University is to be commended for its international study programs and the social work programs for their active and effective involvement in supporting students in their overseas experiences.

- Commendation 5. The quality of the residential programs is to be commended. These were highly rated by all students and social workers in the community who contribute their time and expertise. They contribute significantly to the high standing of the programs in the community and the strong sense of identity students and new graduates have with CSU.

- Commendation 6. The coverage of child protection, Indigenous issues, cross cultural work and rural practice is impressive. It is noteworthy that material in each of these areas reinforces the other areas – this is particularly evident in the integration of child protection and Indigenous issues.

## The Origns of CSU Social Work

Social Work at CSU opened its doors in 1991 when CSU was a new university, benefiting from the mentorship of the University of New South Wales (UNSW). At that time UNSW provided a mentoring role for many of the new courses at CSU. An important plank of UNSW's advocacy for social work was the external Course Advisory Committee (1989–1990), which strongly supported the proposal to the professional body (the AASW), arguing that CSU would provide a high-quality distance education program that was capable of educating social work students to the required standards. Members of the first Course Advisory Committee were eminent scholars and senior practitioners in social work and sociology (CSU, 1990: 82):

- Professor Betsy Wearing, UNSW;

- Professor Brian English, UNSW (later founding Professor of social work at Newcastle University);

- Ms Colleen Jackson, Regional Social Work Advisor, Bathurst Community Health;

- Ms Renee Koonin – UNSW;

- Dr Rob Watts – Phillip Institute of Technology (later RMIT);

- Ms Sheila Truswell, Senior Social Worker, Royal North Shore Hospital.

Internal support for the new social work course came through the Dean of the School of Humanities and Social Sciences Riverina which would host the program – Professor Richard Johnstone, Principal Lecturer Dr Ross Chambers (later Head of the school, Dean of the Faculty of Arts and Deputy Vice Chancellor (Academic) CSU), Senior Lecturer Mr Lew Wilson and Lecturer Mr Mike Collingridge (later Head of School and long term academic and supporter of the social work program).

Mrs Claire Bundey, formerly of UNSW, and unofficial 'mother' of the group work discipline in Australian social work, was the nominated AASW consultant for the CSU proposal. Claire's advocacy for and consistent support of social work at CSU during its early years in a variety of roles, was key to the successful establishment and growing reputation for excellence, of social work at CSU.

In 1995 at the first graduation of CSU educated social workers, Claire was awarded an Honorary Doctorate in recognition of her services to social work in Australia, an award to be added to her many other awards. Claire continued to be a committed advocate for CSU's distance education program for many years: as an active member of the Social Work Board of Studies, travelling to Wagga Wagga to teach group work at the residential schools, and mentoring academic staff across the School of Humanities and Social Sciences. As one of the key people working in partnership with Chinese academics to establish social work in China, she also advocated for CSU to be the preferred provider of 'top-up' higher education courses for overseas qualified social workers wanting to practise in Australia. Claire introduced an international perspective to our programs which has only strengthened over the years, culminating in the recent contributions to international social work by Professor Manohar Pawar and acknowledged international student mobility programs led by Associate Professors Karen Bell and Susan Mlcek, commended by the 2015 Accreditation Review Panel.

The other leading figure in establishing social work at CSU was Dr Richard Roberts. Richard was initially employed by CSU in 1990 as a consultant to the course to write the first 'mail packages' as they were called. He then accepted a two-year secondment from UNSW to CSU Wagga Wagga in 1991, to oversee the first two years of the program. Together with the first social work academics at CSU, Richard laid the foundations of scholarly rigour and high professional standards which have continued as the hallmarks of CSU social work.

Twelve students took the courageous step of enrolling in the first year of CSU's social work distance education program in 1991. Richard Roberts and Wendy Bowles were employed as the first social work academics, both of whom moved to Wagga Wagga from UNSW. Noel Azar, a CSU academic already located at Bathurst campus, taught one social work subject from there.

Richard and Wendy were also joined by a group of eminent social work scholars and senior Wagga-based practitioners who wrote subjects and taught into the first residential schools. Famous social work names who contributed to CSU's early social work program in these ways include Prof Martin Mowbray (UNSW and later Professor of Social Work and Dean of Arts, RMIT), Ms Elspeth Browne (UNSW), Ms Helen Murray (University of Melbourne), Ms Anne Hollands (CEO Relationships Australia), Ms Val Clark (senior clinician who later joined the CSU staff before taking a position at Newcastle University), and Dr Michael Wearing (UNSW). This innovative approach of bringing in leading academics and senior practitioners to teach into residential schools and write learning materials has remained a feature of the program ever since.

In 1992 Margaret Alston and Jennifer McKinnon joined the social work staff at CSU, while Richard Roberts concluded his contract and returned to UNSW. Noel Azar also retired from the university at that time. By the third year of the program demand for the course was growing and the university became more confident to employ social work staff: in 1993 Margaret Alston, Wendy Bowles and Jennifer McKinnon were now employed full time with Bill Anscombe also appointed as a full time social work academic (CSU, 1994: 3–5). CSU's next submission to the AASW for the following accreditation review (CSU, 2000) records a doubling of the social work staff over the following period to the year 2000 with Val Clark, Karen Bell, Manohar Pawar (joined in 1998) and Rohena Duncombe joining the 4 staff members already at Wagga Wagga.

Since this tentative beginning staff numbers have swelled to 27 people supported by hundreds of sessional staff employed on a casual basis. Significantly, most of the founding staff members remain connected to social work at CSU through bonds of friendship, research and scholarship.

Social Work Board of Studies

An important and ongoing part of the social work story at CSU is the role of the Social Work Board of Studies, which has consistently supported and advised social work staff about course structure, curriculum content and external environmental issues from the first days of our program. Members of the original Course Advisory Committee, Professor Brian English, Ms Colleen Jackson and AASW Consultant Mrs Claire Bundey formed the heart of external advisors in the first Board of Studies. Over the years the Board of Studies has been privileged to include eminent scholars and senior social work managers from state, national and non-government organisations.

## Organisation of the book

This book is organised into three parts. The first part *Innovations in Conceptualising Social Work* comprises five chapters exploring innovations in social work theory, learning and teaching. Wendy Bowles' chapter describes the integrated model of social work that frames the curriculum at CSU. This model captures the complexity of the social work endeavour and it has been useful for students and academics alike as a 'map of social work'.

Following this, the chapter by Karen Bell describes a post-conventional philosophy of social work, one that challenges the constraints of conventional, modernist approaches. She argues for a re-envisioned foundation for social work theory and practice – a foundation that values interdependence, cooperation, diversity and equity. Such a post-conventional philosophy of social work provides a sound rationale for contemporary global social work and ecosocial work.

Manohar Pawar, Richard Hugman, Andrew Alexandra and Bill Anscombe's chapter on virtues in social work outlines some of the findings from their Australian Research Council project. Their focus on virtues is innovative in that it explores not only aspects of thinking and doing in social work but also the '*being*' aspect of social work – what does it take to *be* a social worker and how can virtue-led social work be applied in practice?

In Susan Mlcek's chapter an adaptive framework for culturally responsive practice is proposed. Susan promotes critical whiteness as a way to practise knowingly, to challenge power and privilege, and to re-think the white ontological base of dominant forms of social work.

Heather Boetto's chapter on ecosocial work describes the multidimensional, transformative possibilities of ecosocial approaches to practice in terms of thinking, doing and being. Heather's work emphasises the centrality of interdependence of all living things on the natural environment.

Thus all chapters in the first part of this book, challenge conventional approaches to social work theory and practice. The authors urge us to practise knowingly and to take into account the ontology, methodology and epistemology of social work as we work for transformative social change, and for sustainable social justice and human rights.

The eight chapters in the second part: *Innovations in Social Work Education and Practice*, discuss applied innovations in social work education and practice. It begins with Karen Bell and Susan Mlcek's overview of the impressive range of study abroad programs offered to social work students at CSU, between 2010 and 2016. This program has been acclaimed by external accreditation panels and national research projects into the impact of international mobility programs for students.

Ndungi Mungai and Ignatius Chida follow this with their account of the innovations introduced through the human rights subject which is compulsory in the social work program. Understanding human rights, they contend, is not only core to social work education but is vital in contributing to citizens' capacity to enact democratic processes. Human rights subjects also contribute to fulfilling the national and international human rights obligations of universities.

The next three chapters in Part 2 showcase innovations in field education practice. *Benefits of a research-focussed social work placement* by field educator John Burns, is a case study of how social work students on field education placements participate in and contribute to real world research evaluating programs that make a difference in the lives of families involved in a child protection service, while also learning a great deal themselves. In the following chapter, Karen Dempsey outlines how she integrates principles of non-violence into her supervision practice as a field educator, and the way this enhances student learning.

Rohena Duncombe's chapter explores Rohena's long term innovation of 'adding value' to the liaison role, by holding student dinners in northern NSW during field education liaison visits. These dinners bring otherwise isolated online students and field educators together, and offer networking and professional development opportunities.

In their chapter, Cate Thomas, Monica Short and Heather Barton challenge readers to critically reflect on the implications of hidden disabilities for practitioners and service users alike, through an auto-ethnographic exploration of society's norms.

Bruce Valentine and Wendy Bowles then outline CSU's reimagining of recognition of prior learning in field education as a professional development opportunity for experienced practitioners in their chapter *Recognition of prior learning in practice.* In the process they challenge the current credentialist approach promoted in accreditation policy.

The final chapter in Part 2 addresses an area of concern for all social workers: wellbeing at work. In this chapter Fredrik Velander discusses the growing epidemic of mental health issues at work and argues that systemic as well as individual responses are urgently needed.

Together these eight chapters offer a glimpse of the diversity of applied innovations in social work education and practice that CSU social work has initiated or inspired. They provide only a taste of the many and varied innovations that have emerged over the last 25 years.

The final part of the book has six chapters, each highlighting innovations in applied social work research. Bronwyn Hyde's chapter shows how social work practitioners as researchers can contribute to building knowledge from the inpatient mental health setting. She discusses the contested meaning of recovery in mental health, the innovative research design, hermeneutic phenomenology, and how it dovetails well with social work ethos. Her analysis and arguments should inspire many practitioners to undertake research in the field of social work and beyond.

In the next chapter, Monica Short discusses her experiences of using the cooperative inquiry method. Unlike other research methods, the cooperative inquiry method allows for researchers, practitioners and research participants work together in a cooperative manner on a chosen research problem. Based on her research experience, Monica systematically discusses four phases of the cooperative inquiry method and its limitations. She points out some of the innovative aspects of this method and its benefits, if we use it carefully and appropriately.

By employing an auto-ethnographic approach, John Paul Healy in an innovative way explores how older people may be engaged in Bluegrass and Old Time music and how they can informally learn. John also discusses how this experience has informed and enhanced his own teaching of adult learners. His chapter argues that different types of informal learning have implications for our formal teaching practices, and John demonstrates how he has innovatively employed these informal learning insights in his own teaching.

In their chapter, Sabine Wardle and Ndungi Wa Mungai explore ageing and age-related issues amongst migrant population in Wagga Wagga in the Riverina region of rural New South Wales (NSW). Their research shows unaddressed issues relating to the concept of ageing and aged, language and culture, and understanding and perceptions of service providers. They make recommendations to offer culturally sensitive and needs-based services to the aged.

Although a lot of research has been undertaken on migrants, there is very little research on migrants settled in rural and regional areas. This is what Ignatius Chida, Ndungi Wa Mungai and Manohar Pawar have explored in their chapter that looks at opportunities and challenges experienced by southern-African skilled migrants in rural and regional New South Wales. It brings out the role of economic, social and cultural factors in settling migrants in rural and reginal areas and the need for governments' proactive policies and programs and the people's participation in them.

In his chapter, George Rafael tells the courageous and successful story of how he fought cancer and survived. His experiences of social work service provider to social work service receiver are instructive to social work practitioners, cancer patients and their families. The chapter underscores the importance of cultivating hope and the role of social work in multi-professional teams.

We hope you enjoy your journey through some of the innovations in social work thinking, education, practice and research that CSU has inspired. We are honoured to be part of such a creative social work community and look forward to the next 25 years.

## References

AASW. (2015). Final Review of the HEP Accreditation Review Panel, 9 October 2015. Available from School of Humanities and Social Sciences, CSU.

CSU – see Charles Sturt University

Charles Sturt University (1990). *Bachelor of Social Work Course Document*, April 1990. Available from School of Humanities and Social Sciences, CSU.

Charles Sturt University (1994). *Social Work Accreditation Report*. Available from School of Humanities and Social Sciences, CSU.

Charles Sturt University (2000). *Bachelor of Arts/Bachelor of Social Work Internal Program Accreditation Report 2000*. Available from School of Humanities and Social Sciences, CSU.

European Commission (2010). This is European social innovation. Retrieved from http://ec.europa.eu/enterprise/flipbook/social_innovation/

Grimm, R., Fox, C., Baines, S., & Albertson, K. (2013). 'Social innovation, an answer to contemporary societal challenges? Locating the concept in theory and practice', *Innovation: The European Journal of Social Science research*, 26(4), 436–55.

Howaldt, J., & Schwarz, M. (2010). *Soziale innovation. Konzepte, forschungsfelder und internationale trends. Trend study of the international monitoring project (IMO)*. IMA/ZLW & IfU: RWTH Aachen University.

Mumford, M. D. (2002). 'Social innovation: Ten cases from Benjamin Franklin', *Creativity research journal*, 14(2), 253–66.

Murray, R., Caulier-Grice, J., & Mulgan, G. (2010). The open book of social innovation. Retrieved from http://youngfoundation.org/wp-content/uploads/2012/10/The-Open-Book-of-SocialInnovationg.pdf

Pawar, M. (2014). Social Challenges and Policy Innovations by Social Workers in Australia. Retrieved on 8 February 2018 from http://csd.wustl.edu/Publications/Documents/WP14-10.pdf

Phills, J. A., Deiglmeier, K., & Miller, D. T. (2008). 'Rediscovering social innovation', *Stanford Social Innovation Review*, 6(4), 34–43.

Pol, E., & Ville, S. (2009). 'Social innovation: Buzz word or enduring term?' *Journal of Socioeconomics*, 38, 878–85.

Young Foundation (2007). Social innovation: What it is, why it matters, how it can be accelerated. Retrieved from http://youngfoundation.org/wp-content/uploads/2012/10/Social-Innovation-whatit-is-why-it-matters-how-it-can-be-accelerated-March-2007.pdf.

PART I

# INNOVATIONS IN CONCEPTUALISING SOCIAL WORK

# TWO

# The CSU Integrated Model of Social Work

*Wendy Bowles*

## Abstract

This chapter discusses the integrated model of social work developed at CSU. The early conceptual development of social work pedagogy at CSU is partly attributed to the novel requirements for this first distance education social work program to produce written subject materials for non-traditional learners who were 'at a distance' from the university. Principles underlying the model are explored, the 'model' itself is explained, and some of the ways this approach may have influenced CSU scholars and graduates is discussed.

## Introduction and Context

Since its small beginning in 1991 as the first separately accredited social work course by distance education in Australia, social work at CSU has grown steadily, adapting its programs to meet the changing needs of its communities, as well as complying with the evolving and increasingly detailed accreditation standards set by the professional body: the Australian Association of Social Workers (AASW). From the beginning and in order to develop a distance education course (now termed 'online'), CSU staff had to respond to two imperatives.

First, teaching was primarily through the written word – a quantum change from the traditional aural pedagogies of face-to-face classes. In those early days Australian social work academics rarely published about social work education, tending to focus on research into social work issues, practice and theory. However, in the CSU context, before subjects could be taught, complete, detailed study guides and books of selected readings had to be prepared. Intellectual rigour and clarity were pre-requisites for teaching as much as for research at CSU.

The second pressure was the necessity to explain social work to a widely diverse group of students. Up until the 1990s the large majority of social work students were drawn from Australia's urban Anglo-European middle classes: either young people whose parents could afford to support them through full time study, or middle-aged people – mostly women – who were in a financial position not to be in paid employment and thus able to study full time on campus. Further, social work courses were only offered fulltime and in cities, where populations were large enough to draw sufficient students.

In contrast, the opportunity to study part time by distance education meant that CSU opened social work's doors to a different range of students who had previously been excluded from social work education either due to location or inability to study fulltime. This diverse range of students included people from regional, rural and remote areas as well as city-based mature-aged students. Many students were and still are the first in their family to attend university education; many were experienced practitioners with a variety of educational backgrounds. Whatever their background, the vast majority of students had never had the luxury of attending full time on-campus social work studies.

On the other side of access and equity is the issue of demand. A key driver for the establishment and continuation of the social work programs at CSU has been to address the long-acknowledged difficulty of recruiting and retaining social work and human services personnel in regional and rural/remote areas of Australia (see for example, Lonne & Cheers, 2004). Our distance education and on-campus programs in the regional areas of Wagga, Dubbo and Port Macquarie allow people to remain at home while they study. This not only enables people to maintain existing work and family responsibilities while studying social work, it also assists them to develop local professional networks and profiles for future social work employment in their local area through our field education program.

Evidence that CSU has been successful in contributing to the social work and welfare workforce in western NSW was supplied by an independent evaluation on the impact of place of tertiary study carried out by the Western Research Institute in 2010 (WRI, 2010). Key findings included that 46% of respondents who graduated since 1995 (when the first CSU social work graduates completed their studies), held a base qualification from CSU. Almost half of all respondents (47%) had experienced a rural placement or work experience that had encouraged them to pursue rural work opportunities. An ongoing commitment to remain working in the regions was also demonstrated by these people. The Executive Summary concluded:

> The study highlights however, that the strongest contributor to this region has been Charles Sturt University. In particular this is evidenced by the level of supply of more recent graduates to the regional workforce, the significant contribution of Charles Sturt University graduates to the diversity of roles within the workforce and Charles Sturt University's status as preferred provider of future education for the workforce. Additionally, the results highlight the critical role that Charles Sturt University and other regional universities play in transitioning members of the regional community into the social work and social welfare professions. (WRI, 2010: 6)

These three imperatives: to write conceptually and comprehensively about social work in plain English, to inspire a diverse group of students ranging from novices to experienced practitioners, and to create curriculum directly relevant to regional, rural and remote practice, impelled staff to conceptualise social work teaching in ways that were not so apparent in face to face social work courses. For example, CSU staff were amongst the first to publish directly from background research undertaken to develop subjects (see for instance: Pawar, 2000), or to publish Australian texts for particular subjects (for example: Alston & Bowles, 1998, on research methods; Alston & McKinnon, 2001 on Australian fields of practice). CSU staff were also early innovators co-authoring with postgraduate students (for example: Alston et al., 2005) and with field education students (for example: Pawar, Hanna & Sheridan, 2004).

## Principles Underpinning an 'Integrated Model'

Within this context it was a 'natural development' for an integrated model of social work / social work education to emerge. By the mid-2000s, and with the impetus of a complete revision of course structures, staff were ready to develop a coherent approach that was consistent right across the social work program. Over the previous decade the discipline had consolidated its vision and mission and developed a series of pedagogical principles underpinning social work education. At the heart of all three (vision, mission and principles) are social work values and ethics, as expressed by the International Federation of Social Workers (IFSW) and International Association of Schools of Social Work (IASSW) *Statement of Ethical Principles* (IFSW & IASSW, 2004) and the Australian Association of Social Work's *Code of Ethics* (AASW, 2010). This has remained consistent since 2005, notwithstanding regular reviews and changes in national accreditation standards.

CSU social work's vision since 2005 is: *Informed action for social justice and human rights.*

Its mission is committed to provide leadership in the human services sector by:

Advancing social justice and human rights,

Promoting thriving regional, national and international communities and,

Providing quality leadership in distance education, research, ethical practice and partnerships. (CSU, 2015a)

Guided by these vision and mission statements the social work program aims to prepare students for practice that is ethical, knowledgeable, effective and multi-dimensional. The program recognises that the student group is a diverse group of students when they commence the degree and throughout their studies. Having its origins in the impetus to prepare social workers for rural and regional practice, respect for Indigenous knowledges and learning to work with Indigenous colleagues and communities have been important principles underpinning CSU's integrated approach to social work education. This is eloquently expressed in the recent expression of CSU's ethos gifted to the university by Wiradjuri Elders: 'Yindyamarra Winhanganha' (a Wiradjuri phrase meaning, 'the wisdom of respectfully knowing how to live well in a world worth living in' – CSU, 2015b).

Following the national accreditation standards (AASW, 2012, 2017a) social work education at CSU is broad, holistic and action-oriented. It encapsulates knowledge from a variety of disciplines including knowledge about the individual, knowledge about groups and communities, knowledge of the society, the environment, knowledge of ethics, commitments to human rights and social justice, processes of how to get things done and the social worker's life experiences (being). This plethora of influences, knowledge and aims are both its strength and its weakness: a strength that the whole person in the environment can be considered; a weakness in that it can lead to tensions between priorities and /or lead to the accusation: 'jack of all trades and master of none.'

As educators who have reflected upon the definitions of social work and its highly commendable aims, the depth and breadth of social work practice and the contested nature of its work, our educational philosophy is founded on the belief that social work requires a capacity for thinking and the ability to articulate one's epistemology, a capacity for doing and being clear about methodology and a quality of being (ontology). The emphasis on thinking and doing and being helps to adequately prepare students (especially rural students) for practice across the micro, meso and macro levels. It seeks to expose students to theoretical approaches and diverse areas of practice. It aims to develop critical, systemic, analytic and lateral thinking capacities and to progressively build knowledge and understanding to enable graduates to practice effectively and ethically and contribute to clients across multiple levels of societies.

Within the social work program, we have always been committed to lifelong learning and continuing professional education, opportunities for mutual learning by both student and educators and the integration of theory and practice. Adult learning principles – including experiential learning and learning styles – underpin the whole program and are most clearly articulated in the field education subjects which are assessed via collaboratively negotiated learning plans and include analysis of adult learning styles for both students and field educators. Field education, now termed workplace learning at CSU, offers explicit opportunities for mutual learning for both students and educators through this collaborative approach to learning and assessment and in the various forms of professional development offered to field educators and academic liaison staff. More broadly, educators and students have opportunities for mutual learning as subjects and courses evolve and are evaluated using student feedback mechanisms and through peer review within teaching groups.

Theory and practice is integrated throughout the program; all subjects have a strong practice-based education focus using both inductive and deductive approaches. Our commitment to integrating theory and practice is demonstrated in all subject structures, most explicitly in the social work theory and practice subjects.

Throughout the Bachelor of Social Work program, learning objectives specified in subject outlines demonstrate balance between skills and knowledge. Skills-based teaching occurs in the theory and practice subjects, the four core curriculum subjects, policy and research subjects in on-campus classes, in residential schools, in some online teaching strategies and in field education subjects. Small workshop groups are utilised in all modes, including the online environment.

One of the advantages of CSU's integrated model is its ability to incorporate new approaches as social work evolves. Most recently principles of ecosocial work, sustainability and the interdependence of human and natural worlds are being incorporated as principles underlying CSU's integrated model (see for example Boetto 2017, 2016; Boetto & Bell, 2015).

## An Integrated Model

The term 'integrated model' is actually a misnomer. In effect the so-called 'integrated model' is really two complementary frameworks that sit side by side. One was initially developed by Karen Bell and colleagues for the first social work theory and practice subject, building on the work of Maidment & Egan (2004); and Kirst-Ashman (2007) – please see Figure 2.1. This diagram illustrates how social work professional identity draws from personal characteristics, foundational knowledge and social work practice theory to enable a holistic, ethical approach to social work practice across micro, meso and macro levels or systems. Together with the theory and practice foundational subject, these three levels now form the basis for how the social work theory and practice subjects are structured.

This framework integrates concepts of thinking, doing and being across the three levels of practice, as shown in in Figure 2.1. For a full account of the need to develop a coherent post-conventional approach to social work thinking (how and what we know – also termed epistemology), doing (how and what we do – or methodology) and being (who we are – also termed ontology), see Bell (2012).

The accompanying and complementary model, initially developed by Wendy Bowles and colleagues for the second social work theory and practice subject, offers a different view of these links via nested circles. This framework maps the key curriculum content across the program, highlighting the relational context of social work (see Figure 2.2).

In both frameworks all levels of the models overlap, interact with and influence each other. The boundaries between these layers are permeable, fostering notions of integration, and of the importance of coherence between being (ontology), knowing (epistemology) and doing (methodology).

Figure 2.1: A CSU Model of Social Work

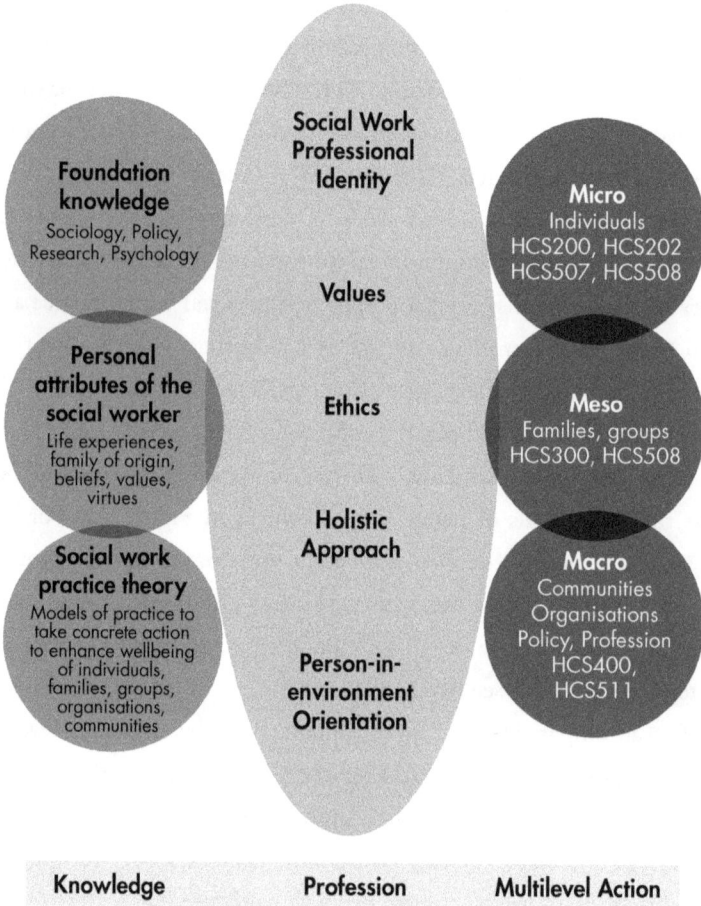

| Foundation knowledge | Social Work Professional Identity | Micro |
|---|---|---|
| Sociology, Policy, Research, Psychology | | Individuals HCS200, HCS202 HCS507, HCS508 |
| | Values | |
| Personal attributes of the social worker | | Meso |
| Life experiences, family of origin, beliefs, values, virtues | Ethics | Families, groups HCS300, HCS508 |
| Social work practice theory | Holistic Approach | Macro |
| Models of practice to take concrete action to enhance wellbeing of individuals, families, groups, organisations, communities | Person-in-environment Orientation | Communities Organisations Policy, Profession HCS400, HCS511 |

**Knowledge** **Profession** **Multilevel Action**

Adapted from Maidment & Egan (2004); and Kirst-Ashman (2007)

## Figure 2.2

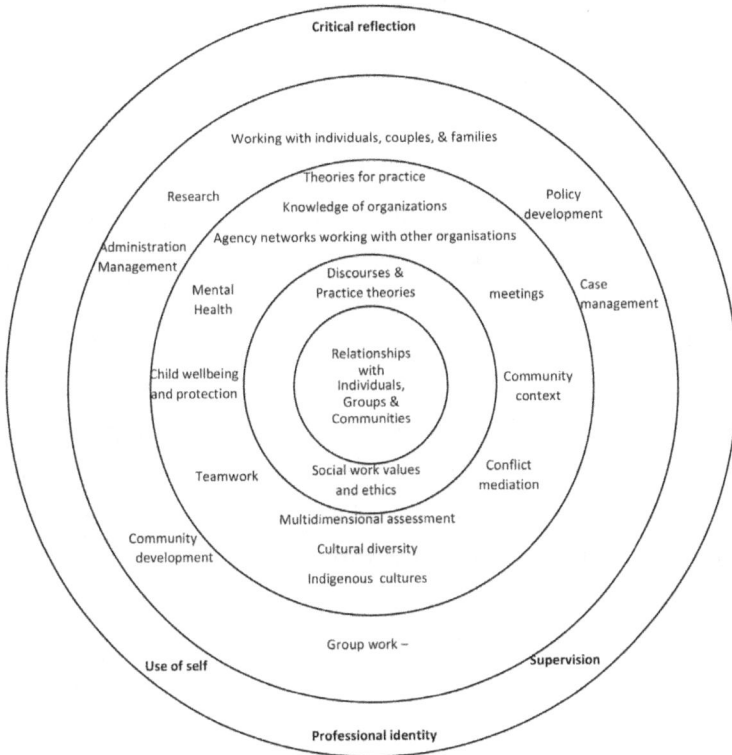

Relationships lie at the heart of Figure 2.2, illustrating how social work first and foremost is about relationships whether these are with individuals, couples, families, groups, communities, organisations or the wider society in the case of policy workers. This focus is reflected in all the subjects in the curriculum, beginning with the foundational subjects.

The second ring from the centre of the diagram represents social work values and ethics, discourses and theories (both theories for practice and practice theories) as these form the lenses through which social workers understand client situations and the practice issues that confront them on a daily basis. Theories and values inevitably influence how social workers understand and assess clients' situations and subsequently how they prioritize and undertake interventions and evaluations. This ring surrounds the heart of the diagram to depict the fundamental influence of theory and values on what we understand as 'reality' and how we act in the world. Ethics is both a 'golden thread' woven through many subjects including the field education and theory and practice subjects, as well as comprising a subject in its own right. Social work discourses and theories are introduced in the first social work theory and practice subject then explored in more detail in the following theory and practice subjects.

The third ring encompasses the skills and knowledge for social work practice that all social workers use no matter what their focus, specialization or job description may be. These include: the four core curriculum areas mandated in the AASW standards (AASW, 2012) – mental health competences, practice with Aboriginal and Torres Strait Islander people and communities, cross-cultural practice and child wellbeing and protection. These core fields of practice are currently being broadened to include areas such as disability, ageing and ecosocial practice. This is in response to the changing professional and service environments as well as the publication of new education and accreditation standards (AASW, 2017a).

Specific skills such as interpersonal and communication skills (both oral and written), data collection and management, advocacy, negotiation and mediation, knowledge of client groups and populations, teamwork, and understanding the contexts of power and social structures on human experience are also part of this layer of the diagram. The skills and knowledge listed in this ring are examples only of the range of skills and knowledge that are taught throughout the course. These are introduced in stages – initially in the foundational subjects and then in greater depth in the social work theory and practice subjects, social policy, law, research methods, human rights and ethics subjects.

The fourth ring depicts the major methods and roles of social work practice from micro level casework or counselling practice with individuals and families through meso level practice with groups and organisations including management and administrative practice, through to macro level practice in community development, reflecting the re-structured theory and practice subjects. Policy and research work is included here, each with respective subjects in the social work program.

The outer ring 'holds everything together'. It represents the aspects of professional identity and competence that social work students develop throughout the course. Skills of critical thinking and analysis, reflective and reflexive practice, use of self and constructive use of professional supervision are included in this ring as defining characteristics of good social work practice and effective social workers. They are introduced gradually throughout the theory and practice subjects, with greatest emphasis in the final capstone social work theory and practice subject.

By applying these frameworks across the curriculum, the social work programs aim to develop our students' abilities for reflective and reflexive practice, structural analysis, critical thinking, ethical professional behavior and the other graduate attributes specified by both AASW (AASW, 2012, 2017a) and CSU's Graduate Learning Outcomes and other pedagogical policies.

## Influences of the Integrated Model

The early development of CSU's integrated approach to social work education, partly as a result of pressures to produce written learning materials for a diverse range of non-traditional learners, as discussed in the introduction to this chapter, has meant that CSU has led the way in conceptualising practice-based education in social work. Some examples of how the integrated approach has influenced CSU scholars conclude this chapter.

From its first year CSU was a leader in developing national field education pedagogy in Australia (also known as practicum or work integrated learning). CSU's approach to field education, initially developed by Wendy Bowles in consultation with colleagues, gained its scholarly reputation 'organically' as the model was distributed via CSU-published learning materials to students, field educators and diverse academic liaison staff, who in turn shared it with staff from other universities. From here it was a relatively small step for CSU to lead the first national research project into field education supervision supported by a grant from the Australian Learning and Teaching Council. This remarkably successful collaboration between seven universities, the professional body (AASW) and an employer, developed a conceptual framework for student supervision including online supervision resources and postgraduate subjects in student supervision (Bowles et al., 2011; Agllias et al., 2010). These outcomes in turn led to the establishment of the first national networks in field education as well as recommendations for standards for supervisor training which were incorporated into national accreditation standards (AASW, 2012, 2017a). Both the handbook and the online postgraduate supervisor training subjects produced from this project are still promoted nationally through the AASW's website (AASW, 2017b). As a side note, many other CSU field education policies and processes have found their way into successive versions of the AASW's field education accreditation standards (AASW, 2012, 2017a) due to the national reputation of CSU's field education program and CSU staff participation on national field education advisory bodies.

The influence of CSU's integrated approach to social work can also be seen in many of the chapters in this book as well as in other scholarly publications and research projects by CSU staff. For example, Manohar Pawar and Bill Anscombe's book *Reflective Social Work Practice – Thinking, Doing and Being* (Pawar & Anscombe, 2015) draws many of the elements of the integrated approach into a reflective social work practice model, as might be expected from two people who have shared in developing the integrated approach at CSU over many years.

## Conclusion

CSU's integrated model of social work with its underpinning principles, which was first developed in the early 2000s, has stood the test of time and proven itself to be flexible enough to adapt to and incorporate innovations from the ever-changing terrain of social work theory, practice and pedagogy. For instance the model remains the basis for the social work curriculum now that the theory and practice subjects are organised according to micro-meso-macro divisions, even though it was originally designed with the earlier more holistic configuration of engagement-intervention-evaluation (which attempted to integrate the micro, meso and macro levels of practice at the various stages of social work intervention) in mind. Similarly, various combinations of fields of practice and settings may be prioritised in the 'third ring' of the circular part of the model. The model can also support the increasing focus on environmental and sustainability issues or ecosocial work, with its imperative to shift social work's foundation to being eco-centred rather than person-centred for the survival of the planet (for example Boetto, 2017). Having worked with and contributed to this model over many years, it is little wonder that CSU's social work academics and graduates are making leading edge contributions to social work education, theory and practice locally, nationally and internationally.

## References

Agllias, K., Bowles, W., Cassano, B., Collingridge, M., Dawood, A., Irwin, J., Maywald, S., McKinnon, J., Noble, C., O'Sullivan, J., Wexler, J., & Zubrzycki, J. (2010). *A Guide to Supervision in Social Work Field Education* (rev. edn.). Strawberry Hills, Sydney: Australian Learning and Teaching Council. Available from: http://socialworksupervision.csu.edu.au/resources/.

Alston, M., & Bowles, W. (1998). *Research for social workers: an introduction to methods.* St Leonards, NSW: Allen & Unwin.

Alston, M., & McKinnon, J. (2001). *Social Work: Fields of Practice.* Melbourne: Oxford University Press.

Alston, M., Allan, J., Bell, K., Brown, A., Dowling, J., Hamilton, P., McKinnon, N., Mitchell, R., Whittenbury, K., Valentine, B., Wicks, A. and Williams, R. (2005). '"SERPS up": Support, engagement and retention of postgraduate students – a model of postgraduate support', *Australian Journal of Adult Learning,* 45(2), 172–90.

Australian Association of Social Workers (AASW) (2010). *Code of Ethics.* Canberra: AASW.

Australian Association of Social Workers (AASW) (2012). *Australian Education and Accreditation Standards (ASWEAS) 2012 V1.4 Revised January 2015.* Canberra: AASW, Retrieved from: https://www.aasw.asn.au/document/item/3550.

Australian Association of Social Workers (AASW) (2017a). *Australian Education and Accreditation Standards (ASWEAS).* Melbourne: AASW.

Australian Association of Social Workers (AASW) (2017b). *Field Education Resources.* AASW. Retrieved from: https://www.aasw.asn.au/professional-development/field-education

Bell, K. (2012). 'Towards a Post-Conventional Philosophical Base for Social Work', *British Journal of Social Work*, 42(3), 408–23.

Boetto, H. (2016). 'Developing ecological social work for micro level practice'. In J. McKinnon & M. Alston (eds.), *Ecological social work: Towards sustainability* (pp. 59–77). Houndmills, ENG: Palgrave Macmillan.

Boetto, H. (2017). 'A transformative eco-social model: Challenging modernist assumptions in social work', *British Journal of Social Work,* 47(1), 48–67.

Boetto, H., & Bell, K. (2015). 'Environmental sustainability in social work curricula: A pilot study of online course content', *International Social Work,* 58(3), 448–62.

Bowles, W., Collingridge, M., McKinnon; J., Agllias, K., Dawood, A., Irwin, J., Maywald, S., Noble, C., O'Sullivan, J., Zubrzycki, J. (2011). *Online Student Supervision Training – Accessible and cooperative learning in Social Work.* Strawberry Hills, NSW: Australian Learning and Teaching Council.

Charles Sturt University (CSU) (2015a). *Higher Education Provider Submission for Reaccreditation.* Available from School of Humanities and Social Sciences, Wagga Wagga.

Charles Sturt University (CSU) (2015b). *Yindyamarra Winhanganha* Retrieved from:https://www.csu.edu.au/csu-live/csu-live/category/my-csu-experience/videos/yindyamarra-winhanganha?iPKdujyOMBp9hoIh.99.

International Federation of Social Workers (IFSW) & International Association of Schools of Social Work (IASSW) 2004. *Statement of Ethical Principles.* Retrieved from http://ifsw.org/policies/statement-of-ethical-principles/.

Kirst-Ashman, K. K. (2007). *Introduction to Social Work and Social Welfare: Critical Thinking Perspectives,* Belmont, California: Thomason Brooks/Cole.

Lonne, B., & Cheers, B. (2004). 'Retaining Rural Social Workers: An Australian Study', *Rural Society*, 14(2), 163–77.

Maidment, J. and Egan, R. (2004). *Practice Skills in Social Work and Welfare – More than just Common Sense.* Crows Nest, NSW: Allen & Unwin.

Pawar, M. (2000). 'Social development content in the courses of Australian social work schools', *International Social Work*, 43(3), 277–88.

Pawar, M., & Anscombe, B. (2015). *Reflective Social Work Practice – Thinking, Doing and Being.* Melbourne, Victoria: Cambridge University Press.

Pawar, M., Hanna, G., & Sheridan, R. (2004). 'International social work practicum in India', *Australian Social Work, 57*(3), 223–36.

Western Research Institute (WRI), 2010. *Professional and Educational Profile of the Social Work and Social Welfare Workforce in Western NSW.* Western Research Institute.

# THREE

# Post-Conventional Social Work

*Karen Bell*

## Abstract

Social work, as a global profession, has human rights and social justice at its heart. However it is argued that foundation theory at the ontological level has been somewhat neglected in social work at times resulting in a reliance on conventional, modernist theoretical perspectives. This reliance is highly problematic for social work in that conventional approaches are typically comprised of a series of hierarchical dualisms. These can serve to naturalise individualism and oppression and as such, conventional approaches are at odds with core social work aims and values. It is a challenge for twenty-first century social work to consolidate a distinct foundation theory for social work efforts towards social justice and human rights. This chapter explores the capacity of post-conventional theory to conceptualise collectivity, diversity, equity, interdependence and sustainability. It is argued that post-conventional theory is more consistent with social work in the twenty-first century at ontological, epistemological and methodological levels.

## Introduction

Globally, Social Work is characterised by a commitment to work with individuals, groups, communities and organisations for empowerment, equity and social justice. While there may be contextual variations in how social work is constructed as a profession and as an academic discipline from country to country, this overarching focus is fundamental to the profession and is reflected in the International Federation of Social Work (IFSW, 2014) definition. However, the dominant form of Social Work particularly in Euro-Western contexts, while not homogenous, grew out of a modernist tradition largely based on individualism and a positivist theoretical mode (Bell, 2012; Sin, 2010; Yellow Bird, 2010). This is at odds with key aspects of the IFSW (2014) definition relating to collective responsibilities, diversity, indigenous knowledges and liberation (IFSW, 2014). Social Work theorists have explored the shortcomings of conventional approaches and note the fundamental issues that conventional foundation theory poses for contemporary Social Work (Bell, 2012; Boetto, 2017; Dominelli, 1996; Fook, 2002; Healy, 2014; Ife, 1997; Ling How Kee, 2010; Mafile'o, 2010; Parton & O'Byrne, 2000). These challenges centre on the limitations of conventional approaches in conceptualising collectivity, diversity, interconnectedness, intersectionality, indigenous knowledges, sustainability, human rights and social justice. Thus it is imperative for Social Work to have a clearly articulated, consistent philosophical foundation to underpin efforts to promote equity, empowerment and truly emancipatory social change (Anastas, 2012; Bell, 2012; Faith, 2010; Green & McDermott, 2010; Morley & Macfarlane, 2012; Noble & Henrickson, 2014; Parton & O'Byrne, 2000; Pease, 2009; Peile & McCouat, 1997).

Broader, global patterns of colonisation are also mirrored in the development of social work as a profession over time. Dominant modes of Euro-Western Social Work colonised diverse, non-Western contexts around the world as if Euro-Western forms of social care were universal and somehow inherently superior to indigenous forms of social care. Through colonisation, indigenous ontologies and epistemologies were (and arguably continue to be) generally devalued or ignored completely. Even in contexts with ancient traditions of social service such as India (Nimmagadda & Martell, 2010: 143; Faith, 2010) and Australia (Bennett, Green, Gilbert & Bessarab, 2013; Fejo-King, 2014), colonisation marginalised indigenous forms of care.

Twenty-first century Social Work has been described as 'slow' in valuing and adopting indigenous world views and knowledge (Gray, Coates

& Yellow Bird, 2010) and 'slow' to thoroughly consider its ontological foundations *vis a vis* our stated mission (Dominelli, 2002; Bell, 2012). The modernist tradition tends to silence and marginalise voices and to position itself as the 'centre and wellspring of knowledge' (Gray, Coates & Yellow Bird, 2010: 2). This construction legitimates the epistemological disadvantage of the marginalised and underpins the 'invisibility' of indigenous and other forms of social care.

The marginalisation of non-Western, indigenous practice is a form of epistemic ignorance and results in epistemic injustice for those thus marginalised. Those colonised by dominant forms of conventional Euro-Western social work often have their epistemic agency undermined thorough processes of 'testimonial quieting' (Dotson, 2011). Testimonial quieting occurs when the dominant discourse lacks the will and/or capacity to recognise non-traditional, non-dominant forms of knowledge. Within this frame of reference, even if non-dominant, non-traditional theory and practice is acknowledged, it is typically not fully validated if it does not easily fit conventional forms. Whether there is complete or partial testimonial quieting, this constitutes an 'active process of unknowing' so as to maintain the dominant paradigm (Dotson, 2011: 243).

Even in the face of dominance however, there is often resistance to epistemic injustice as marginalised knowledges and alternative paradigms retain their quiet strength and resilience. So while dominant discourses, based on competition and mastery, act to maintain dominance, non-dominant discourses are preserved in pockets of resistance. As these 'quietened voices' struggle for recognition, the struggle itself can be a unifying force as it gathers momentum towards potential change. The ongoing existence of non-dominant forms of knowledge despite the powerful colonising efforts of conventional Euro-Western social work is testament to the power of resistance that can emerge in the face of oppression. Thus, the dominant, conventional approach fundamentally impacts on social work ontology, epistemology and methodology and as such, these foundations deserve further exploration as we work to transform the conceptual framework of social work as a non-oppressive, emancipatory discipline.

Figure 3.1: The conceptual framework of social work

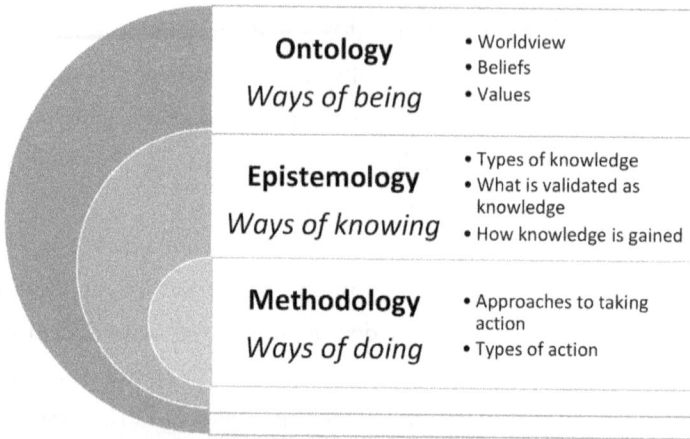

| | |
|---|---|
| **Ontology**<br>*Ways of being* | • Worldview<br>• Beliefs<br>• Values |
| **Epistemology**<br>*Ways of knowing* | • Types of knowledge<br>• What is validated as knowledge<br>• How knowledge is gained |
| **Methodology**<br>*Ways of doing* | • Approaches to taking action<br>• Types of action |

## Some Limitations of Conventional Theory

Conventional theory – meaning modernist traditions based on linear, individualised subjectivity and a series of binaries and hierarchical dualisms – is highly problematic for social work. Conventional theory uses the individual subject as its central reference point and ontological base. This individual subject is typically constructed as male, white, middle-class, educated, heterosexual and Euro-Western (Bell, 2013; Braidotti, 2005; Cuomo, 1996; Ife, 2010; Shildrick, 1997). The subject is generally constructed as engaged in competition with other subjects with dominance and mastery being central in this approach (Braidotti et al., 2004; Code, 1991). The standpoint of the individualised subject is generalised as representative of all human experience and it becomes the 'standard' reference point. This marginalises non-male/non-white/non-middle-class/'uneducated'/non-heterosexual/non-Euro-Western 'others' to a subordinate position in this system of dualistic hierarchies. Thus, privilege is constructed with some categories of humans placed in a position of entitlement and 'others' being cast as subordinate, 'vulnerable', less entitled or even un-entitled and unworthy of being recognised as a legitimate holder of knowledge. Using the generic conceptual framework from the previous section (Figure 3.1), some of these limitations are illustrated in Figure 3.2:

**Figure 3.2: Some limitations of the conventional paradigm.**

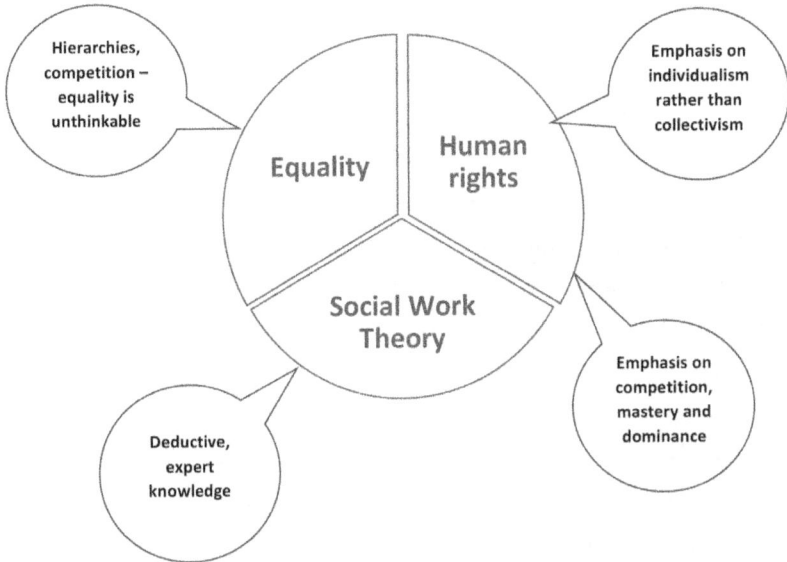

The individualised subject is also constructed as rational and 'objective' knowledge is valued most highly. The conventional subject is disembodied and detached, capable of dominance, focused on self-interested profit as well as individualised self-determination. Within this ontological frame, the natural environment, other (subordinate) humans and other living creatures become resources for exploitation as part of this naturalised order. Likewise, this ontology underpins the aforementioned colonisation and 'development' of non-Western countries thereby creating a global pattern of domination, dependence and social injustice.

This ontological foundation of dualistic hierarchy typically ensures that those constructed as dominant are privileged with agency. These active agents occupy privileged positions in relation to power, authority, resources and knowledge. Subordinated subjects and disempowered objects are relegated to positions of vulnerability and disadvantage. This naturalisation of privilege is highly problematic for social work. Working within this conventional, modernist ontology means that transformative, alternative worldviews are difficult to comprehensively conceptualise and validate.

Diversity, equity, collectivity and interconnectedness of equal human (and non-human) subjects are also unthinkable within the limitations of conventional theory (Plumwood, 1993).

Without a thorough, transformative reconceptualisation of the philosophical foundation of social work, there is a risk for example, that the focus will remain largely on what oppressed people can do to ameliorate their situation. Likewise, there will also be too little focus on the reproduction of privilege and oppression. Privileged groups are too often left unchallenged and the responsibility to trigger and sustain change for social justice is arguably too often focused on what the underprivileged must do (Pease, 2010). As Pease (2010) argues, it is vital for social work to understand the construction and maintenance of privilege in order to make intersecting sources of oppression and privilege visible. Without a sustained shift in focus in this direction, how can social work hope to redress disadvantage with under-developed ontological, epistemological and methodological tools to identify and take action against unearned advantage? How can the profession work for equity when inequity has been 'naturalised' and remains largely invisible and under-scrutinised in conventional theory? How can advocacy on behalf of oppressed people be effective and sustained without truly addressing sources of intersectional oppression at all levels (Morley & Macfarlane, 2012)? How is it possible to address under-privilege if privilege is not deconstructed and re-envisioned at all levels (Pease, 2010)?

To genuinely pursue the admirable aims of social work, a foundation theory with the capacity to conceptualise the interconnectedness of all – people, all other living things, and the natural environment – is needed; not a foundation theory dependent on inequity via a series of hierarchical dualisms that only serve to normalise oppression. Social work theory in the twenty-first century must possess the capacity to identify unearned privilege if meaningful action is to be undertaken to restore rights, ensure equity, preserve the natural environment and respect diversity. As a distinct profession with noble aims, it must have a coherent basis for social justice activities; *being* and *thinking* must correspond with *doing*. Ethical social work action for emancipatory outcomes must be founded on an adequate ontological base and not on one that legitimises oppression through its hierarchical dualisms. Social Work simply must have the conceptual capacity to 'unmask' privilege (Pease, 2010: ix). Likewise, to move beyond descriptive theory to explanatory theory in social work the profession must also be able to explain the genesis and intersectionality of oppression, its maintenance in order to have the capacity for truly transformative practice in a diverse range of settings.

If action for human rights and social justice focuses only on epistemology and methodology, leaving ontology unattended, real progress on transformative, sustained social change is unlikely. And disturbingly, well-intentioned action might only soften the edges of oppression and effectively act as a means of social control. Dominelli (2002) describes this as an incorporationalist response in that incremental change may be enacted but fundamental, transformative change is unaddressed, thereby maintaining systems of oppression. Does twenty-first century social work aim to challenge or reinforce the status quo (Pease, 2010)? Faith (2010: 255), referring to Einstein, observes that no problem is 'solved by the same consciousness that created it'. For example, if there is a desire to enhance gender equity, any number of programs and strategies can be implemented and they may produce successful, ameliorative outcomes in the short term. While this is of some value, it follows that if the major causes of gender oppression remain unaddressed – such as the dominant habit of thinking of men as the 'standard' form of human existence and women as 'other'– for these social justice outcomes are unlikely to be sustained in the long term.

Dominelli (2002) argues, social work should be egalitarian and reject the dominant theory that grants some humans privilege over others. Without a clear, post-conventional theory, dominant forms of Euro-Western social work risk will remain as being part of the problem rather than as a solution and by default or design, a participant in the reproduction of oppression rather than a change agent for human rights and social justice. Further, there is a need to ensure that the focus is not solely on 'the vulnerable', 'the disadvantaged', 'the oppressed' because an exclusive focus on those impacted by domination and mastery removes the one's gaze from the sources of oppression, reinforcing the 'invisibility of privilege' (Pease, 2010: 6). Thus, foundation theory cannot be ignored and theorists and practitioners cannot simply hope that good intentions are enough to achieve sustainable change.

## The Foundations of Post-Conventional Theory

Post-conventional theory in social work is largely based on post-structural feminism (Bell, 2012; Braidotti, 2005; Haraway, 2004; Irigaray, 1984; Plumwood, 1993; Shildrick, 1997), embodiment theory and complex systems theory in social work (Cameron & McDermott, 2007; Green & McDermott, 2010). These theoretical foundations have the capacity to conceptualise subjectivity as diverse, equitable, interconnected and fluid. The individual, hegemonic subject of conventional theory is disrupted and restored as an equal in relation to all subjects – not entitled to unearned privileged or legitimised as dominant and transcendent. This is a key ontological positioning of subjectivity in post-conventional theory and is the basis of the conceptual capacity of this theory for meaningful social work theory and practice, represented in Figure 3.3:

Figure 3.3: The power of post-conventional approaches.

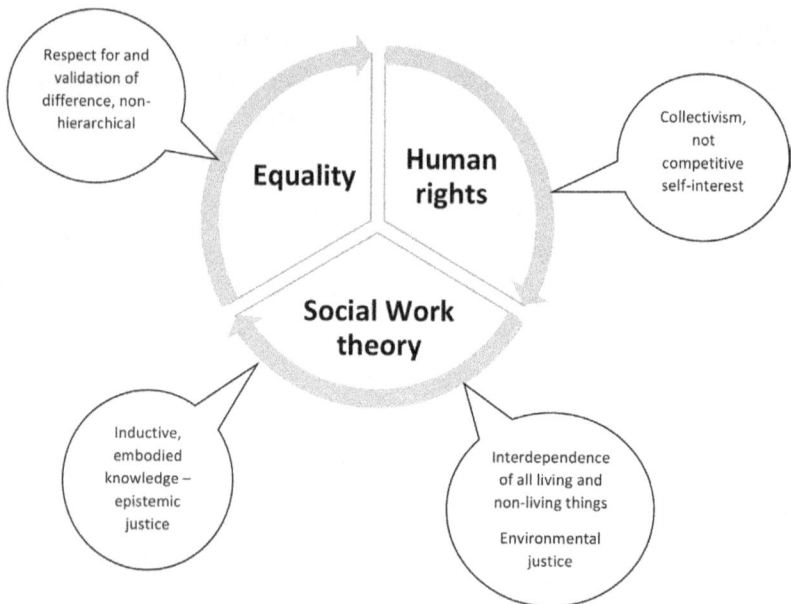

Respect for and validation of difference, non-hierarchical

Collectivism, not competitive self-interest

**Equality**

**Human rights**

**Social Work theory**

Inductive, embodied knowledge – epistemic justice

Interdependence of all living and non-living things

Environmental justice

Subjectivity in post-conventional theory is interactive and embodied – not individualised and disembodied, as in conventional theory – this is highly significant for the philosophy of social work. Recognising the embodied nature of subjectivity means that lived experience is validated as are diverse ways of experiencing the world. This grounded approach to ontology more effectively captures the complexity, fluidity and interconnections of existence. Humans move as part of the natural environment, in different roles and intersecting contexts. Human subjectivity is not fixed, static or dominant in hierarchical relation to other living things and the natural environment. Humans engage in ontological choreography (Thompson, 2005) as interactions with other humans and the natural environment need to be adapted in different situations and in different contexts. As interdependent entities, we are at times in need of help and sustenance, and at times we are the helpers and sources of sustenance.

Constructing subjectivity in this way could arguably lead to a relativist nightmare, however this is not inevitable; it would be a risk only if subjectivity remains under-examined and if subjectivity continues to be constructed as competitive, individualised, disembodied and hierarchical (Morley & Macfarlane, 2012). If the linear, disconnected, individual subject is maintained as the 'standard' ontological base, then there is indeed a risk in reinforcing rampant individualism and the privilege of some at the expense of many others. As subjectivity in post-conventional theory is recognised as fluid, interconnected and interdependent, collectivism is validated and necessary due to the interconnectivity of subjects and all things. Diversity is valued and difference between subjects is recognised and validated. The adequate conceptualisation of difference is important as in conventional theory, difference is constructed with reference to the standard individual subject in a hierarchical dualism (difference *from*). The 'standard' subject is typically cast as uppermost in the hierarchy. Using post-conventional ontology, difference *between* equal subjects can be conceptualised and there is no need for literal or figurative hierarchy. Indeed the very act of theorising difference is an act of resistance to conventional, oppressive constructions (Sin, 2010).

If subjectivity is thoroughly re-imagined and reformed as fluid, interconnected and 'nomadic', the capacity to fully conceptualise collectivity is possible. That which was unthinkable in conventional ontology becomes thinkable in a post-conventional ontology (Braidotti, 2005; Plumwood, 1993); what seemed dichotomous can be seen as more fluid, more permeable. Collective concern for welfare is the key; taking one's fair share (rather than competing to take as much as one can in order to dominate) becomes the validated mode of existence.

## Implications for Social Work Practice

While conventional theory offers a predominantly mechanical, technical-rational approach to social work, in post-conventional theory there is capacity for a range of worldviews to be validated along with a range of practice modes focused on social justice. The capacity exists for respectful, culturally authentic practice based on local knowledge, creativity and connectedness in Euro-Western and non-Western locations (Nimmagadda & Martell, 2010). In re-imagining its foundation theory along post-conventional lines (Figure 3.4), social work could actively engage in a transformative decolonisation of practice and gain as a whole from the validation of pre-colonial systems of care and indigenous knowledge (Faith, 2010).

**Figure 3.4: The conceptual framework for post-conventional social work.**

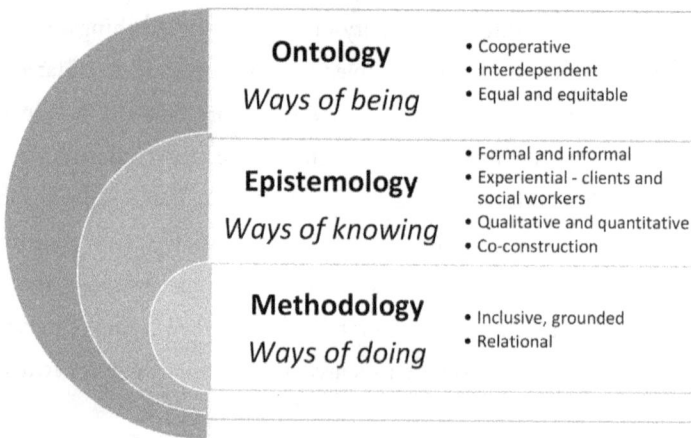

| Ontology<br>*Ways of being* | • Cooperative<br>• Interdependent<br>• Equal and equitable |
| Epistemology<br>*Ways of knowing* | • Formal and informal<br>• Experiential - clients and social workers<br>• Qualitative and quantitative<br>• Co-construction |
| Methodology<br>*Ways of doing* | • Inclusive, grounded<br>• Relational |

# Conclusion: The Potential of Post-Conventional Theory to Sustain Social Work

In terms of sustainability, while the ongoing reliance on conventional ontology would ensure the longevity of mainstream social work it would not be for admirable reasons; a form of social work unreflectively reliant on conventional theory typically reacts to the symptoms of inequity and rarely effects fundamental change at the causal level of ontology. Social work action would remain compromised by conventional thinking that naturalises disadvantage and privileges some at the expense of others. It is acknowledged that often such work is of immediate relief to marginalised people, but in the longer term, little may have been achieved to effect fundamental change in the construction of oppression. Thus without transformative action, the amelioration of the symptoms of oppression results in social control.

Thus, in order to take purposeful action for sustained, holistic ecological and social justice outcomes, it is necessary to be able to map systems of oppression, starting from the way humans' place in the world is constructed (Cuomo, 1996; Pease, 2010). Transformative, sustainable change can only be achieved when the mechanisms of oppression are decommissioned. This unification of ontology and methodology is more consistent with the core values of global social work and contributes to a rich epistemology and practice wisdom in the profession. This epistemology validates a range of epistemic agents and sources of knowledge including marginalised, non-dominant knowledge. It is grounded, rich and multidimensional. This is a firmer, more appropriate base for meaningful social work in the twentieth first century. Post-conventional theory has the potential to underpin a form of global social work with liberation and equity as central themes. This provides an ontological foundation congruent with the core values of social work and would enhance social work epistemology and methodology, sustaining efforts for holistic ecosocial change through the twenty first century.

# References

Anastas, J. (2012). 'From scientism to science: How contemporary epistemology can inform practice research', *Clinical Social Work Journal*, 40, 157–65.

Bell, K. (2012). 'Towards a post-conventional philosophical base for social work', *British Journal of Social Work*, 42(3), 408–23.

Bell, K. (2013). 'Post-conventional approaches to gender, climate change and social justice'. In M. Alston & K. Whittenbury (eds.) *Action and Policy: Addressing the Gendered Impacts of Climate Change* (pp. 53–62). Dordrecht: Springer.

Bennett, B., Green, S., Gilbert, S. & Bessarab, D. (2013). *Our voices: Aboriginal and Torres Strait Islander Social Work*. South Yarra: Palgrave Macmillan.

Boetto, H. (2017). 'A transformative eco-social model: Challenging modernist assumptions in social work', *British Journal of Social Work*, 47(1), 48–67.

Braidotti, R. (2005). 'A critical cartography of feminist postmodernism', *Australian Feminist Studies,* 20 (47), 169–80.

Braidotti, R., Charkiewicz, E., Hausler, S. & Weiringa, S. (2004). *Women, the environment and sustainable development: Towards a theoretical synthesis.* London: Zed Books.

Cameron, N. & McDermott, F. (2007). *Social work and the body.* Houndsmills: Palgrave Macmillan.

Code, L. (1991). *What can she know? Feminist theory and the construction of knowledge.* New York: Cornell University Press.

Cuomo, C. (1996). Toward thoughtful ecofeminist activism. In K. Warren (ed.), *Ecological feminist philosophies.* Bloomington: Indiana University Press.

Dominelli, L. (2002). *Anti-oppressive social work: Theory and practice.* Basingstoke: Palgrave Macmillan.

Dotson, K. (2011). 'Tracking epistemic violence, tracking practices of silencing', *Hypatia, 26*(2), 236–57.

Faith, E. (2010). 'Indigenous social work education: A project for all of us?' In M. Gray, J. Coates & M. Yellow Bird (eds.), *Indigenous social work around the world: Towards culturally relevant practice* (pp. 245–56). Abingdon: Ashgate.

Fejo-King, C. (2014). 'Indigenism and Australian social work'. In C. Noble, H. Strauss & B. Littlechild (eds.). *Global social work: Crossing borders, blurring boundaries* (pp. 55–68). Sydney: Sydney University Press.

Fook, J. (2002). 'Theorising from practice: Towards an inclusive approach for social work research', *Qualitative Social Work*, 1, 79–95.

Gray, M., Coates, J. & Yellow Bird, M. (eds.). (2010). *Indigenous social work around the world: Towards culturally relevant practice.* Abingdon: Ashgate.

Green, D. & McDermott, F. (2010). 'Social work from inside and between complex systems: Perspectives on person-in-environment for today's social work', *British Journal of Social Work,* 40, 2414–30.

Haraway, D. (2004). 'Situated knowledges: The science question in feminism and the privilege of the partial perspective'. In S. Harding (ed.), *The feminist standpoint theory reader: Intellectual and Practical controversies.* London: Routledge.

Healy, K. (2014). *Social work theories in context: Creating frameworks for practice.* Houndmills: Palgrave Macmillan.

Ife, J. (1997). *Re-thinking social work: Towards critical practice.* Melbourne: Addison Wesley Longman.

Ife, J. (2010). *Human rights from below: Achieving rights through community development.* Cambridge: Cambridge University Press.

International Federation of Social Workers (IFSW) (2014). *Global Definition of Social Work.* Retrieved from http://ifsw.org/policies/definition-of-social-work/.

Irigaray, L. (1984). *An ethics of sexual difference.* New York: Cornell University Press.

Ling How Kee, (2010). 'The development of culturally appropriate social work practice in Sarawak, Malaysia'. In M. Gray, J. Coates & M. Yellow Bird (eds.), *Indigenous social work around the world: Towards culturally relevant practice.* (pp. 97–107). Abingdon: Ashgate.

Mafile'o, T. (2010). 'Tongan social work practice'. In M. Gray, J. Coates & M. Yellow Bird (eds.), *Indigenous social work around the world: Towards culturally relevant practice.* (pp. 117–28). Abingdon: Ashgate.

Morley, C. & Macfarlane, S. (2012). 'The nexus between feminism and postmodernism: Still a central concern for critical social work', *British Journal of Social Work,* 42, 687–705.

Nimmagadda, J. & Martell, D. (2010). 'Homemade social work: The two-way transfer of social work practice knowledge between India and the USA'. In M. Gray, J. Coates & M. Yellow Bird (eds.), *Indigenous social work around the world: Towards culturally relevant practice* (pp. 141–52). Abingdon: Ashgate.

Noble, C. and Henrickson, M. (2014). 'Towards clarifying a philosophical basis for social work'. In C. Noble, H. Strauss & B. Littlechild (eds.). *Global social work: Crossing borders, blurring boundaries.* (pp. 3–15). Sydney: Sydney University Press.

Parton, N. & O'Byrne, P. (2000). *Constructive social work: Towards a new practice.* New York: St Martin's Press.

Pease, B. (2009). 'From evidence-based practice to critical knowledge in post-positivist social work'. In L. Allan, L. Briskman and B. Pease (eds.), *Critical social work: Towards critical pluralism in clinical practice.* Crows Nest: Allen and Unwin.

Pease, B. (2010). *Undoing privilege: Unearned advantage in a divided world.* London: Zed Books.

Peile, C & McCouat, M. (1997). 'Emotional and embodied knowledge: Implications for critical practice', *Journal of Sociology and Social Welfare,* 25(4), 39–59.

Plumwood, V. (1993). 'The politics of reason: Towards a feminist logic', *Australian Journal of Philosophy,* 71(4), 436–62.

Shildrick, M. (1997). *Leaky bodies and boundaries: Feminism, postmodernism and (bio) ethics.* London: Routledge.

Sin, R. (2010). 'Reconfiguring 'Chineseness' in the international discourse on social work in China'. In M. Gray, J. Coates & M. Yellow Bird (eds.), *Indigenous social work around the world: Towards culturally relevant practice.* Abingdon: Ashgate, pp. 166–78.

Thompson, C. 2005. *Making parents: The ontological choreography of reproductive technologies.* Cambridge: MIT Press.

Yellow Bird, M. (2010). 'Terms of endearment: A brief dictionary for decolonising social work with indigenous peoples'. In M. Gray, J. Coates & M. Yellow Bird (eds.), *Indigenous social work around the world: Towards culturally relevant practice.* (pp. 275–92). Abingdon: Ashgate.

# FOUR

# Virtue-Led Social Work Practice

*Manohar Pawar, Richard Hugman,*
*Andrew Alexandra and Bill Anscombe*

## Abstract

By presenting the genesis of the research idea and delineating and developing the concept of virtue in social work practice, this chapter brings out the significance of virtue-led practice and how it strengthens 'being' of social workers along with their thinking and doing. It summarises research methods employed and major findings of an Australian Research Council discovery project, 'Virtuous Practitioners: Empowering social workers' and discusses implications for social work education, research and practice.

## Genesis of the Idea

As we celebrate 25 years of Charles Sturt University's (CSU) Social Work program, tracing the genesis of the idea of virtue-led social work practice has a special significance as the idea was born in a social work residential school (intensive teaching sessions) lecture in a CSU classroom, though researching virtue-led social work previously been discussed by a number of authors, prior to our project, including most recently McBeath and Webb (2002) and also Banks (2004; Banks & Gallagher, 2009). Birth or conceptualization of a new, good idea not only symbolizes some kind of purity or sacrosanct of CSU classrooms (like the birth or beginning of springs of water in the first author's culture), but also it shows how our social work residential schools are powerful in facilitating meaningful discussion and debate with our co-learners, students, generating new ideas and disseminating them for the larger benefit of the society, what we now call impact on and engagement with end users.

Elsewhere, the first author remembers that in one of his history and philosophy classes at the Tata Institute of Social Sciences (TISS), Mumbai, India, nearly four decades ago, Professor M. S. Gore, then director of the TISS, stated, social work makes a better 'human being' and social work is not a 'readymade meal', you have to make what you want from it (Pawar, 2014). These words often contemplatively reverberate in his mind since he has heard them in 1981 as student of social work. He questions himself, 'Have I become a better human being? Have I made what I want from social work?' Answers to these questions are evolving every day. On the other hand, some are of the view that it is not sure whether social work does always make a better human being, though they may aspire to that.

With these questions at the first author's back of mind, when he was new to CSU social work teaching, out of curiosity, he attended residential school lectures to reorient himself to CSU social work education. In one of such lectures, his colleague, Dr Bill Anscombe stated, 'if you think and do not do anything, you are useless; if you do without thinking, you are dangerous; and central to your thinking and doing is being' (Pawar and Anscombe, 2015). This statement triggered his thought process and he began seriously reflecting about 'being' in social work practice. Later, Dr Bill Anscombe and Pawar had a great opportunity to work together on a doctoral thesis entitled *Consilience in Social Work: Thinking, doing and being*. In the thesis, 'being' was conceptualized in terms of qualities and character and it looked at how being can be employed while working with individuals, families, groups, communities, administration/management, and while conducting research (Anscombe, 2009; Pawar and Anscombe, 2015). The conceptualization of virtue-led social work practice is further extension of this research work, which, as stated earlier, originally emanated from the CSU social work residential school lectures and they are proud to state so on the occasion of the silver jubilee of CSU social work.

## Conceptualization of the Project

The project was conceptualized on the basic premise that 'being', though crucial for social work practice, is mostly neglected in social work practice, research and education. In social work, although the phrase, thinking, doing and being is often used, most of the time we are preoccupied with thinking and doing, at the neglect of being. Thinking refers to theory and doing refers to practice. Most of the time, we emphasise in our education, practice and research either theory to practice or practice to theory in a binary form. While both are important, theory to practice and practice to theory, equally important is being. If so, what is being? How the concept can be developed and applied in social work education, practice and research.

The dynamic concept of being is constructed in terms of the physical/organic, mental/emotional, social/relational and spiritual/existential dimensions of it. Being involves recognising that humans are both shaped by and shapers of the environment – physically, socially, ecologically and spiritually (see Anscombe, 2009; Pawar and Anscombe, 2015). The terms 'being', 'self', 'identity', 'integrity' and 'character' are also sometimes used interchangeably in different contexts. Being involves concepts of personhood and the self. Heydt and Sherman (2005: 25–6) argue that the self is an instrument and in fact the primary instrument that a social worker has to facilitate change. They say that the conscious use of self purposefully and intentionally used allows for:

> ... his or her motivation and capacity to communicate and interact with others in ways that facilitate change... the skilled worker is purposefully making use of his or her unique manner and style in relating to others and building positive helping relationships with clients is fundamental to social work practice.

Further, the term 'use of self' has been applied to honesty and spontaneity (Davies, 1994), to genuineness, vulnerability and self-awareness (Edwards & Bess, 1998), mindfulness of one's belief system and judicious self-disclosure (Dewane, 2006). Thus, self is an important part of being and it is developed over a period of time in interaction with others.

One significant aspect of self-development and being is character, qualities or virtue development, which is closely connected to virtue ethics. The conscious construction of being based on virtues is important because social work thinking and doing are dominated by deontology (the study of what is morally obligatory, permissible, right, or wrong) (Kant, 1964), which focuses on moral rules for action based on reason/rationality, objectivity, impartiality, unbiasedness, duty and respect for others, and the ethic of consequentialism (based on the tenets of hedonism – maximising pleasure and minimising pain) and utilitarianism (greatest happiness to greatest number of people). Here the consequence or the outcome is more important, though the action or the process of producing the outcome has to be morally right. These ethical frameworks focus on rule-bound actions and outcomes and ignore the actor.

Countering the influences of deontology and consequentialism/ utilitarianism and to overcome their weaknesses, McBeath and Webb (2002) contend that social work ethics and thereby practice needs to significantly draw on virtue ethics. Social workers on a daily basis deal with complex, unpredictable and uncertain situations and ways of doing or intervening in such situations cannot be defined and prescribed in terms of strict rules, procedures, and duties for conduct. Rather than only focusing on the action and outcome, it is useful to focus on the social worker. Once the core virtues are developed in social workers, those virtues will help them to effectively deal with unpredictable and uncertain situations.

McBeath and Webb (2002: 1020) state, 'virtue ethics can be used to offer an account of the modes of moral existence shaping *the being* of a good social worker'. More simply then, the basic question is not what is good social work, but rather what is a good social worker? A small number of social work ethicists also of the view that virtue ethics is relevant for social work practice (see Hugman and Smith, 1995; Banks, 2004; Bowles et al., 2006). The virtue theory is broadly influenced by the Platonic and Aristotelian notions of what is excellent (arête), what is practical and wise (phronesis) and what typifies human flourishing (eudaimonia), though Aristotle first emphasised good of the larger community and then good of the individual (Aristotle, 1976). Aristotle's doctrine of mean provides the basis for virtues. Prudence or temperance of a worker helps to choose between two extremes in a balanced way that suits the situation.

Conceptualizing being in terms of virtues of social workers, it is useful to look at what McBeath and Webb (2002: 1020) further observe:

> The virtues are the acquired inner qualities of humans – character – the possession of which, if deployed in due measure, will typically contribute to the realisation of the good life or 'Eudaimonia'. The role of the virtuous social workers is shown to be one that necessitates appropriate application of intellectual and practical virtues such as justice, reflection, perception, judgement, bravery, prudence, liberality and temperance. This 'self flourishing' worker, in bringing together the capacity of theoretical and practical action makes possible a hermeneutic or interpretive praxis best appraised in dialogue with fellow practitioners and clients.

Despite the significance of virtue-led practice, the literature shows that social workers' 'being' is peripherally referred to, inadequately researched, underdeveloped and underutilised. Except for theoretical discussions in texts and journal articles (Bowles et al., 2006; Hugman, 2005; Banks, 2004, 2009; McBeath and Webb, 2002; Webb, 2010), to date the use of virtues in social workers' practice has been largely unexplored.

To address this gap in social work education, practice and research, this project was conceptualised: to identify and analyse core virtues which professional social workers need to have and demonstrate in their practices;

to explore whether and how social workers develop and apply virtues in their practices; and to look at approaches to cultivating core virtues in terms of characters within their (professional) socialisation so as to make social work practices more impactful and meaningful in the lives of Australian people and communities. Some of the research questions raised were:

- What are the core virtues which need to be used in social work practice?

- Do social workers use the virtues in their practice?

- How do social workers develop and demonstrate their virtues in practice?

- What roles do virtues and character play in social workers' practice outcomes?

- Will the conscious development and use of virtues and character result in sound judgements, appropriate decisions and better social work practice outcomes?

- How should social workers go about improving their virtues and overcoming virtue flaws/deficiencies?

- Why does the social work profession not draw on virtue ethics?

## Research Methods and Design

Both qualitative and quantitative research methods were employed to conduct this research. In particular, biographic narrative interview method (BNIM, Wengraf, 2001; Rosenthal, 2004), which is an approach within a narrative research methodology (Liamputtong, 2013), focus group discussion, survey, interview and case practice analysis methods were used. A purposive method was employed to select participants and the data were collected from the following seven sources under three phases. To collect data from these sources, six data collection instruments were developed as presented in Table 4.1.

Table 4.1: Data collection sources and instruments

| | Data collection sources | | Data collection instruments |
|---|---|---|---|
| | Phase I | | |
| 1 | Biography of individuals | 1 | Biographic data collection guidelines and open questions and BNIM |
| 2 | Secondary data elated to biographies | | Referring to relevant secondary data |
| 3 | Workshop and focused group discussion | 2 | Focus group discussion guidelines and focused questions |
| | Phase II | | |
| 4 | Interviews with social work practitioners | 3 | Semi-structured and open-ended interview guides |
| 5 | A practice case of social work practitioners | 4 | A practice case pro forma |
| 6 | Social work practice supervisors | 5 | Semi-structured and open-ended interview guides |
| | Phase III | | |
| 7 | Social work ethics educators and their curricula | 6 | A questionnaire |

In the first phase, by employing three criteria (significant contribution to community; public record and recognition in some form; and consistent track of work for the community) ten Australian social work practitioners were interviewed so as to develop their biographies. The biographic interviews were analysed by focusing on life history, important stages of life, the nature of engagement in practice, important socio-cultural influences, and prime factors that have contributed to practice with a view to identifying character formation and core virtues. Where relevant, secondary data, articles, books, letters, and internet sources were accessed to develop biographies. The ten draft biographies were presented in a workshop, in which biographic analysers, philosophers, theologians and social work practitioners contributed to focus group discussion and helped to improve biographies and identify virtues.

In the second phase, 50 social work practitioners and 15 social work practice supervisors from the six states, the Australian Capital Territory and the Northern Territory were interviewed. Interviews with social work practitioners involved discussing one of their practice cases. With the help of NVivo software, these data were analysed by focusing on the virtue formation process of social workers and the absence or presence of virtues in practice. Analysis of social work practice supervisors' interviews focused on the use of virtues and the development of virtues in supervision sessions.

In the third phase, data collected through questionnaires from 22 social work ethics educators (69% response rate) and 22 social work ethics curricula were manually analysed by looking at core themes and contents to explore whether or not virtue ethics is covered in social work ethics education and training. In the curriculum objectives and outcomes, ethics content, assessments and suggested and prescribed reading material were analysed. A brief summary of results is presented below.

## Summary of Findings

As clarified in the introduction, although 'being' encompasses physical, social and spiritual aspects, for the project purpose it was defined in terms of personal virtues, qualities or character, from a virtue-led practice perspective. Our discussion in the workshop/focus group discussion and interviews with social work supervisors and practitioners suggested that in social work practice we need to question and clarify the meaning of virtue so that it can be meaningfully employed in social work education, practice and research. Through such questioning and clarifying process, the project has developed and used the concept of virtue in terms of overlapping four dimensions. These are values/principles, qualities and attributes, roles and functions (see Pawar et al., 2017). Our project experience suggested that the meaning of virtue cannot be just limited to qualities and character. In social work these need to be understood in terms of values and principles such as human rights and social justice, qualities and attributes such as courage, commitment, conviction, determination, and so on, and the range of roles and functions through which these are performed. Indeed, in this sense 'being' is not divorced from 'doing', but rather is demonstrated through the practice that it underpins. We consider this conceptual development of virtue for the field of social work is an important contribution from the project, though it may be further refined in the future.

Employing this concept of virtue, ten biographies of social workers were developed and analysed to explore what kind of virtue-led practice they had in their careers (see Pawar et al., 2017). These biographies include eight women and two men, of whom one is Aboriginal and the other nine are non-Aboriginal. In particular, seeking to include an Aboriginal social worker was purposive sampling, as was the gender balance and the wide geographical spread of the participants across the Australian states and territories in terms of current location, career history and early life. The range of practice experience was also wide, with diversity across government and non-government organisations, and with more than half having worked in both at some stage in their careers. In this way, a diversity of social work is included in the range of biographies. However, the biographical approach is qualitative, not statistical, in its 'representativeness' of exemplars of good social work.

Our analysis shows that there are particular values/principles and qualities/attributes that stand out among this group of leading social workers (Pawar et al., 2017: 194–202). For the purpose of discussion, we have concluded that these can be considered in seven groups: social justice (including the pursuit of human rights); commitment, courage and resilience; compassion and empathy; respect for others and humility; competence; responsibility and accountability (in relation to the exercise of power); integrity and practical wisdom. In addition, there were a number of instances where virtues, as we have defined them, were seen in the biographies of one or two individuals, but were not more widely articulated (such as love, hope, generosity and creativity). Key examples of virtues that were shared among all 10 biographies include a concern with social justice (in the form of the inequities of social divisions, exclusion and discrimination seen in phenomena such as sexism, racism, homophobia, ageism, ableism and so on) and integrity (in the sense of the integration of moral character) in which the various values/principles and qualities/attributes are woven into the roles and functions of social work.

Of the groups of virtues that are evident in only some of the biographies, those that are most widely seen are: courage; commitment; responsibility; and humility. Our analysis linked courage and commitment with resilience (Pawar et al., 2017: 196). In practice, it appears that the virtue of asking difficult questions and challenging powerful others (both people and institutions) is often combined with both a 'doggedness' in focusing on what is seen as right and the capacity to 'hang on in there' in pursuing such goals. Humility takes many forms, including putting others first when important contributions are made to social work, but more generally it also blends with respect, in which the valuing of others is seen throughout a person's practice. Similarly, compassion and empathy are often regarded as virtues that can inform good practice, but which appear quite differently in the lives of each practitioner. This points to the importance of role and function in the development of such values/principles and qualities/attributes, although this relationship is dynamic, not simply a causal progression.

A further grouping of virtues is seen in the values/principles and qualities/attributes of responsibility and accountability (in relation to the exercise of power). Although in some of the biographical narratives, power in this sense is that exercised by others (whether as individuals or through institutions) and it may also be the power these social workers themselves were aware that they exercised in their work. Given that some social work requires that the practitioner exercised power, the virtue of being able to recognise and deal with this with responsibility and accountably is one that might be said to be crucial for good practice (Bowles et al., 2006; Banks, 2008).

Although the capacity to practice is generally highly regarded in social work, less than half the biographies explicitly identify competence as a virtue. Yet, not only do all biographies implicitly reveal the way that competence is valued in a concrete sense, but it also connects values/principles and qualities/attributes with roles and functions (Pawar et al., 2017: 199).

Finally, the virtues of love, hope, generosity and creativity, which were evident each in only a few biographies, nevertheless display values/principles and qualities/attributes that provide an important dimension of good social work, at least in the careers of those particular social workers. Again, the dynamic relationship between these elements of virtues and roles and functions may mean that it is people's biographies that influence whether such aspects of who they are (their 'being') become evident.

In addition to these in depth biographies, our interviews with social work professional supervisors and practitioners suggested that there is a great variance in providing professional supervision to practitioners and the need for professional supervision is not adequately met in the field. Although social work practitioners assume important roles, irrespective of their designation is social work or not, and perform a range of functions in adherence to social work values and principles, their conscious use of attributes and qualities was not well pronounced in our interviews, though they may be implicit.

Similarly, the survey of social work ethics curriculum and educators explored the curriculum content, resources and learning and teaching methods used to teach social work ethics subjects and the coverage and teaching of virtue ethics to social work students. The analysis showed that although there was a great diversity in the curriculum content, textbooks used, teaching methods followed and assessment methods/practices, the greatest degree of commonality was the focus on ethical dilemmas and decision-making and Australian Association of Social Work code of ethics. The curriculum explicitly reflected values and principles and some qualities such as critical thinking and reflection, but the same was not true in relation to virtue qualities and character. Some social work ethics educators clearly stated that they do not cover virtue ethics in their curriculum and teaching. On the other hand, a great majority of the educators were of the view that it is necessary to have a virtue ethics perspective and virtues/qualities have a role in social work practice, and more needs to be done.

Overall, these findings have important implications for social work research, education and practice from a virtue perspective. First, further research is needed to systematically explore the role of virtue ethics in social work practice. Second, social work education and training needs to focus on developing virtues in social workers by revising the curriculum and the code of ethics, where necessary. Finally, it is crucial to see how social workers can consciously use virtues in practice so that they can flourish.

## Conclusion

As stated in the introduction, by presenting the genesis of the research idea and clarifying the concept of virtue, in this chapter we have discussed the significance of being in terms of qualities and character and the need to understand the social worker's being as it has been mostly unexplored. The summary of the research design and findings show the innovative aspects of the project and implications for virtue-led practice. In social work, it is practical to understand virtues in terms values and principles, attributes and roles and functions. A biographic narrative and interview method employed in the project has helped to bring out virtues of social workers. A survey of social work ethics educators and social work ethics curriculum suggests the need to systematically focus on virtue-led practice. Compared to other professions, the social work profession has lagged behind in focusing on virtue-led practice and this project has helped to bridge this gap, at least to some extent. Due to the word limit, as this chapter has tried to capture only the zest of the research project, those who crave for details and depth will not be satisfied. Thus we recommend them to refer to our book, *Empowering Social Workers: Virtuous Practitioners* (Pawar et al., 2017), to find details of any of these biographies summarised here. Another limitation of this research was that it did not include biographies of young social work practitioners. Despite such limitations, we hope it has underscored the application and usefulness of virtue-led practice in social work, and social work practitioners and researchers will further contribute to this vital area.

# References

Anscombe, A.W. (2009). *Consilience in social work: reflections on thinking doing and being*. A PhD thesis. Wagga: CSU.

Aristotle (1976). *Nicomachean ethics,* Harmondsworth: Penguin.

Banks, S. (2004). *Ethics, Accountabiity and the Social Professions,* Basingstoke: Palgrave Macmillan.

Banks, S. (2006). *Ethics and Values in Social Work,* Basingstoke: Palgrave Macmillan.

Banks, S. & Gallagher, A. (2009). *Ethics in Professional Life: virtues for health and social care,* Basingstoke: Palgrave Macmillan.

Bowles, W., Collingridge, M., Curry, S. & Valentine, B. (2006). *Ethical practice in social work: An applied approach,* Sydney: Allen and Unwin.

Davies, M. (1994). *The essential social worker: A guide to positive practice,* Vermont: Arena.

Dewane, C. J. (2006). 'The use of self: A primer revisited', *Clinical Social Work Journal,* 34 (4), 543–57.

Edwards, J. A., & Bess, J. M. (1998). 'Developing effectiveness in the therapeutic use of self', *Clinical Social Work Journal,* 26(1), 89–105.

Heydt, M. and Sherman, N. (2005). 'Conscious use of self: Tuning the instrument of social work practice with cultural competence', *Journal of Baccalaureate Social Work,* 10 (2), 25.

Hugman, R. (2005). *New approaches in ethics for the caring professions.* Basingstoke: Palgrave/Macmillan.

Hugman, R. & Smith, D. (1995). 'Ethical issues in social work: An overview'. In R. Hugman & D. Smith (eds.), *Ethical issues in social work* (pp. 1–15). London: Routledge.

Kant, I. (1964). *The Groundwork of the Metaphysics of Morals.* New York: Harper and Row.

Liamputtong, P. (2013). *Qualitative research methods.* Melbourne: Oxford University Press.

McBeath, G. and Webb, S. A. (2002). 'Virtue ethics and social work: Being lucky, realistic, and not doing one's duty', *British Journal of Social Work,* 32, 1015–36.

Pawar, M. (2014). *Social and Community Development Practice.* New Delhi: Sage.

Pawar, M. and Anscombe B. (2015). *Reflective Social Work Practice: Thinking, doing and being.* Melbourne: Cambridge University Press.

Pawar, M., Hugman, R., Alexandra, A. and Anscombe, A. W. (eds.) (2017).

*Empowering social workers: Virtuous practitioners.* Singapore: Springer.

Rosenthal, G. (2004). Biographical research. In C. Seal, G. Gobo, J. F. Gubrium & D. Silverman, *Qualitative research practice*, London: Sage.

Webb, S. (2010). 'Virtue ethics'. In Gray, M. & Webb, S. A., *Ethics and value perspectives in social work* (pp. 108–19). Basingstoke: Palgrave Macmillan.

Wengraf, T. (2001). *Qualitative Research Interviewing. London: Sage.*

# FIVE

# Combating Whiteness Behaviours Through Culturally Responsive Practice

*Susan Mlcek*

## Abstract

How do we channel new understandings about the negative impact of whiteness behaviours in order to progress developing cross-cultural competencies for social work students? The answer lies in new trends in adaptive social work practice that problematizes the idea that cultural competence is a framework that incorporates a 'one-size-fits-all' set of strategies that can be used in any context with different cultures, including work with Indigenous Australians. However, both the Australian Association of Social Workers (AASW) and the Indigenous Allied Health Australia (IAHA) suggest adopting a new way of working that asks practitioners to be more *culturally-responsive*. Cultural responsiveness in action, is a framework developed by the IAHA to respond to a '... need for practical strategies to build cultural safety using strengths-based and action-oriented approaches ... This capability framework provides guidance around what we need to know, be and do in order to be culturally responsive' (IAHA Chairperson, Ms Faye McMillan, 6 August 2015). The central tenets and principles of the above framework can be used to inform any human services situation, for example: *culture* is a primary consideration for all engagements with individuals and communities; *holistic* and *inclusive* views of the best outcomes for diverse peoples; adopting a *rights-based culturally responsive approach*; recognising *leadership, strength, resilience* and *self-determination*; understanding the *unique professional and cultural perspectives of Indigenous peoples*; acknowledging the *diversity of individuals, families and communities*; and undertaking rigorous *education, evidence-based practice* and *research*. Will this be enough, going forward into the future? How can we measure its success? This paper suggests social workers undertake the development of an 'adaptation framework', using all the relevant and authentic 'tools' they can, to assist in developing their own cultural responsiveness focus.

## Introduction and Background

In 2013, I asked the question, *Are We Doing Enough to Develop Cross-Cultural Competencies for Social Work?* (Mlcek, 2013). The article with this same name was published in the *British Journal of Social Work*, and since then, there have been several opportunities, through seminars and conference presentations, and other publications, to try to answer that question. In just four years, further development along these critical lines has taken the exploration from just thinking about, 'outdated ideas that have as their source prejudice, racism, whiteness behaviours, fear and mistrust, and a lack of knowledge and understanding about the complex layers in understanding situations of access and equity, discrimination and the abrogation of human rights for marginalised communities' (Mlcek, 2013: 1), to action. As social workers, we continue to scrutinise our own biases and entrenched worldviews that are often developed out of an ethnocentric monoculturalism, as well as whiteness behaviours dominated by unearned privilege and power.

At Charles Sturt University, Australia, the social work curriculum addresses all four components of cultural competence (O'Sullivan, Hill, Bernoth, & Mlcek, 2016; Sue, 2006): becoming aware of one's own assumptions, values and biases about human behaviour; understanding the worldview of culturally diverse clients; developing appropriate intervention strategies and techniques; and understanding organisational and institutional forces that enhance or negate cultural competence (Sue, 2006; Sue & Sue, 2008). The curriculum also looks at the specific condition of cross-cultural situations. For example, one of the fallouts through looking at the political dimensions of social work is the extent to which marginalised people are defined through social and ethnic constructs. With these parameters in mind, the beginning journey for students studying cross-cultural competencies is to acquire historical knowledge about the situations of disadvantaged groups and to question the reification of culturalism (Booth, 1999; Jamrozik, 2009) that allows for the continuation of abusive and oppressive practices, 'all in the name of cultural integrity' (Ife, 2008: 79).

Progressing the development of cross-cultural competencies for social work students requires a new paradigm and approach that is not just about developing cultural competencies, but about being culturally responsive to numerous cultural diversity contexts.

## The Source of Adaptive Social Work Practice

Many social workers are engaged in developing or refining capabilities and capacity when working responsively and inclusively with Aboriginal and Torres Strait Islander peoples. Some of these areas include respecting, understanding and valuing Indigenous knowledges, but the Australian Association of Social Workers (AASW) (2016) recognises the further ongoing importance of at least two critical components of being responsive: to be aware of the particular protocols of entering Aboriginal and Torres Strait Islander communities, and to actively engage in understanding the concepts of whiteness and white privilege (p. 7). Fundamentally, there is a need to engage in a life-long journey of not just culturally responsive, but decolonising practices as well; such as critical reflection of one's own racial identity and self-awareness, challenging the status of one's own professional knowledge (Pease, 2002), and responding appropriately to racial information (Bender, Negi, & Fowler, 2010).

# Authentic Tools

An innovative model of social work practice that can be used to inform a culturally-responsive one is necessarily made up of critical pedagogy; a way of working that transforms social relations and raises awareness about issues in society at large. Freire (2000; 2004) likens this stance to a 'pedagogy of indignation' and the problem of neutrality; when it is not enough to 'wash one's hands of the conflict between the powerful and the powerless', because to do so, 'means to side with the powerful, not to be neutral' (Freire, 1985: 122). Another stance relates to a 'pedagogy of discomfort' (Boler & Zembylas, 2003), whereby social workers blend emotional intelligence with mindfulness to engage meaningfully and respectfully with individuals and diverse communities. We utilise our discomfort in situations of difference, to reflectively re-envision our ability to construct new emotional understandings of the ways we can live with others, through *praxis*.

The supposed neutrality of silence is problematic, and at least the above pedagogies, as well as others, become the cornerstone of anti-oppressive practice, and are used to build an adaptive framework for social work. The element of praxis becomes critical here, because intentional knowing will inform the adaptation that needs to occur, depending on the cultural context. That is, the practical consequences of being adaptable from a place of discomfort and indignation may not be appropriate, or even ethical, for all situations because cultural contexts can be diverse, complex and layered.

An adaptive framework can be used to counter discriminatory practices, and to do otherwise is to be negligent. A good place to start is through a capability engagement that includes constant scrutiny and awareness of self, through rigorous education, evidence-based practice and research.

# Indigenous Worldviews

In 2015, Indigenous Allied Health Australia (IAHA) included *self-awareness* (Capability 2), as the continuous development of self-knowledge, including understanding personal beliefs, assumptions, values, perceptions, attitudes and expectations, and how they impact relationships with Aboriginal and Torres Strait Islanders peoples (IAHA, 2015: 15). This type of activity is part of IAHA's culturally responsive Capability Framework, and seen as being achieved through means such as: *rigorous education, evidence-based practice* and *research*.

From that research, two relevant themes can be seen as constant, re-occurring capabilities to add to an adaptive framework for social work practice: knowledge about wise practice, and the transformative qualities that come from living every aspect of life with deep respect on all levels of engagement. Central to these themes is an understanding of how Indigenous worldviews are no less applicable than a non-Indigenous worldview. Taking an Indigenous worldview into account ought to be a benchmark for many cross-cultural situations, because at its heart is the extent and level to which cultural perpetuity is reinforced and maintained. Indigenous worldviews are deeply cultural; spiritual; communal; collective, and respectful. They implicitly challenge the notion of evidence-based practice, which is a Western concept that often equates to 'best practice' (Wesley-Esquimaux & Calliou, 2010), and must be evaluated against the need to make a space for Indigenous knowledges, experiences, and stories, 'learned on the frontlines through socio-cultural insight, ingenuity, intuition, long experience, and trial and error' (Thoms, 2007: 8).

*Yindyamarra Winhanganha* – 'the wisdom of respectfully knowing how to live well in a world worth living in' (Charles Sturt University, 2018), is a phrase gifted by the local Indigenous Australian Wiradjuri Peoples of New South Wales, Australia, to Charles Sturt University. The significance of its message suggests a 'trial and error' endeavour that is a genuine part of life-long learning about the application of respect and wisdom throughout life's journey. When Indigenous writers highlight the importance of wise practice, it is with the emphasis on culture as the all-embracing standard that matters for a culturally-responsive practice. When social workers develop practice wisdom, we do so with the intent to be community-engaged and effective through, 'locally-appropriate actions, tools, principles or decisions that contribute significantly to the development of sustainable and equitable conditions' (Wesley-Esquimaux & Calliou, 2010: 19). When social workers are culturally-responsive, we acknowledge that wise practices recognise the wisdom in each diverse Indigenous community and in that community's own stories of perpetuity.

## Storying

In order to develop critical awareness in social work, critical reflection cycles can present as useful learning opportunities through storying.

Bolton (2014) suggests that stories make sense of who we are and our world. This world and our lives within it are complex and chaotic: seemingly governed by forces not only beyond our control, but beyond our understanding. We tell and retell episodes both minor and major to colleagues, loved ones, therapists and priests, strangers on the train, even an acquaintance perhaps. Storytelling is a dynamic way of making meaning and grasping understanding; we become the pivotal link in events seemingly beyond our control. Caution and awareness are features of effective storying; whereby the 'leaving out' is just as important as the 'leaving in'; in the story telling, *story making* can sometimes hijack realities by weaving together only those safe and self-affirming accounts: our stories can only too easily become essentially uncritical. Or, even worse, they are censoring tools: 'cover stories' (Sharkey, 2004). This self-protectiveness can ensure our stories do not explore sensitive issues, but are expressions of what we feel comfortable with, or would like to be. Combating whiteness behaviours in any profession is challenging, and in social work, particularly difficult.

## Autoethnography

When we engage in storying – in telling our own stories, we place ourselves squarely and subjectively within the places and spaces of our work and contact with individuals and communities. However, we can make our stories more powerful and meaningful when we acknowledge and engage in challenging layers to those stories. There is a distinction between the two types of stories we might share – life stories, and life histories – 'The life history pushes the question of whether private issues are also public matters. The life story individualises and personalises; the life history contextualises and politicises' (Goodson, 1998: 11). To illustrate these ideas from Goodson, in presenting the following story, not only am I indicating who I am, but I am engaging in an auto ethnographic process of deconstructing the way that I and my family were treated as the 'racialised other' in two separate but connected events; the first in the 1950s and the second in 2006. In presenting my own story, I am also being very careful to not appropriate the knowledges of other Indigenous Peoples' stories; a common incentive should be that we are always mindful of addressing a 'colonial legacy of ignorance, fear, inadequacy, and loss of control' (Fejo-King & Mataira, Eds. 2015: 3).

## A Decolonising Story

I am Māori; this is my *Pepeha* [Māori introduction of self], and I welcome all to a small part of my story:

> KO MATAATUA TE WAKA [The Mataatua is my Canoe; my ancestors came to Aotearoa by this means]
> KO MAUAO TE MAUNGA [Mauo is my Mountain – my geographical focal point of where I am from]
> KO TAURANGA TE MOANA [Tauranga is the surrounding area of that place, and incorporates the waters and sea]
> KO NGAI TE RANGI TE IWI [Ngāi te Rangi is my Tribe]
> KO NGAI TUKAIRANGI TE HAPU [Ngaitukairangi is my sub-Tribe]
> KO HUNGAHUNGATOROA TE MARAE [Hungahun-gatoroa is the name of the resting place of the Albatross, and it is also the name of my Marae]
> KO TAAPUITI TE TUPUNA WHARE [Tapuiti is the

name of my direct Ancestor, and the principal name of the main house on my Marae].

In the 1950s, I was born in a tiny hospital in the small town of Te Puke, New Zealand, which is now a 28-minute drive from the main city/town of Tauranga. At that time however, the distance would have taken much longer to cover, and without a car, taking the bus would have incurred several hours, or even the best part of a day. In fact six siblings were all born in Te Puke. My Mother is Māori, and my Father is non-Maori (*Pākeha*). The interesting thing about this situation is that Tauranga was the main town/city, with a much bigger and more-modern hospital, and yet for my Mother and father to get to Te Puke, they would have had to walk to Tauranga from our own home community, wait to catch a regional bus, and drive past the front door of the Tauranga hospital to get to Te Puke. When my older brother was completing his research for a Master of Social Work degree in NZ, he shared an interesting question from that research – *why were we all born in Te Puke? Why did my Mother have to go there; why not to Tauranga, which was far closer and more convenient?* Apparently at that time, Māori were not allowed to have their babies born in Tauranga; they had to go to Te Puke.

Why this happened, I have no reasons from any specific records except the experience of my Mother and all her siblings, and *whānau* (family). I can also speculate that without knowledge of any definitive official strategy to segregate on the basis of race, we had in fact been categorised and racialised as the 'other'. For me, this is an example of the social engineering of Indigenous communities (Mlcek, 2017), and at the heart of these practices, are whiteness behaviours.

Fast forward to 2006 when my Mother was admitted for medical care, although this time to the same Tauranga hospital denied her all those years ago; of course she had been there since, but now she was in the last stages of her life. I wrote an essay about observing the frailty of my Mother and the culturally-responsive care I witnessed being provided by her Pākeha nurses (Mlcek, McMillan, & McMillan, 2017: 51–72). An excerpt from that essay is worth recounting here:

My Mother was a Māori Kaumatua [*Elder*] and revered matriarch of a well-known whanau/family in the local Mount Maunganui [*Mauol*]Tauranga community. Her married name would not have provided that link or knowledge to others… But once the nursing staff knew of my uncle's name, they could make that connection to his sister [*my Mother*] and they were in awe to be in her presence. The information spread throughout the hospital and nursing staff would visit to stand at the door of her room and respectfully watch the scene playing out in front of them. They were never obtrusive or more than one at a time; they became part of the [*culturally safe and responsive*] vigil with those of us watching over her … (Mlcek, McMillan, & McMillan, 2017: 68, my italicized words added in brackets)

On reflection, I like to think that the *mana* (respect) that was minimal or even non-existent in the first part of the story was very much present in the second encounter. The abuse of power and privilege, or worse, the lack of awareness of these as insidious components of whiteness behaviours, has the potential to leave a legacy of pain and disorientation. Social workers have an enormous responsibility in helping to maintain the sense of *mana* where cultural ties are profound because they come from a place of genealogy/ancestry, spirituality, and communality. The loss of respect for an individual through any lack of care and cultural safety, is actually a loss for all who are involved in an engagement.

## Discussion – Decolonising Methodologies – An Ongoing Project

*Mana* (respect) can be endurable, and indestructible, but through negligence in communication, acknowledgement, kindness, information and skills, *mana* can be easily-trampled. One powerful decolonising activity with which we can all identify is through the stories that we reclaim from our past, and ensure that the truthful telling of these is maintained into the present and future. This is an ongoing project for Indigenous Peoples around the world, and especially for Indigenous Australians who are still affected by contemporary colonisation and appropriation of their knowledges, by white people. The project requires not just an acknowledgement of anti-colonialism strategies, but a deep awareness and understanding of the way that whiteness behaviours allocate and entrench positions of privilege and power.

Fejo-King (2013: 144–7) provides a stark and startling example of the playing out of whiteness behaviours, as she recounts the experience of growing up in Darwin amidst the racial segregation imposed on Indigenous Australians wanting to attend a movie night with the rest of the townspeople; including those from different cultural groupings. There were certain demarcation lines in terms of which group could sit where, from the fenced outside areas only ever used by the Aboriginal people, to the sheltered tiered nice seats that were only ever occupied by the 'fair-skinned'. Her example perfectly illustrates Frankenberg's (1993: 1) three dimensions of whiteness. First, 'Whiteness' is a location of structural advantage of race privilege'. Second, there is a 'standpoint', 'a place from which white people look at ourselves, at others, and at society', and third, that whiteness refers to 'a set of cultural practices that are usually unmarked and un-named'.

Whiteness language is akin to 'white noise', manifested in white sound that includes someone saying all the 'right' things; making the 'right' statements. This language is steady like rain, but is also dehumanising, unvarying, unobtrusive, drone-like, drip-like, and masking or obliterating unwanted sounds. Whiteness is a socially and politically constructed behaviour. It represents a position of power where the power holder defines social categories and reality. It provides the stage for the 'master narrator' to perform. Furthermore, examples of unearned privilege are *denumerable* (Deleuze & Guattari, 2013).

The *rhizomatics* (Deleuze & Guattari, 2013) of privilege and critical whiteness here in Australia, are tied to the fact that White Australia has a Black History. When we look at the dismantlement of Indigenous communities, there are ever-present comparative considerations that are part of the personal and political spheres: post-colonialism compared to ongoing contemporary colonisation; cultural perpetuity and responsiveness (O'Sullivan, Hill, Bernoth, & Mlcek, 2016) compared to cultural submersion; inclusion and acceptance compared to diasporic anomie (Mlcek, 2017b); decolonising methodologies to claim stories compared to social engineering that annihilates the narratives of people. The problematic for many, is that there is often quietness associated with the arrogance of some behaviours rather than a shouting from the rooftops when systemic silence allows the perpetuation of stereotypes, tokenistic acknowledgement of 'community', and simplistic views on cultural difference. That is, '... *it is not difference that immobilises us, but silence. And there are so many silences to be broken*' (Lorde, 1984: 84).

In the moment of exposure and disclosure, whiteness behaviours are often grounded in 'technical rationality' (Schön, 1983), grasping for the 'right answers' on how to proceed (Thompson & Thompson, 2008). However, this is not about having a scientifically correct answer (Schön, 1983), but about the complexity and diversity of the other person's experience. Whiteness behaviours serve white needs and do not truly take in and absorb the depths of what the other person is communicating, or their situation.

A much better way to approach the situation is as a reflexive practitioner who engages in *reflection-in-action*, from a professional knowledge base, including the AASW (2013) *Code of Ethics*, and previous experience/s as a jumping-off point from which responses can be tailored to suit the unlimited range of variables operating at any moment in order to having a sense of ease to both self and the other person (Thompson & Thompson, 2008) (combat is an exhausting state to be in). This line of thinking forms part of the journey of taking competency levels and critical reflection, from technician to professional (Kaye, 2007).

# Adaptive Social Work

Based on the information and discussion of the above concepts, what additional ideas can be used to define adaptive social work practice? To a large extent, it is generated from an intuitive framework for practice; built on solid ontological, epistemological and axiological personal grounds. That is, the critical reflection that is integral to this framework is built on an attitude that is fueled by intuition. The attitude we bring to critical reflection requires responsibility by which Freire (2000) meant careful consideration of the consequences to which an action leads. This is an integral part of every social worker's intuitive framework.

Furthermore, the use of an adaptive framework calls for dynamic engagement; not static work, through a blended critical reflection framework for practice that must include dialogue. This comprises the use and application of Autoethnography to inspire us to critically reflect upon our own privilege and power within a socio-cultural context, through storying. That is, the framework also includes sharing sociologically-informed personal stories; sharing life-stories and life-histories that are significant ways to talk about patterns of privilege and oppression, and an awareness of the importance of critical social theory which can help to identify class positioning. There is a distinction between the two types of stories, as noted above, but being culturally-responsive challenges ideals and long-held beliefs that are conveyed through a lack of problematisation; a lack of questioning and critique, which is what the telling of a life-history story can rectify.

Adaptive social work involves performative practice (Mlcek & Hill, 2016), which is not simply related to the way that practitioners perform, but rather about the way that choices are made, and the reasons why. It is the kind of practice that asks practitioners to justify their *praxis*; their intentional practice (Mlcek, 2013). Performative practice is opposed to propositional behaviours whereby bias and assumptions overshadow good performance in establishing relationships. Rather, performative practice is intentionally focused work that generates opportunities to find out things; to explore possibilities and to capitalise on situations with service users that may at first appear to be limiting. The social worker must overcome such 'limit-situations' (Freire, 1972). For Viero Pinto (1960, cited in Freire, 1972), limit-situations are not 'the impassable boundaries where possibilities end, but the real boundaries where all possibilities begin (they are not) the frontier which separates being from nothingness, but the frontier which separates being from being more' (p. 71). When deep listening; *dadirri* (deep listening) is called for, engaging in sitting quietly with someone is not about doing nothing, but a way of helping to live in two worlds (Ungunmerr-Baumann, 2002). Listening deeply to what is being said is not about mindless contemplation, but a deliberate act of respectful engagement in relationship-building in order to generate trust and pragmatic endeavours. To recognise that people have strengths which they can bring to achieving solutions in their situation is also an act of unselfish practice. Ultimately, having cultural courage (Zubrzycki & Bennett, 2006) is part of the process whereby social workers acknowledge that their being this way with people is 'the being with, not the doing to' (Bennett et al., 2011: 34).

Autoethnography – as part of an innovative Capability Framework progresses the development of cross-cultural competence via cultural responsiveness. Initially, when thinking about practice, there is a need for constant reflecting on reflection; when writing about practice, there is a through-the-mirror (Bolton, 2009) exposure of ideas that moves the reflection metaphor related to looking in a static mirror, to being creative in taking those reflections right through the glass and right past the silvering that is at the back of the mirror. The critical reflection required for culturally-responsive practice is highlighted through the level and extent to which practitioners engage in reflexivity. That is,

> Reflexivity is a *stance* of being able to locate oneself in the picture, to appreciate how one's own self influences [actions]. Reflexivity is potentially more complex than being reflective, in that the potential for understanding the myriad ways

in which one's own presence and perspective influence the knowledge and actions which are created is potentially more problematic than the simple searching for implicit theory. (Fook, 2002: 43)

Essentially, using auto-ethnography with Indigenous and other diverse cultures, is about sharing information and stories with people, and part of that process is to facilitate a safe space so that individuals can rename that knowledge in a conscious act of claiming stories from the past; naming stories from the present, in order to deliberately reclaim heritage. The social worker's part in this reclamation of heritage by sharing stories should be undertaken through a profound and essential decolonising lens that involves deep and respectful listening, as well as an understanding that this kind of engagement has the capacity for healing.

## Conclusion

The legacy of colonisation lives on in the cycle of brokerage and enticement, where those of the oppressed group can be easily-enticed to fit the shoes of the oppressor; as 'agents of change', and in many cases not even knowing that is what is happening. However, social engineering is a scourge; we cannot promote resilience, empowerment, safety and respect for others, if we are not constantly mindful of inappropriate and unchallenged behaviours towards communities; we cannot practise unknowingly when positions of power and privilege impact the social and cultural wellbeing of individuals, families and communities.

We need to use a critical whiteness framework to interrogate and problematise those things we know to be wrong. When we try to engineer Indigenous communities – *we reap what we sow* in terms of continued loss and grief, as well as the disengagement of individuals from whole-of-community endeavours. We need to rethink the influences of a white ontological frame, a white epistemological frame, and a white axiological frame, that, at their most basic, privilege the individual over the collective strength of Indigenous communities.

Over twenty years ago, writers and researchers started publishing about the connections between whiteness and privilege; they also advised on the ideal endeavour of checking positive case studies in order to develop similar qualities and skills required to enable best practice in social work. At the same time, however, as the importance of cultural considerations came into play, these ideals of best practice were also problematised in favour of wise practice. That is, the concept of wise practice recognises that culture matters, and rather than trying to adopt universal 'best practices' that may still include inherent inequities when applied – *universally* – wise practices are best defined as, 'locally-appropriate actions, tools, principles or decisions that contribute significantly to the development of sustainable and equitable conditions' (Wesley-Esquimaux & Calliou, 2010: 19). They are 'idiosyncratic, contextual, textured, and not standardized' (Davis, 1997: 4). Furthermore, Davis suggests that wise practice is textured and probably inconsistent, as well as definitely not a one-size-fits-all concept. Wise practices originate from the wisdom held in Indigenous communities and in those community's own stories of achieving success; it makes sense that such practices can be added to an adaptable social work practice framework, in order to help counter whiteness behaviours. Wise practices in an adaptation framework for social work, are thus based on what so many Indigenous scholars have argued; the importance of identity and strong cultural ties (Cowan, 2008). From these Indigenous ideals for engagement; based on wisdom and respect, we can draw attention to the negative and destructive behaviours of whiteness, and we must always do so; having whiteness does not exempt people from exploitation, it reconciles them to positions of power and privilege. It is for those who have and see nothing else, but in a spirit of praxis, our social work students must pursue something much more relevant and authentic. As Samson (2015: 119) suggests,

> Practice wisdom is the foundation for effective practice and encompasses both the *art* and *science* of social work. The divide

between practice and theory has existed since the profession emerged and practice wisdom is the bridge to this gap. The epistemology and ontology of practice wisdom highlights its importance for research, education and practice for the next generation of social workers.

# References

Bender, K., Negi, N., & Fowler, D. N. (2010). 'Exploring the relationship between self-awareness and student commitment and understanding of culturally responsive social work practice', *Journal of Ethnic and Cultural Diversity in Social Work*, 19(1), 34–53.

Bennett, B., Zubrzycki, J., & Bacon, V. (2011). 'What do we know? The experiences of social workers working alongside Aboriginal people', *Australian Social Work*, 64(1), 20–37.

Boler, M., & M. Zembylas (2003). 'Discomforting truths: The emotional terrain of understanding difference'. In P. Trifonas (ed.). *Pedagogies of difference: Rethinking education for social change* (pp. 110–36). New York: Routledge Falmer.

Bolton, G. (2014). *Reflective practice: writing and professional development*. Melbourne, Australia: Sage.

Booth, K. (1999). 'Three tyrannies', in T. Dunne & N. Wheeler (eds.), *Human Rights in Global Politics* Cambridge, England: Cambridge University Press.

Cowan, D. A. (2008). 'Profound Simplicity of Leadership Wisdom: Exemplary Insight from Miami Nation Chief Floyd Leonard', *International Journal of Leadership Studies*, 4(1), 51–81.

Davis, O. L., Jr. (1997). 'Beyond "Best Practices" Toward Wise Practices', *Journal of Curriculum and Supervision*, 13 (1), 1–5.

Deleuze, G., & Guattari, F. (2013) (trans. Brian Massumi). *A Thousand Plateaus*. London, England: Bloomsbury Academic.

Fejo-King, C. (2013). *Let's Talk Kinship: Innovating Social Work Education, Theory, Research and Practice through Aboriginal Knowledges*. Darwin, Australia: Magpie Goose Publishing.

Fejo-King, C., & Mataira, P. (eds.) (2015). *Expanding the Conversations: International Indigenous social workers' insights into the use of Indigenist knowledge and theory in practice*. Darwin, Australia: Magpie Goose Publishing.

Fook, J. (2002). *Social Work: Critical Theory and Practice*. London: Sage.

Frankenberg, R. (1993). *White Women, Race Matters: The Social Construction of Whiteness*. Abingdon, Oxon, England: Routledge.

Freire, P. (1985). *Politics of Education*. Westport, CT: Greenwood Publishing.

Freire, P. (2000). *Pedagogy of the Oppressed (30th Anniversary edn.)*. New York, NY: Continuum.

Freire, P. (2004). *Pedagogy of Indignation*. New York, NY: Paradigm Publishers.

Goodson, I. (2001, published online 2009). 'The Story of Life History: Origins of the Life History Method in Sociology', *Identity*, 1:2, 129–42. Retrieved from http://dx.doi.org/10.1207/S1532706XID0102_02.

Ife, J. (2008). *Human Rights and Social Work: Towards Rights-Based Practice*. Port Melbourne: Cambridge University Press.

Jamrozik, A. (2009). *Social Policy in the Post-Welfare State: Australian Society in a Changing World*. French's Forest, Australia: Pearson Education Australia.

Lorde, A. (1984). *Sister outsider*. Berkeley, CA: Crossing Press.

Mlcek, S. (2013). 'Are We Doing Enough to Develop Cross-Cultural Competencies for Social Work?' *British Journal of Social Work*, 44(7), 1984–2003.

Mlcek, S. (2017). 'Decolonising methodologies to counter "minority" spaces', *Continuum, Journal of Media & Cultural Studies*, 31(1), 84–92.

Mlcek, S., & Hill, B. (2016). Chapter 6: Cultural Diversity and Competence: A Culturally Responsive Approach. In E. Moore (ed.), *Case Management: Inclusive Community Practice* (pp. 123–42). Melbourne, Australia: Oxford University Press.

Moreton-Robinson, A. (2011). *Whitening Race: Essays in Social and Cultural Criticisms*. Canberra, Australia: Aboriginal Studies Press.

O'Sullivan, S., Hill, B., Bernoth, M., & Mlcek, S. (2016). 'Indigenous approaches to research'. In Z. Schneider, D. Whitehead, G. LoBiondo-Wood, & J. Haber (eds.), *Nursing and Midwifery Research: methods and appraisal for evidence-based practice* (5th edn.). Chatswood, Australia: Elsevier Australia.

Pease, B. (2010). *Undoing Privilege: Unearned Advantage in a Divided World*. London, England: Zed Books.

Samson, P. L. (2015). 'Practice wisdom: the art and science of social work', *Journal of Social Work Practice: Psychotherapeutic Approaches in Health, Welfare and the Community*, 29 (2), 119–31.

Sharkey, J. (2004). 'Lives Stories Don't Tell: Exploring the Untold in Autobiographies', *Curriculum Inquiry*, 34(4), 495–512.

Sue, D. W. (2006). *Multicultural Social Work Practice*. Hoboken, NJ: John Wiley and Sons Inc.

Sue, D. W., & Sue, D. (2008). *Counseling the Culturally Diverse: Theory and Practice*, 5th edn., Hoboken, NJ: John Wiley & Sons, Inc.

Thoms, M. J. (2007). 'Leading an Extraordinary Life: Wise Practices for an HIV Prevention Campaign with Two-Spirited Men.' Unpublished paper, 2-Spirited People of the First Nations, Toronto.

Ungunmerr-Baumann, Miriam Rose (2002). Dadirri: Inner Deep Listening and Quiet Still Awareness. Retrieved from http://nextwave.org.au/wp-content/uploads/Dadirri-Inner-Deep-Listening-M-R-Ungunmerr-Bauman-Refl.pdf.

Wesley-Esquimaux, C., & Calliou, B. (2010). *Best Practices in Aboriginal Community Development: A Literature Review and Wise Practices Approach*. Retrieved from http://communities4families.ca/wp-content/uploads/2014/08/Aboriginal-Community-Development.pdf.

Young, S. (2008). 'Indigenous Child Protection Policy in Australia: Using Whiteness Theory for Social Work', *SITES, New Series*, 5(1), 102–23.

Zubrzycki, J., & Bennett, B. (In collaboration with an Aboriginal Reference Group) (2006). 'Aboriginal Australians'. In E. Wing Hong Chui, & J. Wilson (eds.), *Best Practice in the Fields of Social Work and Human Services* (pp. 192–210). Annandale, NSW: Federation Press.

# SIX

# Transformative Ecosocial Work: Incorporating Being, Thinking and Doing in Practice

*Heather Boetto*

## Abstract

This chapter explores the emerging conceptualisation of ecosocial work and the need for transformative ecosocial change to challenge inherent modernist assumptions underpinning the philosophical base of conventional social work practice. By adopting a distinct philosophical base emphasising holism and interdependence with the natural world, the profession can reconceptualise an ecologically centred approach across ontological (being), epistemological (thinking) and methodological (doing) dimensions of practice. This chapter summarises the elements of transformative ecosocial change, and considers challenges faced by the profession in pursuing transformative change, including political and organisational constraints. Although a transformative approach enhances the profession's capacity for a coherent and ethical response to environmental and social problems, it represents a starting point only, as the development of ecosocial work requires the collective efforts of practitioners, educators, service users and academics.

# Introduction

Since the turn of the century, the place of the natural environment in social work has gained momentum in response to increasing concerns about the inequitable impact of the environmental crisis on individuals, families and communities. There is worldwide consensus that an environmental crisis of considerable magnitude is taking place, involving a range of factors that threaten the ecology upon which humanity depends. These environmental factors are impacting the balance of Earth's ecosystems, predominantly caused by an increase in greenhouse gas emissions since the industrial revolution (Intergovernmental Panel on Climate Change (IPCC), 2014). Pollution of the atmosphere by greenhouse gas emissions is causing an unprecedented rise in Earth's average temperature trends, and subsequently, an increase in climate variability, sea levels and biodiversity loss (IPCC, 2014). Other environmental factors of concern include an exponential increase in world population, an increase in consumption and consumerism in wealthy nations, an increase in poverty in poorer nations, and ongoing conflict between human societies. These factors indicate the complex nature of the current environmental crisis.

The impacts of the environmental crisis, particularly climate variability, is evidenced by an increase in extreme weather events and natural disasters worldwide. While attributing any one particular climatic event to global warming can be problematic, an increase in long-term temperature trends caused by the build-up of greenhouse gas emissions is undoubtedly intensifying the occurrence of extreme weather events and natural disasters (Steffen & Alexander, 2016). In the Asia-Pacific region, a total of 160 natural disasters were recorded in 2015, which was more than a two-fold increase from the previous year. These natural disasters accounted for 47 per cent of the world's total disasters in that year and resulted in over 16,000 fatalities (Economic & Social Commission for Asia and the Pacific (ESCAP), 2016). In Australia, the number of record hot days has doubled since 1960 resulting in an increase in mortality rates during the summer season compared to those in winter (Hughes, Hanna & Fenwick,

2016). In 2009, the Black Saturday bushfires in Victoria caused 173 deaths and is ranked as one of the world's top 10 most deadly bushfires in history (Steffen, Hughes, & Pearce, 2015; Teague, McLeod & Pascoe, 2010). These extreme weather events result in severe social, environmental and economic loss for individuals, families and communities.

Social work services are part of an important multidisciplinary response to global environmental concerns. In a recent study in the United States, which interviewed 373 social workers, 71 per cent reported working with people facing environmental injustices, including food insecurity, unsafe play spaces, air pollution and extreme weather events (Nesmith & Smyth, 2015). In Australia, the importance of social work services in attending to the impacts of drought has been highlighted by increases in mental health issues, stress-related illnesses, poverty, and gender inequalities (Boetto & McKinnon, 2013; Dean & Staines, 2010). More generally, during a heatwave in 2009, the Victorian state ambulance service recorded an increase in emergency calls 34 times the average, resulting in 34 additional deaths (Hughes et al., 2016). It follows that social workers involved in disaster recovery and secondary health services are also likely to experience an increase in demand for services, including crisis counselling, attending to loss and bereavement issues, displacement of homes and social health issues. In addition, social workers are involved in environmental responses at community and policy levels of practice (Appleby, Bell & Boetto, 2017), for example by creating partnerships with organisations, developing social policy at local, state and federal levels of government, collective and community-based strategies, and research.

## Conceptualising Ecosocial Work

Fundamental to ecosocial work is an understanding that the delicate balance of Earth's ecosystems sustains humanity, and alternatively the disruption of healthy ecosystems threatens life on Earth for all living organisms. Ecosocial work understands humanity as having a mutually interdependent relationship with the natural environment, and represents a move away from a predominantly socio-cultural understanding of the environment in conventional social work. Social work authors have contributed widely to the conceptualisation of ecosocial work, and to the development of key attributes that represent an ecosocial approach. Drawing from several authors (for example, Bell, 2013; Besthorn, 2012; Boetto, 2017; Helne & Hirvilammi, 2017; Narhi & Matthies, 2016) fundamental principles relating to ecosocial work include the following:

*Holistic worldview:* Adopting a holistic worldview perceives every aspect of life as interconnected within a much larger system. Not only is human wellbeing dependent on the health of natural ecosystems, but all living organisms share an interconnected dependency on having a healthy ecosystem.

*Environmental sustainability and de-growth:* Environmental sustainability promotes the health of Earth's ecosystems and ensures that demands placed on the natural environment to meet human needs do not compromise or disrupt the balance of Earth's ecosystems. De-growth recognises that over-consumption and over-production within industrialised and industrialising nations is depleting the Earth's natural and finite resources.

*Indigenous worldviews:* Indigenous worldviews recognise an interdependent relationship between humanity and the larger cosmos, and embraces a deeply spiritual nurturing of Country and 'place'. This integration of spirituality and nurturing of 'place' distinguishes Indigenous knowledges from Euro-Western knowledges, and are expressed through many customs and sustainable strategies that care for Earth.

*Global citizenship:* Global citizenship shifts attention from an individual to worldwide perspective and recognises that the behaviours of people in industrialised and industrialising nations are largely responsible for causing environmental injustice in poorer nations. Wealthy nations, such as Australia and the United Kingdom, have historically profited from industry and big business initiatives, which have placed the livelihoods of communities in poorer nations at risk.

*Eco-feminism and critical approaches:* A critical approach recognises the interplay between the environment and broader social and political systems, which cause exploitation, disadvantage and unequal power relations. In particular, eco-feminism highlights the connection between the domination of nature and the exploitation of women, largely from patriarchal structures in society. The United Nations Sustainable Development Goals identify gender equity as one of 17 goals, acknowledging that gender equity is not only a human right, but also necessary for an environmentally sustainable world (http://www.un.org/sustainabledevelopment/sustainable-development-goals/).

*Relational wellbeing:* A relational perspective of wellbeing recognises the interdependence between humans and the natural world, and shifts attention from individual wellbeing to consideration of other species. When an understanding of 'self' becomes 'part' of the natural world, feelings of responsibility towards the wellbeing of all living organisms in order to fulfil wellbeing for ourselves is encouraged.

*Multidimensional practice:* An ecosocial work approach recognises that problems associated with the environmental crisis are complex and consist of various multi-dimensional factors. Ecosocial practice therefore involves environmentally related work at multiple levels, including personal, individual, collective, community and political levels of practice.

## Transformative Ecosocial Change

Although some of the attributes referred to above reflect principles underpinning social work, other attributes represent a divergence or variance from conventional social work practice. In particular, holism with the natural world contradicts human-centred concepts associated with social work's conventional knowledge base (Besthorn, 2013). Human-centred concepts, such as self-determination, empowerment and social justice, often emphasise human progress and individualist notions of wellbeing, thus neglecting the wellbeing of other living organisms. As a profession born during the modernist era of the nineteenth century, many of the values associated with modernist thinking at the time, such as individualism, positivism and industrial capitalism, were adopted and are today incorporated into conventional social work (Webb, 2007). Various social work authors, have argued that social work is at odds with developing an environmentally sustainable society, due to pervasive modernist roots embedded within the profession (for example, Boetto, 2017; Coates, 2005; Ferreira, 2010; Ife, 2013). For example, increasing participation in the welfare state, and working towards full employment, inadvertently supports industrial capitalism, which is critiqued for contributing to the global environmental crisis through the unsustainable use of Earth's natural resources (Coates, 2005; Ferreira, 2010; Ife, 2013).

As a profession currently in transition towards establishing an ecological centred stance, the co-dependency between social work and the welfare state represents a major dilemma for the profession. This realisation provides the means and opportunity for the profession to challenge modernism through the re-conceptualisation of social work's philosophical base. Transformative change involves the challenging of fixed assumptions within the profession's philosophical base that separate humanity from the natural world towards a reconceptualisation of humans as a holistic part of the natural world (Boetto, 2017; Gray & Coates, 2015). This approach represents a paradigmatic shift in orientation about the place of humans in the natural world. By adopting a distinct philosophical base that emphasises holism and interdependence with the natural world, social work can promote transformative change towards a more sustainable environment.

The philosophical base of practice has received limited attention in literature, yet is foundational for advancing transformative ecosocial change. The meaning of philosophical concepts can be adapted from authors such as Guba and Lincoln (2004) and Staller (2012), who depict ontology, epistemology and methodology as a set of philosophical concepts, consisting of the most abstract (ontology) at the top and the most concrete (methods) at the bottom. Staller (2012) argues that this layered approach is useful for understanding the links between each level. For example, the philosophical base of social work practice is made up of ontological and epistemological assumptions, which inform the methodological or 'doing' aspects of practice (Aymer & Okitikpi, 2000). A transformative ecosocial approach challenges inherent modernist assumptions in conventional social work by reconceptualising a distinct philosophical base, which is consistent with principles underpinning ecosocial work. The figure below (Figure 6.1) represents the proposed ecosocial model for practice, which articulates a consistent philosophical base across the ontological (being), epistemological (thinking) and methodological (doing) dimensions of practice. A brief outline of ontology, epistemology and methodology, and how these relate to transformative ecosocial change will then be outlined.

**Figure 6.1: Transformative ecosocial model (Boetto, 2016: 5)**

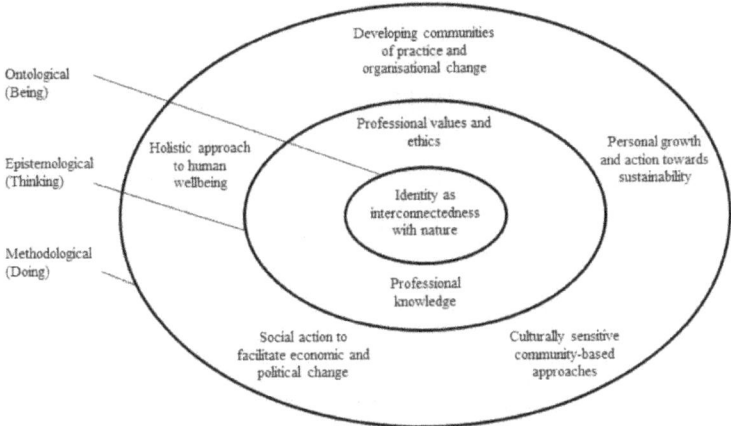

*Ontology (being):* addresses questions about the nature of being, existence and reality. For example, a significant question is 'what is the nature of reality?' For social work, this involves the profession's worldview, and subsequent beliefs and attitudes of the practitioner. Social work's philosophical position concerning the natural environment, as well as the personal dimension of how practitioners relate to the natural environment will determine professional approaches and activities in practice. As a profession, social work has traditionally been associated with a modernist ontological view of nature, which views humans as separate to and independent from nature (Coates, 2005; Besthorn, 2013). In developing a coherent and ethical response to environmental and social problems, social work needs to examine its professional identity and connectedness with regard to the natural environment. Unless social workers are able to personally identify with the natural environment and be consciously aware of the interconnectedness between humanity and the natural environment, then transformative ecosocial work practice at the professional level may be constrained.

*Epistemology (thinking):* addresses questions about the nature of knowledge and how knowledge is created. Relevant questions include 'what counts as knowledge?' For ecosocial work practice, this involves recognising marginalised knowledges, such as Indigenous Knowledges, Global Southern perspectives and eco-feminist perspectives, which challenge prevailing, dominant and oppressive discourses. Thinking also refers to the application of professional knowledge, including theory, values and ethics. Examples of relevant professional knowledge for ecosocial work may include deep ecology, ecotherapy, permaculture and environmental science. Professional values may involve ecological sustainability and ecological justice for all living organisms.

Although the profession has an extensive array of theoretical knowledge (epistemology), for example, anti-oppressive practice, critical social work, and structural approaches, it is argued that social work has an under-developed ontological base (Bell, 2012). If the link between ontology and epistemology are clear, then a weakness of one (ontology) undermines the strength of the others (epistemology and methodology). Essentially, the profession's epistemological knowledge base is at risk of implicitly relying on an inappropriate ontological base informed by modernist ontological assumptions, unless the profession works towards redressing this gap. As discussed, modernist ontological assumptions associated with individualism, positivism, and industrial capitalism are at odds with the emerging principles of ecosocial work. An ontological base emphasising modernist assumptions risks rendering social work's epistemological base as being incoherent and lacking in direction.

*Methodology (doing):* is the plan or approach for undertaking action and lies behind the particular methods being used. For social work, this involves the actions, interventions and strategies used in everyday interaction with individuals, families and communities. These strategies are implemented at multidimensional levels of practice, including the personal (self), individual, group, community, and political levels (Boetto, 2016, 2017). Examples of ecosocial interventions include the development of communities of practice, organisational change, advocacy, social action, sustainable community development, disaster recovery, and ecotherapy. However, as standalone practice strategies, they do not complement a coherent philosophical approach to addressing environmental and social problems. Rather, change at the ontological level of practice integrating principles of holism and interdependence with the natural world has the capacity to bring about broad-based and deep change to the way social work's philosophical base of practice is conceptualised (Boetto, 2017).

## Transformative Ecosocial Change Challenges

Social work operates within the context of society, and is influenced by a range of external factors, including Euro-Western culture, world politics, and organisational policy. These factors, as well as a lack of professional research create barriers for operationalising transformative change within the profession. These factors will be briefly discussed below:

Social work was formed within parts of Europe during the nineteenth century, and has typically characterised Euro-Western traditions, culture and philosophy. Globalisation has led to increasing consideration of distinct knowledges, and ethical responsibilities denote a commitment to cultural diversity and localised approaches to practice. However, despite acknowledgment of Indigenous and Global Southern knowledges, it is important to note that the transformative ecosocial change approach described in this chapter was developed from a Euro-Western frame of reference. This critique acknowledges the dominance of Euro-Western culture pervasive in social work and climate change discourse within broader society. It also acknowledges the invisibility of whiteness and the concept of 'white as normal' embedded within the profession (Bennett, 2015; Walter, Taylor & Habibis, 2013). While many Euro-Western social work practitioners endeavour to remedy socialisation processes relating to modernism, many are unaware of the invisibility of 'separateness from nature' embedded within society and the profession that impedes an understanding of the importance of transformative ecosocial change. For example, many Indigenous cultures share a spiritual unity with the larger cosmos that transcends Euro-Western understandings by being distinctly holistic in such a way that there are no boundaries between people, Earth and the larger cosmos. It is therefore important to acknowledge the epistemological value of Indigenous and other marginalised knowledges to inform a transformative ecosocial approach within the profession.

A relative lack of political will in some parts of the world to address the global environmental crisis, such as Australia and the United States, stifle ecosocial work efforts through reduced resources and funding towards environmental sustainability. In 2017 the United States president withdrew participation from the 2015 Paris Agreement on climate change mitigation, effectively removing one of the world's biggest greenhouse gas emitters from a global committment to capping global temperature rises. The Australian Government has also demonstrated limited interest in developing robust policy to address climate change, developing a range of ad-hoc schemes, rather than implementing a broad-based government comittment towards climate change action. For example, the government has reduced funding allocated to the environment by 14 per cent since 2013 (http://www.climatecouncil.org.au/budget2017). It also abolished the independent advisory group, the Climate Commission, in 2013 (Kenny, 2013). Further, it is argued that the majority of national policies addressing the environmental crisis within industrialised nations operate within the dominant economic model responsible for climate change, emphasising continued economic growth at the expense of broader issues relating to global poverty, social injustice, and depletion of the natural environment (Blewitt, 2015; Castro, 2004). Nevertheless, while nation states grapple with addressing the environmental crisis, local communities and the private sector are leading the way with the development of climate change adaptation and mitigation strategies. Social work therefore, has the opportunity to take leadership and participate in collective and multi-disciplinary approaches to develop ecosocial work, for example by engaging with local renewable energy schemes and grass-roots community projects.

Human services practice also takes place within an organisational context, which influences the priorities and policies of employing organisations. Often, human service workers are faced with competing principles within organisations that constrain or compromise environmental care and concern (McKinnon, 2013). An emerging post-welfare state paradigm has meant reduced funds allocated to social policy projects and short-term competitive-based funding contracts for organisations that operate within a market-centred ideology (Wallace & Pease, 2011). In addition to this, the 'environment' within the welfare sector has traditionally been conceptualised in socio-cultural terms, including institutional, social and cultural systems, rather than recognition of the natural environment as fundamental to human wellbeing. Funding priorities and outcomes therefore often emphasise socio-cultural issues, and short-term outcomes, creating barriers for practitioners concerned with the disproportionate impacts of the environmental crisis on disadvantaged groups. Nevertheless, this practice reality is not dissimilar to other practice challenges faced by social workers that relate to fulfilling the profession's ethical commitments. By understanding the influence of conservative economic ideology on human service organisations, social workers can begin to develop practice strategies that address challenges and create opportunities for ecosocial practice.

Without further research into practice approaches, ecosocial work is at risk of retaining its current marginalised status within the profession. Continuing the momentum for change requires further research with regard to practice approaches that are applicable across a wide range of practice settings. The transformative ecosocial model may have potential, but requires further research into the usefulness and effectiveness of applying this framework in practice. Molyneux (2010) conducted a comprehensive literature review on ecosocial work and concluded that literature relating to practice is vague, lacks application and detail of practice approaches, and is disconnected from everyday interaction with service users. She argues that unless research is undertaken to further develop practice detail then ecosocial work will remain a peripheral rather than mainstream approach in social work. Although ecosocial work has progressed since Molyneux's review in 2010, little empirical research relating to practice has been conducted since then. Future research could take the form of action research and/or cooperative inquiry, which involves collaboration with stakeholders, including practitioners, Indigenous groups and people likely to access social work services, to generate knowledge about ecosocial work practice approaches.

## Conclusion

Transformative, holistic ecosocial change refers to a fundamental re-orientation of human-centred perceptions of the world toward views that reflect a holistic and interdependent view of humans as part of the natural world (Boetto, 2017; Gray & Coates, 2015). This re-orientation requires the profession to acknowledge the influence of the modernist discourse on social work, both from the past and within contemporary society (Ferreira, 2010; Webb, 2007). Various authors contend that social work has contributed to the exploitation of the natural environment by helping people to adapt and participate in a society where the dominant economic model is centred on values of individualism, competition and economic growth. Consequently, the co-dependency between social work and the modernist discourse represents a major dilemma, especially at a time when the profession has recently committed to protecting the natural environment and promoting sustainability. One way to challenge the modernist discourse in social work is to examine the philosophical base of practice and reconceptualise ontological, epistemological and methodological assumptions in such a way that they are congruent with attributes of holistic ecosocial work. While social work is faced with challenges that impede progress towards transformative ecosocial change, it should not deter collective efforts towards developing coherent philosophical change within the profession.

# References

Appleby, K., Bell, K., & Boetto, H. (2017). 'Climate change adaptation: Community action, disadvantaged groups and practice implications for social work', *Australian Social Work,* 70(1), 78–91.

Aymer, C., & Okitikpi, T. (2000). 'Epistemology, ontology and methodology: What's that got to do with social work?' *Journal of Social Work Education,* 19(1), 67–75.

Bell, K. (2012). 'Towards a post-conventional philosophical base for social work', *British Journal of Social Work,* 42(3), 408–23.

Bell, K. (2013). 'Post-conventional approaches to gender, climate change and social justice'. In M. Alston & K. Whittenbury (eds.), *Research, action and policy: Addressing the gendered impacts of climate change* (pp. 53–62). London: Springer.

Bennett, B. (2015). Stop deploying your white priviledge on me! Aboriginal and Torres Strait Islander engagement with the Australian Association of Social Workers. *Australian Social Work,* 68(1), 19–31.

Besthorn, F. (2012). 'Deep Ecology's contributions to social work: A ten-year retrospective', *International Journal of Social Welfare,* 21(3), 248–59.

Besthorn, F. (2013). 'Radical equalitarian ecological justice: A social work call for action'. In M. Gray, J. Coates & T. Hetherington (eds.), *Environmental social work* (pp. 31–45). London: Routledge.

Blewitt, J. (2015). *Understanding sustainable development* (2nd edn.). Oxon: ENG: Routledge.

Boetto, H. (2016). 'Developing ecological social work for micro level practice'. In J. McKinnon & M. Alston (eds.), *Ecological social work: Towards sustainability* (pp. 59–77). Houndmills: Palgrave Macmillan.

Boetto. H. (2017). 'A transformative eco-social model: Challenging modernist assumptions in social work', *British Journal of Social Work,* 47(1), 48–67

Boetto, H., & McKinnon, J. (2013). 'Gender and climate change in Australia: A review of differences', *Critical Social Work.* 14 (1), 15–18. Retrieved from http://www1.uwindsor.ca/criticalsocialwork/system/files/Boetto_McKinnon.pdf.

Castro, C. J. (2004). 'Sustainable development: Mainstream and critical perspectives', *Organisation and Environment,* 17(2), 195–225.

Coates, J. (2005). 'The environmental crisis: Implications for social work', *Journal of Progressive Human Services,* 16(1), 25–49.

Dean, J. G., & Stain, H. J. (2010). 'Mental health impact for adolescents living with prolonged drought', *Australian Journal of Rural Health,* 18(1), 32–7.

Economic & Social Commission for Asia and the Pacific (ESCAP) (2016). Disasters in Asia and the Pacific year in review. United Nations. Retrieved from http://www.unescap.org/sites/default/files/2015_Year%20in%20 Review_final_PDF_1.pdf.

Ferreira, S. B. (2010). 'Eco-spiritual social work as a precondition for social development', *Ethics & Social Welfare,* 4(1), 3–23.

Gray, M. & Coates, J. (2015). 'Changing gears: Shifting to an environmental perspective in social work education', *Social Work Education,* 34(5), 502–12.

Guba, E. G., & Lincoln, Y. S. (2004). 'Competing paradigms in qualitative research: Theories and issues'. In S. N. Hesse-Biber & P. Leavy (eds.), *Approaches to qualitative research: A reader on theory and practice* (pp. 17–38). New York, NY: Oxford University Press.

Helne, T., & Hirvilammi, T. (2017). 'The relational conception of wellbeing as a catalyst for the ecosocial transition'. In A. Matthies & K. Närhi (eds.), *Ecosocial transition of societies: Contribution of social work and social policy* (pp. 36–53). Abingdon, ENG: Routledge.

Hughes, L., Hanna, E., & Fenwick, J. (2016). The silent killer: Climate change and the health impacts of extreme heat. Climate Council. Retrieved from https://www.climatecouncil.org.au/uploads/b6cd8665c633434e8d0291 0eee3ca87c.pdf.

Ife, J. (2013). *Community development in an uncertain world: Vision, analysis and practice.* Port Melbourne, VIC: Cambridge Press.

Intergovernmental Panel on Climate Change (IPCC) (2014). *Climate change 2014 synthesis report: Summary for policy makers*: Author. Retrieved from https://www.ipcc.ch/pdf/assessment-report/ar5/syr/AR5_SYR_FINAL_SPM.pdf

*Kenny, Chris (Sept. 2013).* 'Coalition delivers on promise to axe Climate Commission', *Australian.* Retrieved from https://www.theaustralian.com. au/national-affairs/climate/coalition-delivers-on-promise-to-axe-climate-commission/news-story/d937226cac1ddf655ebb518a75a49c3e.

McKinnon, J. (2013). 'The environment: A private concern or a professional practice issue for Australian social workers', *Australian Social Work,* 66(2), 156-170.

Molyneux, R. (2010). 'The practical realities of eco-social work: A review of literature', *Critical Social Work,* 11(2), 61–9. Retrieved from http://www1. uwindsor.ca/criticalsocialwork/the-practical-realities-of-ecosocial-work-a-review-of-the-literature

Närhi, K., & Matthies, A. (2016). 'The ecosocial approach in social work as a framework for structural social work', *International Social Work.* Online access 14 June 2016.

Nesmith, A. & Smyth, N. (2015). 'Environmental justice and social work education: Social workers' professional perspectives', *Social Work Education,* 34(5), 484–501.

Staller, K. M. (2012). 'Epistemological boot camp: The politics of science and what every qualitative researcher needs to know to survive in the academy', *Qualitative Social Work,* 12(4), 395–413.

Steffen, W., & Alexander, D. (2016). 'Super-charged storms in Australia: The influence of climate change', Climate Council of Australia. Retrieved from https://www.climatecouncil.org.au/uploads/3ca765b1c65cb52aa74eec2 ce3161618.pdf.

Steffen, W., Hughes, L., & Pearce, A. (2015). *Climate change 2015: Growing risks, critical choices,* Climate Council of Australia. Retrieved from https:// www.climatecouncil.org.au/uploads/153781bfef5afe50eb6adf77e650cc71.pdf.

Teague B, McLeod, R. & Pascoe, S. (2010). 2009 Victorian bushfires royal commission: Final report: Parliament of Victoria. Retrieved from http:// www.royalcommission.vic.gov.au/finaldocuments/summary/PF/VBRC_ Summary_PF.pdf.

Wallace, J., & Pease, B. (2011). 'Neoliberalism and Australian Social Work: Accommodation or resistance', *Journal of Social Work,* 11(2), 132–42.

Walter, M., Taylor, S., & Habibis, D. (2013). 'Australian social work is white'. In B. Bennett, S. Green, S. Gilbert & D., Bessarab (eds.), *Our voices: Aboriginal and Torres Strait Islander social work* (pp. 230–47). South Yarra, VIC: Palgrave Macmillan.

Webb, S. A. (2007). 'The comfort of strangers: Social work, modernity and late Victorian England, Part 1', *European Journal of Social Work,* 10(1), 30–54.

PART II

# INNOVATIONS IN SOCIAL WORK EDUCATION AND PRACTICE

# SEVEN

# International Student Mobility Programs 2010–16

*Karen Bell and Susan Mlcek*

## Abstract

This chapter provides an overview of the range of study abroad programs offered to social work students at Charles Sturt University (CSU), 2010–16. With several years' experience facilitating these short-term programs and drawing on our research findings, we outline the impacts of these initiatives on students and host communities along with our guiding principles. We also outline some of the challenges and future potential of these programs for social work education at CSU.

## Overview of International Mobilitiy Programs

Many Australian universities now offer opportunities for outbound international learning in order to comply with the internationalisation agendas of their own university and government initiatives, and to enrich students' learning (Zuchowski et al., 2018). International engagement in social work education includes a range of activities such as visiting scholar programs for academics, international placements, semester-long study and full-year student exchanges as well as short-term study abroad programs of two to four weeks duration (VeLure & Fisher, 2013). These activities can potentially provide transformative learning experiences in addition to the standard curriculum and standard modes of course delivery for participants to: enhance cultural awareness, explore privilege, to contribute to social justice initiatives, to expand worldviews and to appreciate the global nature of social work (Bell, Moorhead & Boetto, 2017).

Despite their brevity, short-term international programs led by experienced academic facilitators offer opportunities for transformative experiential learning. The intensity of these programs can serve to unsettle students' beliefs and to challenge frames of reference, especially in relation to ethnocentrism (Wehbi, 2009). As long as opportunities for guided reflection are integral to the program, paradigm shifts can be encouraged, neo-colonialism can be discouraged and global citizenship can be enhanced (Macias, 2013).

Another important aspect of program delivery is the nature of our engagement with host agencies and communities. Effective academic facilitation here too plays a key role in ensuring our programs are offered in an ethical manner, based on respectful partnerships with host entities rather than on neo-colonialism (Nuttman-Shwartz & Berger, 2012). Students have various motivations for participating in these programs including; altruism, personal development, professional development and cultural curiosity (Nuttman-Shwartz & Berger, 2012).

## International Programs at CSU

Our academic staff work with CSU Global to plan and deliver our international education opportunities. As a division of the university, the team at CSU Global manages the administrative, logistical and procedural aspects of a range of international education opportunities, including the mobility programs. This enables academic staff to focus on the educational aspect of the programs. CSU Global also works closely with academics on applications for Commonwealth government funding.

Prior to 2010, most student-centred international social work education had been in the form of semester-long and year-long exchange study (Bell & Anscombe, 2013). These types of programs are typically more accessible for younger students studying full time, on-campus. Opportunities for extended international engagement also favour those with more resources rather than those from lower socioeconomic backgrounds. Taking these issues into consideration and given the profile of social work and human services students at CSU, we were motivated to provide a wider range of international opportunities. We were keen to offer opportunities that were more accessible for part-time, mature age students, often from lower socioeconomic backgrounds and studying by distance education mode. Thus, working in partnership with CSU Global, the short-term programs were initiated in an attempt to enhance the extra-curricular activities for all students. A 'short-term program' is defined as any program in which the active, in-country phase is less than a semester (VeLure & Fisher, 2013). The duration of programs at CSU has generally been 10–14 days.

To improve the accessibility of CSU short-term programs, most programs are offered only after external funding is secured in order to reduce the cost of participation. Academic staff interested in facilitating a program liaise with CSU Global to submit applications for federal government funding, usually through the Department of Foreign Affairs and Trade (DFAT) and the Department of Education and Training (DET). The DFAT funding is offered as part of its New Colombo Plan to support undergraduate students to engage in a range of longer term as well as shorter term international programs in the Asia-Pacific region (DFAT, 2018). The DET funding is offered via its Endeavour Funding scheme with the objective of supporting undergraduate and postgraduate students (in coursework programs) to engage in study overseas and to encourage Australian universities to develop international partnerships for research and teaching purposes (DET, 2018). Since 2010, CSU has had sustained success in securing funding for international programs and this enables CSU Global to significantly reduce the cost of each program for participating students.

In addition to our partnership with CSU Global, some programs have also involved partner organisations in host locations. The host organisations typically manage the on-site program for our groups and these programs usually involve visits to community agencies, local orientation, cultural awareness workshops, and practical arrangements in relation to accommodation, transport, security and the like.

# Study Abroad Programs for Social Work Students

In the years 2010–17, we facilitated programs to India, Samoa, Indonesia, Malaysia and South Korea. For 2018–19, there are plans in place to facilitate programs to Ireland, China and India. The first study abroad program for social work students in 2010 was co-facilitated by Bill Anscombe and Karen Bell. This program consisted of a two-week visit to the rural village of Malavli, in India and was run in partnership with the India Study Abroad Centre (ISAC) (Anscombe & Bell, 2013). Malavli is approximately 2–3 hours by road, east of Mumbai in the state of Maharashtra. The aim of this program was to provide students with an international experience through which they could engage in cross-cultural issues through field work in local community welfare agencies. It was also hoped that the group's involvement with local agencies would result in positive contributions to the host community, however modest. The mobility program also enabled the social work discipline to make a significant contribution to the University's Strategic Plan as well as the Faculty of Arts Operational Plan in relation to internationalisation objectives. The 2010 program was also systematically evaluated with pre-program and post-program surveys and in summary, the findings indicated positive outcomes for students in relation to their conceptualisation of social work as a global profession (Bell & Anscombe, 2013).

A particularly pleasing outcome of the inaugural program was that two students applied, post-program, for a small grant through the School of Humanities and Social Sciences Lila Kirilik Social Justice Fund. The application was successful and the small grant was delivered to a community child welfare agency in 2012 to fund the installation of a water filtration system. The students' initiative in attaining the grant resulted in significant benefits to the agency and the children it serves, as well as providing CSU students with experience in writing a submission for funding and delivering a tangible, ecosocial outcome.

In 2011, Heather Boetto, Bernadette Moorhead and Karen Bell co-facilitated another program to Malavli, again in partnership with ISAC. In addition to the generic program of agency visits, de-briefing sessions and guided discussions, the co-facilitators also offered a series of three workshops for critical reflection each focused on a key theme – ecosocial work, gender and professional identity. Drawing on decolonising approaches to international field work, the pedagogical foundation for this program was based on the work of Rotabi et al. (2006) and VeLure (2013). The format for the workshops was based on Fook and Gardner's (2007) structured approach to critical reflection, to encourage students to draw on specific concrete experiences as they considered intersecting macro-level issues and their own professional and personal development. The outcomes of these workshops are detailed in Moorhead, Boetto and Bell (2014), Boetto, Moorhead and Bell (2014) and in Bell, Boetto and Moorhead (2017).

In 2012, Heather Barton and Bill Anscombe co-facilitated a third visit to Malavli. A parallel project funded by 'CSU Green' was run in conjunction with this program, with Heather Boetto and Karen Bell leading the research team. The research team also included colleagues from divisions of CSU, including CSU Travel as well as CSU Green. The focus of the program was on environmental sustainability and part of the funding was used to develop a series of six optional online workshops for social work students on environmental issues and global citizenship. Funding was also used to support a series of tree-planting workshops as a measure to offset the carbon emissions generated through international air travel. Students and colleagues were encouraged to participate in tree-planting sessions at various locations on the CSU Wagga Wagga campus. To date, we have also offered one other program to Malavli, facilitated by Therese Jones-Mutton and Heather Barton. It is envisaged that at some stage, we will work again with our host partner – Beyond Borders (formerly ISAC) – to return to Malavli.

In 2014, Susan Mlcek led a program to Indonesia, supported by the Bandung School of Social Welfare. The focus of this program was disability and participants had opportunities to observe how an assets-based model of community development could be applied 'on the ground' utilising indigenous knowledges. The group of ten students undertook a cross-cultural orientation program at the International Language College in Bandung in the first week of the visit and engaged in field work during the second week. The field work in particular highlighted the differences between individualist and collectivist societies. The power of experiential learning *in situ* can be discomforting, especially as participants negotiate with and adapt to the communities in which they are located. The centrality of praxis-oriented program facilitated is once again highlighted, as students are reminded that they cannot practise unknowingly (Mlcek, 2014).

In 2015, we offered our first program to Samoa, facilitated by Garth Norris and Karen Bell. The focus of this program was on community engagement and environmental sustainability. This program was run in partnership with Projects Abroad as the host-country agency, with an office and several support staff based in Apia. Twelve students participated in the two-week program with agency visits to Apia Hospital, Tafaigata Prison facilities (Upolu and Savaii), the Office of the Ombudsman and National Human Rights Institution, community mental health, acute mental health, Victims Support, a school for children living with disabilities and a mainstream primary school. Staff and students had experiential learning opportunities in community development work through a nutrition program delivered on-site at the local market through a 'zumba' exercise workshops. Opportunities for group work and session leadership were also offered at a local school, through Project Abroad's nutrition program. Students and staff also engaged with service users at the Tafaigata Prison facilities. The group developed and delivered a professional development program for workers at the prison. Staff and students were fortunate enough to stay with local families for the duration of the program and this provided many rich experiences for cultural immersion and learning from host families.

A program specifically for a small group of coursework masters-level students was offered in 2016 when Karen Bell facilitated a program to Seoul, South Korea. As part of this program, students attended the International Social Work and Social Development conference in week 1 and then participated in a partnership program for international students at Soongsil University in week 2.

Also in 2016, Belinda Cash and Ndungi Wa Mungai facilitated a program to Malaysia, run in partnership with the Universiti Sains Malaya in Penang. This program focused on ageing and disability policy and service delivery, with students visiting agencies to observe programs in action. This program also involved liaison with the Malaysian Association of Social Workers and there is potential for ongoing relationships and research collaboration in the fields of ageing and disability.

Programs have also been offered to other locations in India, including several programs to Kerala in 2015 and 2017, in partnership with Rajagiri College, facilitated by Heather Boetto and Belinda Cash. Also in 2017, Bernadette Moorhead and Lava Kohaupt worked with Beyond Borders to facilitate a program in Goa. Plans are underway for programs to Ireland and China in 2018 and in 2019, we will return to Rajagiri College in Kerala for the Dyuti conference.

## What Frames Our Study Abroad Programs in Social Work?

In developing opportunities for our students to gain international field experience, social work academics are guided by the vision and mission of the social work discipline, the university's ethos and the university's commitment to ethical engagement and global citizenship – *Yindyamarra Winhanganha*.

### Figure 7.1: Guiding principles

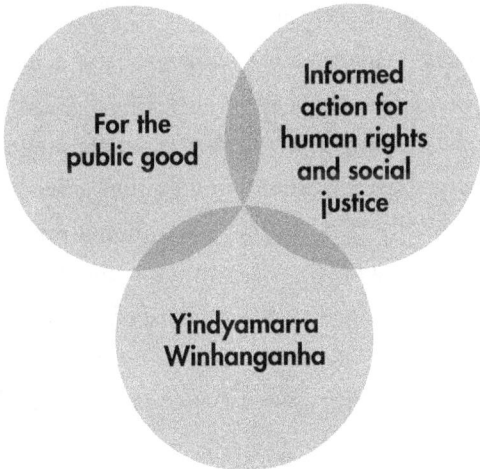

For the public good

Informed action for human rights and social justice

Yindyamarra Winhanganha

*Yindyamarra Winhanganha* is a Wiradjuri phrase gifted to the university by Wiradjuri elders and adopted by CSU to represent the university's approach to education. The phrase means 'the wisdom of respectfully knowing how to live well in a world worth living in'. This ethos is central to our international mobility programs as we encourage our students' commitment to global citizenship.

The university motto – 'for the public good' – also sits well with the broad aims of social work and our professional code of ethics. The social work and human services' vision statement – 'informed action for human rights and social justice' – is another important reference point for our international programs. The vision statement emphasises the need for purposeful, active engagement by well-informed social workers, with capacity for understanding and articulating theory as it underpins ethical practice. These guiding principles are utilised as we work with students at all stages of our international programs – from the recruitment phase through to the post-program phase.

## Preparing Our Students

From our initial involvement in 2010, we have developed and refined a system of pre-departure orientation and post-program follow-up as well as academic facilitation during the actual program. Participants are generally recruited at the start of each academic year, when information about upcoming programs is circulated via online subject sites and during classes on-campus. After students' applications are assessed and participant groups confirmed, the participant group is notified about pre-program orientation. The pre-program/preparation phase typically runs across at least 8 weeks prior to the departure date. We have a dedicated online site for our international programs and this sits within our standard online learning environment, so students are familiar with the online platform. From this site, academic facilitators offer at least three pre-departure (synchronous online) meetings and a range of asynchronous text-based, video and other resources (see Figure 7.2):

## Figure 7.2: Pre-departure phase

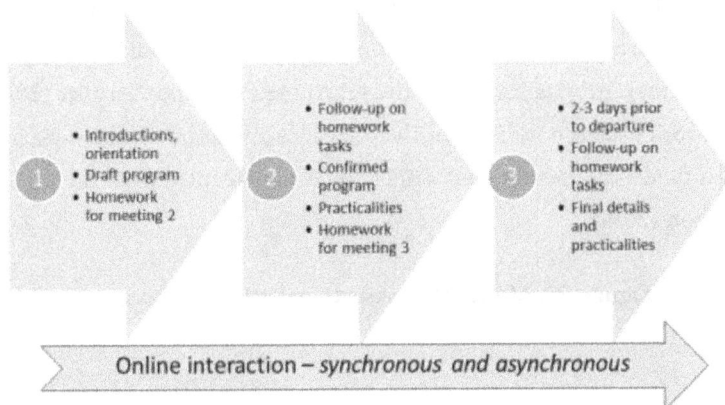

## The Active Phase of International Programs

Most of our programs have been offered over two weeks, with week 1 focused on community orientation, cross-cultural awareness and basic language skills. Week 2 typically involves a range of field work opportunities – some observational and some quite 'hands-on'. Over the years, participants have engaged with local community welfare agencies in the various fields of practice including: out-of-home care for young children, services for people living with disabilities, mental health facilities, sexual health services, women's community development programs, health services, environmental protection agencies, 'slum' projects and human rights organisations working at a macro-level of practice.

Despite the brief nature of the field work immersion, students have made some tangible contributions to host communities over the years. For example, students have worked with agencies: on applications for external funding, the development of policy and procedure manuals, updating service-user records, delivering presentations to client groups, assisting agency workers in day-to-day activities, fund-raising and other practical tasks.

Facilitators typically offer to students a range of opportunities for de-briefing and guided critical reflection. The de-briefing is at times informal and 'as-needed' and at other times, it is offered as part of a scheduled, structured group activity. Opportunities for guided reflection are also built-into most programs to encourage students to reflect in multidimensional ways on their experiences. Over the years, the Fook and Gardner (2007) framework has been utilised for these sessions and at other times, we have used a model of intersectional, critical reflection adapted from the work of Mattsson (2014):

Figure 7.3: Model of Intersectional critical reflection

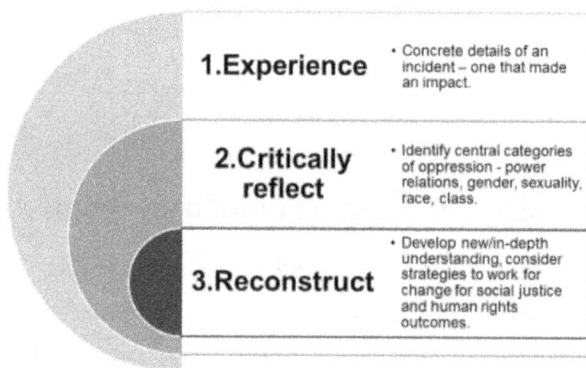

Toward the end of each program, facilitators work with students to provide feedback to the host agencies as requested and in some instances, students are also invited to provide formal, written feedback to the academic facilitators for official CSU projects (with ethics approval in place). In the post-program phase, facilitators hold at least one online meeting with participants as a way to officially 'end' the program and to gain verbal feedback from students. CSU Global also requests feedback from students and academic facilitators. Many students from past programs have been involved in subsequent promotional activities to raise awareness amongst their peers as to the opportunities on-offer and the impacts of these experiences on their learning. For example, students have become CSU Global ambassadors during orientation week, and some students have participated in presentations at residential schools and on-campus classes.

# Outcomes for Participants, the University and Host Communities

Over the years, Social Work academics have systematically gathered data on international programs, provided structured, ethical educational opportunities for students, conducted research projects and published in high quality, peer reviewed outlets. Efforts are ongoing to sustain international research collaborations and to consolidate partnerships with universities, community welfare agencies and social justice enterprises in host locations.

From the research, key ingredients for success centre on the active cultivation of students' awareness of global social work issues. As these programs are intense, active academic facilitation, along with experiential learning and opportunities for guided, critical reflection are critically important. Without careful, structured and systemic academic facilitation, there is a risk to the quality of these programs and a risk to the university's reputation as an ethical global citizen.

> The power of this type of experiential learning is enhanced when opportunities for guided reflection during the on-site phase along with consistent academic facilitation by faculty can be extended beyond the life of the programme and holistically woven throughout social work curricula. With careful planning, sustained facilitation and adequate resourcing, short-term study abroad programmes can make a positive contribution to ethical, social work professional development and global citizenship. (Bell, Moorhead & Boetto, 2015: 12)

The university's reputation as a provider of structured, ethical international programs in social work has resulted in collaborations with other universities and in international research projects, such as the *Going Places Project* (see Mlcek & Bell, 2018). Publications emerging from our international program have explored some specific themes such as professional identity (Moorhead, Boetto & Bell, 2014), environmental issues (Boetto, Moorhead & Bell, 2014), gender (Bell, Moorhead & Boetto, 2017) and online ecosocial work education (Boetto & Bell, 2015). In addition, several CSU social work academics have also published on other aspects of international social work education (Cox & Pawar, 2013; Johnson & Moorhead, 2010; Pawar, Hanna & Sheridan, 2004; Pawar 2010, 2013, 2014, 2016; Trede, Bowles and Bridges, 2013).

In relation to outcomes for host communities and agencies and plans for consolidating partnerships with host organisations and communities, the following table provides an overview:

**Table 7.1: Examples of engagement with international partners**

| Organisation | Nature of engagement | Potential for ongoing engagement |
|---|---|---|
| **India** Beyond Borders (formerly India Study Abroad Centre, ISAC) – Malavli and Goa. | Multiple programs since 2010 – ongoing (Malavli). 2017 – Goa. Seminars, community orientation, cultural workshops, opportunities for professional engagement and research collaboration. | Consolidation of partnerships with Beyond Borders and agencies in Malavli and Goa. |
| **India** Rajigiri College, Kerala. | 2015, 2017, 2019 – In partnership with Social Work academics from Rajigiri College and community workers – co-facilitation of conference workshops, presentations, research projects. | January 2019 – program to Kerala to attend conference and co-facilitate workshops, engage in meetings to plan research projects and co-publication. |
| **South Korea** Soongsil University, Seoul. | 2016 – one-week program of seminars, community agency workshops, cultural orientation, engagement with international relations team and social work academics. | Research – potential research and publication partnerships with social work staff at SU, Social Work Department/ gender projects. |

| Malaysia Universiti of Malaya, Kuala Lumpur Malaysian Association of Social Work National Council Social Welfare. | 2016 – Engagement with social work academics and professional association leadership team. | Potential for research collaboration in relation to aged care, disability service delivery. |
|---|---|---|
| Indonesia Bandung School of Social Welfare, Indonesia. | 2015 – Partnership with Bandung, community visits. | Potential for ongoing programs and partnerships. |
| Samoa Projects Abroad Samoan Prison Authority – Tafaigata Prison Samoan Victims Support Group Apia Hospital, Samoa Human Rights Office – Ombudsman Red Cross School for children with disabilities Community mental health | Commenced 2015 during mobility program; student and staff volunteer work at prison – assessment of prisoners, case notes, assessment reports, and development of resources. Academic staff organised and co-facilitated a professional development session for prison staff. | Provision of resources for case management of clients, professional development of staff, rehabilitation of clients. Potential for research and placement opportunities with future programs. Negotiation of placement opportunities for students at Apia hospital; CSU academics provide professional development and liaison. Potential for partnership with CSU-qualified social worker (and HRD student) based in Fiji. |
| Ireland Limerick University, department of social work | 2018 program, details to be finalised, field program with partner university – Limerick University, attendance at the IFSW/IASSW *Social Work and Social Development* conference, Dublin. | For development, post 2018. |
| China | 2018 program, details to be finalised, partner university and/or professional association involved. | For development, post 2018. |

# Conclusion

Our international programs provide multidimensional opportunities for critical reflection as participants are immersed in an intense experience in unfamiliar locations. Participants' usual reference points are disrupted as they actively engage in a range of intercultural interactions and guided reflection; worldviews can be challenged and cross-cultural awareness can be further developed. The international programs thereby supplement curriculum content across our social work and human services degrees as they create spaces for critical discourse and provide sites for the critique of values, priorities and behaviours for future professional practice.

# References

Anscombe, B. & Bell, K. (2010). *India Study Tour: International social work volunteer programme 2010.* Wagga Wagga: CSU.

Bell, K. & Anscombe, A. (2013). 'International field experiences in Social Work: Outcomes of a study abroad program', *Social Work Education: The International Journal,* 32(8), 1032–47.

Bell, K., Moorhead, B. & Boetto, H. (2017). 'Social work students' reflections on gender, social justice and human rights during a short-term study programme to India', *International Social Work,* 60, 132–44.

Boetto, H. & Bell, K. (2015). 'Environmental sustainability in social work education: An online initiative to encourage global citizenship', *International Social Work – Special issue: Climate Change,* 58, 448–62.

Boetto, H, Moorhead, B. & Bell, K. (2014). Broadening the 'environment' in social work: Impacts of a study abroad program. *Critical Social Work,* 15(1), 2–7.

Cox, D. and Pawar, M. (2013). *International Social Work: Issues, strategies and programs.* California: Sage.

Department of Education and Training (DET) (2018). *Endeavour Mobility Grants,* retrieved from https://internationaleducation.gov.au/Endeavour%20 program/studentmobility/Pages/International%20Student%20Mobility%20 Programs.aspx.

Department of Foreign Affairs and Trade (DFAT) (2018). *New Colombo Plan: Connect to Australia's Future, Study in the Region,* retrieved from http://dfat.gov. au/people-to-people/new-colombo-plan/pages/new-colombo-plan.aspx

Fook, J., & Gardner, F. (2007). *Practising critical reflection: A resource handbook.* Maidenhead, Oxford University Press.

Johnson, S., & Moorhead, B. (2010). Melbourne, Darwin, next stop Dili: Social workers on the loose. *AASW National Bulletin,* 20(1), 19–20.

Macias, (2013). '"Bursting Bubbles": The Challenges of Teaching Critical Social Work', *Affilia,* 28(3), 322–4.

Mattsson, T. (2014). 'Intersectionality as a useful tool: Anti-oppressive social work and critical reflection', *Affilia,* 29(1), 8–17.

Mlcek, S. (2014). 'Are we doing enough to develop cross-cultural competencies for social work students?' *British Journal of Social Work,* 44(7), 1984–2003.

Mlcek, S. & Bell, K. (2018). 'Developing Global Perspectives and Respectful Knowledge through International Mobility Programs'. In T. Hall, T. Grey, G. Downey & M. Singh (eds.) *The Globalisation of Higher Education – Developing Internationalised Education in Research and Practice,* Palgrave Macmillan.

Moorhead, B., Boetto, H. & Bell, K. (2014). 'India and us: Student Development of Professional Social Work Identity through a Short-term Study Abroad program', *Journal of Social Work Education,* 33(2), 175–89.

Nuttman-Shwartz, O. and Berger, R. (2012). 'Field education in international social work: Where we are and where we should go?' *International Social Work,* 55(2), 225–43.

Pawar, M. (2010). *Community Development in Asia and the Pacific,* New York: Routledge.

Pawar, M. (2016) 'Reflective Learning and Teaching in Social Work Field Education in International Contexts', *British Journal of Social Work,* 47, 198–218.

Pawar, M. (2013). International Community Practice: Local-Global issues and strategies. In Marie, Weil, Michael Reisch and Mary Ohmer, *Handbook of Community Practice.* California: Sage.

Pawar, M. (2014). *Social work practice with local communities in developing countries: Imperatives for political engagement.* SAGE Open, Jun 2014, 4(2).

Pawar, M. Hanna, G. & Sheridan, R. (2004). 'International social work practicum in India', *Australian Social Work,* 57(3), 223–36.

Rotabi, K., Gammonley, D. & Gamble, D. (2006). 'Ethical guidelines for study abroad: Can we transform ugly Americans into engaged global citizens?' *British Journal of Social Work,* 36 (3), 467–84.

Trede, F., Bowles, W. & Bridges, D. (2013). 'Developing intercultural competence and global citizenship through international experiences:

Academics' perceptions', *Intercultural Education,* 24(5), 442–55.

VeLure, R. and Fisher, C. (2013). 'Expect the Unexpected: International Short-Term Study Course Pedagogies and Practices', *Journal of Social Work Education*, 49(1), 48–65.

Wehbi, S. (2009). 'Deconstructing motivations: Challenging international social work placements', *International Social Work*, 52 (1), 48–59.

Zuchowksi, I., Miles, D., Howard, E., Harris, N. and Francis, A. (2018). 'Sustaining quality learning abroad opportunities in Australian schools of social work', *International Social Work*, Retrieved from online first – https://doi.org/10.1177/0020872818757590

# EIGHT

# Teaching Human Rights for Social Workers at Charles Sturt University

*Ndungi wa Mungai and Ignatius Chida*

## Abstract

The aim of this chapter is to provide a critical reflection on why and how social work and human rights have influenced the development of a key subject at Charles Sturt University (CSU). The chapter demonstrates why the teaching of a specific human rights subject is a critical requirement for social work and how human rights are an integral part of the social work profession. The chapter addresses the unique history of the subject at CSU and the innovations in teaching the subject. By integrating the human rights course in its academic curricula, CSU social work and human service discipline fulfils the national and international human rights obligations required of universities in delivering education that leads to a better world for all. It is suggested that teaching human rights in universities is a prerequisite for democratic societies, which highly value principles of mutual understanding, toleration, and the valuing of others' cultures, traditions, and ethnicities. The human rights teaching staff contribution to research is discussed and the future challenges explored.

# Introduction

The overriding objective of teaching social work and human rights is persuading the students to view social work as a human rights profession. The students completing the subject should be able to:

- demonstrate a critical understanding of human rights theories
- understand the history of human rights in national and international contexts
- understand the meaning of human rights instrumentalities
- understand the concepts of anti-discrimination and anti-oppressive practices
- apply human rights concepts to social work and
- understand the implications of human rights to social work practice.

The teaching of human rights in social work is supported by the United Nations, International Federation of Social Workers (IFSW) and International Association of Schools of Social Work (IASSW). These bodies suggest that human rights should be taught in social work courses around the world to engender commitment to human rights protection:

> It is imperative that those involved in the field of social work education and practice have a clear and unreserved commitment to the promotion and protection of human rights and to the satisfaction of fundamental social aspirations. (Centre for Human Rights, 1994: 3)

Social workers support people with unmet needs and in the process realize that these needs relate to human rights violations and they need to address the violations. That requires them to use a human rights-approach in assessing and addressing these presenting needs. A human rights-based approach aims to move beyond addressing the immediate needs. A precise definition of human rights is hard as the Universal Declaration of Human Rights (UDHR) did not attempt to provide such a definition. However, the consensus was that human rights were the intrinsic fundamental rights for all, simply by virtue of being human, and the core of the concept of human rights is shared human dignity (Reichert, 2007).

Human rights are universal, which means that they apply to every single human being without distinction and they confer human dignity and worth to all people on this planet. The universality also means that everyone has a duty to promote them and protect them as they otherwise lose meaning if they are only applicable to some people some of the time. The United Nations Human Rights Office of the High Commissioner (OHCHR) notes that states have the duty, on behalf the citizens, to protect these rights:

> The 1993 Vienna conference on human rights, for example, noted that it is the duty of states to promote and protect all human rights and fundamental freedoms, regardless of their political, economic and cultural system. (OHCHR, 2017, par. 3)

The OHCHR also defines human rights as 'inherent to all humans, whatever our nationality, place of residence, sex, national or ethnic origin, colour, religion language or any other status' (OHCHR, 2017, par. 1). An important principle of human rights is that they are interrelated, interdependent and indivisible (Ife, 2012). This principle is a deterrent from choosing some human rights to uphold and others to ignore.

When the General Assembly of the United Nations issued the Universal Declaration of Human Rights seven decades ago, it aimed at setting, identifying, and valuing the basic rights of human beings. The General Assembly of the United Nations called upon all Member Countries to promote the Universal Declaration of Human Rights 'to be disseminated, displayed, read and expounded principally in schools and other educational institutions, without distinction based on the political status of countries or territories' (United Nations, 1998). Only people who know their rights can claim, promote and protect them.

The Global Standards set by IFSW/IASSW identify advancing human rights as core competency for social workers and this is also applicable to the US Education Policy and Accreditation Standards of the Council of Social Work Education (Berthold, 2015). The Australian Association of Social Workers (AASW), which is responsible for the accreditation of social work courses in Australia, points out in the code of ethics that the 'principles of human rights and social justice are fundamental to social work (AASW, 2010). Calma and Priday (2011) claim that social workers could be defined as human rights workers. This would be applicable if social workers practice human rights-based social work, especially when working with marginalised groups like the Indigenous people. A human rights-based practice promotes realization of human rights and social justice including when working in clinical practice (Berthold, 2015). A human rights-based approach reframes the concept of needs into one of entitlements or rights and hence it rejects pathologising people's difficulties and views the problems in their socio-political and structural contexts and it is these contexts that need intervention (Berthold, 2015; Ife, 2012). Students studying human rights learn to understand the contribution of policies and practices to people's problems and not just take a reactive micro practice approach.

CSU has been teaching social work and human rights since 2005 when Jenny McKinnon and Margaret Alston developed the subject. The subject has since become a compulsory subject for the Bachelor of Social Work (BSW) and Master of Social Work (Professional Qualifying) (MSW (pq). The subject is also offered as an elective in Bachelor of Social Welfare (BSocW). There are few social work courses in Australia that offer human rights as a standalone subject. CSU has therefore been one of the pioneers in this. Human rights teaching at CSU is also embedded throughout the social work course including social work ethics, fields of social work practice and Theory and Practice subjects.

Human rights and social justice are closely interlinked but while human rights are more clearly codified by the UN, various regional bodies and national constitutions, social justice has not had a universal definition. However, social justice is understood to include recognition of human rights for all, more equitable distribution of resources and eradication of poverty. The Australian government recognises social justice as a matter of addressing existing inequalities and defines a socially just Australia as characterised by:

- a fair distribution of economic resources
- equal access to essential services such as housing, health care and education
- equal rights in civil, legal and industrial affairs and
- equal opportunity for participation by all in personal development, community life and decision making. (Department of social services, 2014).

It is clear from this definition then that social justice is about human rights, equal sharing of resources, participatory democracy and working towards a fair and just society.

## Content Social Work and Human Rights

To teach social work or human rights is to teach values, such as: the dignity and worth of the person, all people are equal, and that discrimination is harmful. The dignity and worth of the human person is underscored in the preamble of the UDHR which highlights that the 'recognition of the inherent dignity and of the equal and inalienable rights of all members of the human family is the foundation of freedom, justice and peace in the world' (UDHR, preamble). The United Nations provides a guidance on what rights are to be regarded as human rights and member countries are bound to respect these rights by virtue of their membership. The UN charter commits to 'reaffirm the fundamental human rights ... dignity of the human person ... equal rights of men and women and ... nations large and small' (UN charter, preamble). The concepts of human rights, human dignity and equality are therefore at the core of the United Nations reasons for existence and arise from the experience of extreme human rights abuses during the Second World War.

Social workers in Australia take the cue from the UN in adopting values that uphold, respect and promote human rights. The AASW code of ethics commits social workers to practice in ways that are guided by the principles of human rights and social justice:

> Social workers will promote policies, practices and social conditions that uphold human rights and that seek to ensure access, equity, participation and legal protection for all (AASW, 2010, Part. 5.1.3(i)).

Social work values and ethics are therefore anchored in human rights. Steen and Mann (2015) have noted that there has been a move over the last four decades to integrate human rights into social work literature, positions of professional bodies and accreditation standards. Ife (2012) had the influential book *Human rights and social work: towards rights-based practice* first published in 2001. Human rights-based practice has also been adapted into courses like community development (Ife, 2010), policy practice (Steen & Mann, 2015) or practice approaches such as clinical social work (Berthold, 2015). This clearly demonstrates the growing interest in human rights in social work. What makes human rights so critical is that the world is saturated with conflicting social theories and ideologies. This makes the concept of a shared humanity so critical to social work ethics and practice as 'the idea of human rights provides an alternative moral reference point for those who would seek to reaffirm the values of humanity' (Ife, 2012: 1).

At CSU we teach social work as a standalone subject that in the last review in 2011 was redeveloped to be consistent with the AASW practice standards (AASW, 2012). The four major areas identified in the standards were social work with Indigenous people, children, mental health, refugees and asylum seekers. A brief outline here presents the 10 modules that make up the current content of the subject.

## 1. Introduction

The introduction attempts to define the concept of human rights and underscores the importance of the United Nations in defining human rights and in particular the International Bill of Rights consisting of the Universal Declaration of Human Rights (UDHR) and the two covenants arising from it.

## 2. Three Generations of Human Rights

The work of Karel Vasak in attempting to understand the evolution of the 30 articles of human rights in the UDHR assists the students to appreciate the long history of the struggle for human rights. Critically analysing the human rights this way assists in understanding how some rights have gained prominence over others in different regions, despite the UN position that these human rights are interrelated, interdependent, indivisible and inabrogable.

## 3. Human Rights' Theories

The rights listed in the UDHR were not based on particular theory and this was both a strength and a weakness. A strength in that the drafters were free to pick and choose what they felt was practical and relevant but a weakness in that the choices could not be justified from a theoretical position. Nevertheless theories like natural law may have informed some of the early concepts in human rights. Other influences include culture, religion, law, philosophy and science.

# 4. Human Rights' Instrumentalities

The students are introduced to the concept of instrumentalities as the means to claiming human rights. The UN charter is one such instrumentality as the UN has a global mandate to protect human rights. The General Assembly has the power to conduct a study and make recommendations for 'the purpose of promoting international co-operation in economic social cultural, educational, and health fields and assisting in in the realization of human rights and fundamental freedoms' (Art. 13b). Other instrumentalities include the UDHR and a list of covenants and conventions alongside the effective laws in the country of practice.

# 5. Anti-Oppressive Practice in Social Work

Anti-oppressive social work practice is not easy to define but it is broadly defined as social justice-oriented social work. It recognises multiple oppressions, it is transformative, aims at social change and builds on other social work traditions including feminist, Marxist, postmodernist, Indigenous, poststructuralist, critical constructionist, anti-colonial and anti-racist theories (Baines, 2011). A range of discriminatory and oppressive practises are explored with the idea that these dehumanising practises lead to human rights violations, war crimes and genocide. It is in this context too that the students get to explore the role of privilege and how unexamined privilege can lead to oppression (Pease, 2010).

# 6. Human Rights Practice – Feminist Practice

It was found to be important in this subject to highlight the special human rights issues faced by women around the world. The particular focus here is how private troubles are also public issues. While human rights appear as public issues and social work as private issues, making the connections bridges the gap between social work and human rights (Ife, 2012). In many places around the world, historical mistreatment of women make them a vulnerable group. In those places the female status is perceived as inferior and of lower status compared to the male and this is regarded as the natural order (Reichert, 2006). The role of the Convention on the Elimination of all forms of Discrimination against Women (CEDAW) is noted as the instrumentality to ensure women have equal status as men in all fields of life.

## 7. Human Rights for Indigenous People

Understanding the historical situation in regard to human rights for Indigenous people in Australia is one that the social work profession and the university take seriously as a competency issue for students. The historic and continuing disadvantaged position of the Indigenous people is of concern to social work and has human rights implications. The United Nations Declaration on the Rights of Indigenous People (UNDRIP) asserts that Indigenous people are entitled to all human rights enjoyed by other people and in addition possess collective rights which are critical for their survival and development. It is also noted that for their survival and prosperity, issues of equality, diversity, non-discrimination and respect for their culture, heritage, land and spirituality are fundamental. History shows that 'Aboriginal people have lost their land, language, aspects of their culture, children and have suffered major disruption to their kinship system' (Bamblett & Lewis, 2006: 63). This is the starting point in understanding the human rights abuses suffered by the Indigenous people and the ensuing trauma.

## 8. Children and Human Rights

The unique needs of children make this a very important area of human rights as reflected in the UN Convention on the Rights of the Child (CRC). The CRC is highly rated as a human rights instrumentality for its breadth of coverage, comprehensiveness and theoretical consistency (Melton, 1999). It is used as a guide on all matters involving children such as child protection, welfare and education. The four core principles are:

non-discrimination, devotion to the best interest of the child, the right to life, survival and development and respect for the views of the child. There are some controversies on the rights of parents. While this is an important issue as CRC recognises the responsibilities of the parents, controversy only arises when there are abuses and the 'best interest principle' has to be invoked (Hansen & Ainsworth, 2009).

## 9. Mental Health and Human Rights

People living with mental health are vulnerable to human rights abuses and their plight can remain hidden even in developed countries. The 2008 UN convention on the Rights of Persons with Disability (CRPD) sets out these rights that include 'civil and political rights, the right to live in the community, participation and inclusion, education, health, health and social inclusion' (World Health Organisation (WHO), 2017). WHO notes that neglect for people with mental health is widespread and governments do not spend enough on the required services. WHO recommends that 'human rights-oriented mental health policies and laws can be an effective way of preventing violations and discrimination and promoting the autonomy and liberty of people with mental disabilities and should be put in place' (WHO, 2007: 3). WHO further adds that the aim of CRPD is to 'promote, protect and ensure the full and equal enjoyment of all human rights of persons with disabilities (WHO, 2007: 3). Social workers play a major role in the care of people living with mental health so their sensitivity to their human rights is critical.

## 10. Human Rights for Refugees and Asylum Seekers

The issue of refugees and asylum seekers is a global one and a clear demonstration of the outcome of human rights abuses. Millions of people around the world are forced to flee their homes to escape conflict, discrimination and gross human rights abuses. The principle instrument applicable to their protection is the 1951 Refugee Convention and its 1967 protocol. They specify the rights of the refugees and the obligations of the signatory states. In addition, UDHR recognises the right to seek asylum (art. 14) and the right not to be tortured (art. 5). The UN Convention against Torture and other Cruel, Inhuman or Degrading Treatment or Punishment (UNCAT) (OHCHR, 1984) prohibits refugees and asylum seekers being returned to countries where they would be at risk of being tortured (art.3). Australia has an exemplary record in resettling refugees but also notoriety for detaining asylum seekers and forcing boats carrying potential asylum seekers back before they could make their claims.

It is clearly not possible to cover every aspect of human rights in 10 modules but the students are exposed to some of the important human rights issues that social workers can expect to encounter in their practice. At completion, they are in a position to articulate the meaning of human rights, and their role in advancing, protecting and promoting them. They would also be expected to be able to articulate the applicability of a human rights-based approach to social work practice.

## Innovative Teaching and Assessment

CSU prides itself as a leader in providing online education and this is how this subject is currently taught. This lack of face to face interaction with students deprives them a chance to interact and debate with their teacher and peers. It also makes it difficult to have guest speakers addressing the students. To overcome these hurdles an online presence becomes critical. The online forum offers the students the opportunity to interact with each other and with the teacher. Short, recorded lectures are also posted online and while they are not interactive they provide an opportunity for the students to see and hear their teacher. Other modes of interaction include e-mail and telephone.

One of the assessment items first implemented in 2017, requires each student to produce an audio recording of themselves discussing one of the elective research topics. The current electives topics are human rights issues in: racism and xenophobia, criminal justice, fair trade and international aid, LGBTIQ people, climate change and aged care. The students can access and interact with each other's recordings. The availability and near universal access to technology makes this possible and it is an exciting and innovative way of enabling students to learn from each other.

In the main assessment the students are challenged to identify a current issue in the media and devise a way of intervening. The intervention does not have to be a major or dramatic action but an innovative act such as writing a letter to the local newspaper editor, starting a webpage to promote awareness of a human rights issue or joining an existing human rights group. The students are not directed on what to do but they keep inventing novel ways of being 21st century activists to address current human rights issues. The students are assessed on their description of the human rights issue and on their ability to critically reflect on their proposed intervention.

## What the Students Think of the Subject

Results from student evaluation surveys over the years have been positive and often students indicate that they would have liked to have completed the subject earlier in the course. The subject is one of the final year subjects in the social work degree and it aims to prepare students for professional practice. Students find it both challenging and stimulating as they transform themselves into human rights-based social workers. One student's email summarised what most students have expressed:

> I found the assignments encouraged me to read very widely and learn some very valuable information for my future social work career. In a short space of time, I have gathered a lot of knowledge which I am able to identify very easily in my workspace as it closely relates to this subject.
>
> I have gained a vocabulary that is useful in my professional setting from this subject. This new vocabulary is also helpful to my clients, as I work with very marginalised clients and I am now able to effectively validate the oppression they experience. (Personal comment, name withheld)

# Contributing to Knowledge

In an ideal world teaching, learning, researching and taking action should all happen in a self-sustaining cycle. Steen and Mann (2015) suggest that teaching human rights in educational institutions raises rights awareness and can 'assist educators in creating opportunities for students to identify and address the often times myriad and intersecting issues that can contribute to human rights violations.' More particularly, students who learn human rights in their university education would develop an adequate knowledge that can enable them to build connections between local, national, and international concerns in regard to human rights issues.

The primary role for the human rights team has been teaching and ensuring that the students graduating in social work have an appreciation of human rights and human rights-based social work. Beyond that the team aims to contribute to the promotion of human rights by enhancing their own knowledge, participating in conferences, seminars and workshops. Collaborating with other individuals and centres in researching and writing on human rights is an ongoing commitment.

In 2015, the first author ran two youth workshops on human rights for the UN Youth Conference in Albury and Wagga Wagga. In 2016, the author also ran one workshop at the National Young Leaders' Day Masterclass held on Wagga Wagga campus. On both occasions young people studying at Australian high schools and universities had an opportunity to discuss the meaning of human rights and related issues like social inclusion and what role they could play in creating a world worth living in.

The teaching staff have been active in researching and publishing on human rights issues. A good example of this is Mungai and Pulla (2015) 'Human rights as a cornerstone of resilience and empowerment in addressing poverty in Asia in the 21st century'. Another contribution is 'Forced eviction in Bangladesh: a human rights issue' (Islam & Mungai, 2015). A human rights-informed analysis is also used in a number of other publications, particularly those focusing on refugee resettlement issues in Australia. The commitment to human rights and social justice in the social work and human services discipline is demonstrated by our record of research, publication and teaching.

## Conclusion

Teaching human rights at CSU in the social work and the human services discipline is linked to the advancement of principles of respect, mutual understanding, tolerance, and acceptance of others' cultures, traditions and ethnicities. Teaching human rights at CSU clearly has tangible positive consequences on individuals and communities and prepares students for the challenges they can expect to encounter in the field in areas such as child abuse, sexual assault, homelessness, family violence and all other areas that represent the outcome of human rights violations.

Often students comment how they enroll in the human rights subject assuming they know everything about human rights and ultimately realize there is much more to learn. They also state that they had assumed human rights abuse only happened overseas but through their engagement with the subject material, they recognize that human rights violations also happen in Australia. These are positive outcomes and we believe our graduates are well equipped to understand human rights abuses when they encounter them and are outstanding advocates for human rights.

## References

Australian Association of Social Workers, (AASW) (2010). *Code of Ethics*. Retrieved from: https://www.aasw.asn.au/document/item/1201.

Australian Association of Social Workers, (AASW) (2012). *Australian Social Work Education and Accreditation Standards (ASWEAS)*. Accreditation standards requirement. Retrieved from: https://www.aasw.asn.au/document/item/3550.

Baines, D. (2011). 'An overview of anti-oppressive practice: Roots, theory, tension'. In D. Baines (ed.), *Doing anti-oppressive practice social justice social work*. Black Point, Nova Scotia: Fernwood.

Bamblett, M., & Lewis, P. (2006). 'Embedding culture for a positive future for Koorie kids', *Developing Practice: The Child, Youth and Family Work Journal*, 17, 58–66.

Berthold, S.M. (2015) *Human rights-based approach to clinical social work.* New York, NY: Springer.

Calma, E., & Priday, E. (2011). 'Putting Indigenous human rights into social work practice', *Australia Social Work,* 64(2), 147–55.

Centre for Human Rights. (1994). *Professional Training Series No. 1. Human Rights and Social Work A Manual for Schools of Social Work and the Social Work Profession.* Geneva: United Nations. Retrieved from: http://www.ohchr. org/Documents/Publications/training1en.pdf.

Department of social services. (2014). *Social justice.* Retrieved from: https://www.dss.gov.au/our-responsibilities/settlement-and-multicultural-affairs/programs-policy/a-multicultural-australia/national-agenda-for-a-multicultural-australia/participation/social-justice.

Hansen, P., & Ainsworth, F. (2009). Human rights abuse in respect of child protection, *Australia Journal of Social Issues,* 44(2), 183–93.

Ife, J. (2010). *Human rights from below achieving rights through community development.* New York, NY: Cambridge University Press.

Ife, J. (2012). *Human rights and social work: Towards rights-based practice* (3rd edn.). Port Melbourne, VIC: Cambridge University Press.

Islam, M. R. & Mungai, N.W. (2015). 'Forced eviction in Bangladesh: A human rights issue', *International Social Work,* 59(4), 494–507.

Melton, G. B. (1999). 'Children's rights in the healthcare system: The evolving framework in international human rights law', *Journal of the Children's Issues Centre,* 3(2), 13–17.

Mungai, N.W., & Pulla, V. (2015). 'Human Rights as cornerstone of resilience and empowerment in addressing poverty in Asia in the 21st century'. In V. Pulla & B. Mamdi (eds.), *Some aspects of community empowerment and resilience* (pp. 140–58). Delhi: Allied publishers.

Pease, B. (2010). *Unearned Advantage in a Divided World.* London, UK: Zed Books.

Reichert, E. (2007). 'Human rights in the twenty-first century: Creating a new paradigm'. In E. Reichert (ed.), *Challenges in human rights: A social work perspective* (pp. 1–15). New York, NY: Columbia University Press.

Reichert, E. (2006). *Understanding human rights: An exercise book.* London, UK: Sage.

Steen, J.A., & Mann, M. (2015). 'Human rights and social work curriculum: integrating human rights into skill-based education regarding policy practice behaviours', *Journal of Policy Practice,* 14(3–4), 275–291.

United Nations (1998). Universal Declaration of Human Rights. All Human

Rights for All. *Fiftieth Anniversary of the Universal Declaration of Human Rights*. Retrieved on 27 September 2017 from: http://indigenousrights.net. au/__data/assets/pdf_file/0003/396147/f79.pdf.

UN Human Rights Office of High Commissioner (OHCHR) (1984). *Convention against Torture and Other Cruel, Inhuman or Degrading Treatment or Punishment*. Retrieved from: http://www.ohchr.org/EN/ ProfessionalInterest/Pages/CAT.aspx.

UN Human Rights Office of High Commissioner (OHCHR) (2017). *What are human rights?* Retrieved from: http://www.ohchr.org/EN/Issues/Pages/ WhatareHumanRights.aspx.

World Health Organization. (2007). *Promoting the rights of people with mental disabilities*. Geneva: author. Retrieved from: http://www.who.int/ mental_health/policy/legislation/1_PromotingHRofPWMD_Infosheet. pdf?ua=1.

World Health Organization. (2017). *Mental health, human rights & legislation*. Retrieved from: http://www.who.int/mental_health/policy/ legislation/en/.

# NINE

# Benefits of a Research-Focussed Social Work Placement: Evaluating the Keeping Children Safe Program

*Research conducted with the assistance of CSU social work students on placement*

### *John Burns*

In 2013 the author was managing a Social Work Department in a busy regional referral Health Service at Orange in the Central West of New South Wales.

Since 2004 the author had been partnering with Orange Family Support Service (OFSS) to deliver child protection education, targeting parents of at-risk children. In 2013 the author and partners decided to conduct an outcome evaluation of the education programme with the assistance of social work students on placement from Charles Sturt University.

This chapter describes how the resulting research project was conceived, developed and carried out. Issues about social work practitioner research are explored and the benefits of social work students being involved in the research discussed. For the chapter the students recorded brief reflections on their placements. Some of their comments are reproduced.

# The Research Project

## Background

The author and family worker, Sue Brown, met in 2003 and recognised the need to provide an education programme which could attract and retain parents of children subject to child protection concerns, or at risk of this. Locally these parents were either not going to programmes being offered, or were dropping out from them. Strategies were devised to address the barriers for these parents, by developing a programme run at OFSS by Sue and the author. The six session Uniting Care Burnside programme, Keeping Children Safe (KCS), was chosen for the content delivery. This programme raises the awareness of parents about child protection, informing them about the different kinds of child abuse and neglect, their effects on children and ideas for prevention. It also gives information on the role of NSW Family and Community Services and other agencies. (Uniting Institute of Education, 2016)

At least two programmes a year were subsequently run and through the strategies implemented, had success in attracting and retaining parents in the target group. Through 2004 to March 2015, 232 people had attended the KCS groups, with 83% having attended four or more of the six sessions. 52% of the parents had not attended parenting groups before.

## Evaluation in Child Protection

Lamont (2009) distinguishes three kinds of evaluation in child protection services – process evaluation, impact evaluation and outcome evaluation. Process evaluation focuses on the way a service or programme is delivered and the client's experience of it. Impact evaluation focuses on what the client immediately gained from the programme including knowledge, attitude change and skills.

The leaders were continuously evaluating the KCS programme in terms of its processes, and its immediate impact, as reported by participants. Both kinds of evaluation produced positive results.

Lamont highlighted the importance of the third kind of evaluation in child protection, outcome evaluation, but acknowledged the significant difficulties associated with carrying out such evaluations. Outcome evaluation tries to measure whether a service has made a difference in terms of its long term, underlying goals. In the case of child protection, services are designed to improve parenting and increase child safety. So outcome evaluations need to focus on those more fundamental changes. However, there had been no outcome evaluation of the KCS programme.

## Practitioner Evaluation in Social Work

Alston and Bowles (2003), Soydan (2015), Payne (2005), Harvey et al. (2013) and McNeill and Nicholas (2012) have highlighted the crucial importance and benefits of intervention research and discussed the challenges of such research by practitioners.

Harvey, Plummer, Pighills and Pain (2015) surveyed social workers in health in Northern Qld and identified a positive interest in research but a lack of confidence, time constraints and limited research capacity. These findings were consistent with the context at the Social Work Department at Orange Health Service and in OFSS in 2013.

Joubert and Hocking (2015) reported on a partnership between the School of Social Work at the University of Melbourne and a cancer service, whereby a Senior Research Fellow mentored social work practitioners to build-in intervention research. There were a number of clinical and practitioner benefits reported.

McNeill and Nicholas (2012) reported on research development in a paediatric hospital setting in Toronto, Canada. The authors expressed concern about what they saw as a low priority on research in undergraduate social work training leading to the pre-eminence of direct practice to the exclusion of research in the hospital setting and a lack of research capacity amongst degree social workers. McNeill and Nicholas presented the strategy developed in the Social Work Department at Toronto Sick Kids Hospital where some positions are occupied by 'clinical PhD Social Workers' who carry out research as well as having a direct service role.

## Partnering with CSU School of Social Work

The author approached the Field Education Academic staff at Charles Sturt University (CSU), Wagga Wagga, about the possibility of Social Work Undergraduate or Qualifying Masters students on their first, 'indirect' placements assisting with the development and conduct of a follow-up exploratory outcome study of KCS participants. The University was enthusiastic about the idea, and so three students, in sequence, worked on the project for 18 months from early 2014.

The research project was again a partnership between the Social Work Department and OFSS, and now CSU had effectively become a partner. The students were supervised by the author and they were based at the Social Work Department.

# Research Design and Methodology

The study was an attempt to evaluate the underlying objectives of the KCS programme at OFSS. The research question was 'Has the KCS programme made a more lasting difference to or had an influence on participants' knowledge of child abuse and neglect, their parenting, their relationship with their children, the safety of their children, and how adult conflict is handled in their homes?' The study was consistent with the classic concerns of social work research around the relationship of individuals to society, the possibilities for social change and the situation of vulnerable people (McDermott, 1996).

It was decided to seek the perceptions of participants and referring agencies in addressing the research question. Participants were also given the opportunity to provide other feedback on the programme.

It was not possible to mount a study with a control group, for ethical and other reasons, and the research was exploratory in scope.

Participants who had completed 4 or more KCS sessions at least three months before and as far back as February/March 2011 were followed up. There were 63 participants on the final contact list. The primary source of data was a structured interview of each participant eligible to be contacted for the study.

In addition, a short survey was sent to agencies who had referred clients to the programme.

A mixed method study was agreed. It sought quantitative data through ordinal and nominal scales and qualitative data via the explanations and perceptions of participants and referring agencies. Participants were also asked if they were aware of any new concerns by the child protection authority, Family and Community Services (FaCS), since the completion of the programme. The interview schedule also contained eleven scenarios. Participants had to decide if the children in each scenario were being abused/neglected or not. Finally, participants were invited to make other comments on the KCS programme. No suitable existing interview schedule or questionnaires was identified so it was agreed that one be designed. The resulting participant interview schedule and agency survey were reviewed by a CSU PhD academic and piloted without any major changes.

Ethics approval for the study was given by the Local Health District Human Research Ethics Committee. This was more complex than usual due to the nature of the study with vulnerable clients, another site (OFSS) and the involvement of students. Site specific approvals were granted by the respective organisations. Spreadsheets were designed to enter the data obtained.

## Research Results

Due to the length of the design and approval processes, interviews did not commence until May 2015 and concluded in August 2015. Attempts were made to contact all 63 on the eligibility list. There were 16 interviews completed.

At the same time surveys were sent to 7 referring agencies. Disappointingly, only 4 were returned, and a couple of those after a lot of chasing up.

The results were entered on spreadsheets and qualitative data analysed for themes.

The results of the participant interviews were generally very positive. A number of people interviewed indicated that the programme had made either some or a lot of difference to their parenting, their relationship to their children and the safety of their children. A majority stated the programme had made a difference to how adult conflict is handled in the home. The most influential session seemed to be the one on sexual abuse of children, as participants often spoke about the changes they have made to supervision of their children and other risk management strategies. 13 of the 16 parents stated they were not aware of any fresh concerns by FaCS since completing the programme. The other 3 were 'not sure'. The answers to the scenarios were strongly consistent with the understandings of child abuse presented in the programme. A common comment was that the programme should be more widely available, even compulsory.

The agency survey responses were in the main positive, two were very positive. The other respondent was unable to say whether positive changes noted were attributable to KCS. Two key comments were that the KCS programme influenced participants to work more cooperatively with their case managers and that the programme content was consistent with what the agencies were trying to achieve with the clients.

A comprehensive report on the project was completed in March 2016 and sent to stakeholders. It is also planned to submit a journal paper on this research.

## Social Work Field Education Aspects

As in the case of other Australian universities, Charles Sturt University Social Work students, both degree and qualifying Masters students, complete two placements. The first placement is an 'indirect' placement and the second a 'direct' practice placement. The first placement provides the opportunity for students to be involved in research activities.

# Integration of Theory and Practice on Social Work Placements

Smith, Cleak and Vreugdenhil (2015) reported on a comprehensive study of the learning activities of Australian social work students on placement. The students surveyed had undertaken at least one placement. Part of the article highlighted the importance of students having the opportunity, through observation, of supervised practice and structured reflection, to integrate practice with theory. Of the 263 respondents to the study survey, a solid majority had reflected on practice but only 49% had linked theory to practice. The researchers did not report on the type of activities undertaken by students in terms of direct or indirect, macro, mezzo or micro. So it is not known how many students undertook research-related placements. The authors highlighted the need for clearer standards and strategies for students to be able to more effectively link theory to practice on placement.

Lewis and Bolzan (2007) reported on a study of Australian social work students who had completed their first placement. The findings showed that the students felt ill-equipped for their first placement. Students commented on the variance between theory from 'academia' and the practice setting, and the serious challenge this caused for them. Again in this article there was no coverage of indirect activities. The authors stated 'Students are mostly concerned with direct practice tasks and skills that they are carrying out in the placement' (138). The authors claimed that 'social work writing has provided, at best, only a tenuous bridge between theoretical perspectives of social work and on-the-ground experiences of what social workers do' (140). From a post-modern perspective, they argued the need for students to be engaged in a 'dynamic co-construction of social work' (137).

## Role of Students in the Research Project

For the project at Orange, three students in sequence, on their first, indirect placements assisted with the research as their primary learning activity.

The University's Field Education Coordinator initially selected whom she considered could be a suitable student for each of the placements. The author, as Field Educator, met with the student in a pre-placement interview at the Health Service. This meeting was very important to ensure there was a match between the needs of the placement setting and the needs and expectations of the student. The student was therefore aware of what would be involved in the placement before she started.

The students were based with the General Social Work team at the Health Service. Each student had the opportunity to observe social workers working in the General Hospital, Community Health and Mental Health Service as well as assisting with the research project. This provided a balance of valuable learning experiences. The student also orientated to OFSS where the KCS groups were run. Each student participated as a group member in the KCS programme in which the field educator was a co-facilitator with Sue Brown, Family Worker. The participants were informed of the evaluation, which was discussed in the group, and the role of the student in this.

> It was an incredible experience being involved with this research for my placement. I was able to attend Keeping Children Safe classes and interact with parents who were participating. I was able to consider how those parents might be involved in a research project and the valuable contribution this would make. (Social Work Student Reflection 2, 2017)

The first placement started in February 2014. The first student initially reviewed the literature list for the study and expanded this. She assisted the supervisor in the design of the research and with the application to the Health Service Human Research Ethics Committee (HREC). These were complex undertakings and valuable learning activities for the student. The author and student worked together on the on-line HREC application. This took several sessions.

My role was to assist with the application … to get approval
for the research. The process was a new experience for me. I
was not prepared for the depth of information required nor
the length of the application process. (Social Work Student
Reflection 1, 2017)

It was important for each of the students to become familiar with
ethical and other issues associated with research with a vulnerable, hard-
to-engage population. Completing two tasks, the research design and
HREC application, required the student and supervisor to consider and
apply the core social work values of Respect for Persons, Social Justice and
Professional Integrity. This was therefore an integrative experience for the
student, who also voiced her opinion when she thought the rights of the
research participants needed more protection or consideration. The student
later reflected it had been important for her learning to

have the opportunity to discuss theories in a safe and reliable
manner at supervision, to have permission to put forward my
views of practice, and given the opportunity to support my
views without judgement. (Social Work Student Reflection 1,
2017)

The first student had only limited experience in spreadsheets but still
designed a spreadsheet for the research data collection. She also made
spreadsheets for evaluation data already obtained for the KCS groups,
entered this data and completed some thematic analysis. The completion
of the first placement saw the completion of the research design and the
submission of the HREC application.

The second placement ran for the second half of 2014. There was a delay
in the HREC reviewing the application which impacted the placement.
While waiting for the HREC response the student improved the original
spreadsheets and did a lot of data entry. This was in addition to attending
the KCS group and undertaking other learning activities. One of these

was observing social work in the Mental Health service. In response to the ethics application, the HREC came back with a number of questions. The supervisor and student worked together on these and made required changes to the application. The student already had good research skills but it was still a valuable learning experience for her to be now practising in a Social Work context.

> I obtained real world experience in regards to creating a proposal to conduct research, dealing with the relevant ethic committees to proceed with the research and techniques for conducting the research ... Waiting on comments from the ethics committee and adjusting or considering how to tailor the techniques so the research could proceed. (Social Work Student Reflection 2, 2017)

Ethics approval for the project was given in late 2014.

The third placement commenced in early 2015 and, unlike the previous placements, was part-time, and finished in August. Site-specific approval had to be given for the research, at both sites, and this was not finally obtained till March. Interviews did not commence till May and finished in August. It was the role of the third student to contact participants, conduct the interviews and enter the data. This was in addition to attending the current KCS group. (She would not be interviewing those participants for the research project.) The student did an outstanding job in interviewing 16 of the potential 63 study population and entering the data onto the spreadsheet. The student also did some preliminary work on the research report.

## Student Supervision and Learning

The author directly supervised the students. Formal supervision sessions were held weekly and separately from the sessions that reviewed progress on the research project. The student was expected to have an agenda for supervision. Review of progress on the student's Learning Plan was part of supervision. Reflection on the application of social work values, theories and models was important. The students were more easily able to reflect on the application of social work's values. This included reflection on the partnership's goal of improving the access of a vulnerable group to a baseline parent programme and how this was maintained. It also included the use of participant-centred research methods carried out with respect and empathy. It was important for the student to understand how her work and practice fitted into that.

The students initially had more difficulty identifying the social work theories and models relevant to both the KCS programme and the research. The placement offered a significant opportunity for the students to start to look critically at social work theories and models being applied in a diverse placement setting including the indirect work. Supervision sessions brought up a range of theories and models which the student was encouraged to explore and document.

For example, an early social work systems perspective relevant to the KCS programme explored is the Pincus and Minahan Model (Payne, 2005), which distinguishes client, change agent, target and action systems and the role of the worker in strategically working within that framework. As an example of systems thinking, this model can be particularly helpful to analyse parent education in the child protection context because of the duty of care workers have to children and the concept of working with parents to improve outcomes for children. Systems perspectives are also relevant because of the complexity of the child protection assessment and intervention system. The criticism that systems approaches can lack a value base was raised.

Structural theory was looked at and the student encouraged to think about what aspects of the KCS programme might be consistent or inconsistent with critical social work thinking and approaches. How might the research reinforce social disadvantage or contribute to social change?

Empowerment theory was commonly identified and discussed by the students. This related to the KCS programme as well as the research. The study was not just a process of evaluating the KCS programme, but also of valuing the perspectives and contribution of participants and affirming the improvements reported in their lives. For people who were often disadvantaged and possibly at a low point in their lives, this was important.

> They appeared to have 'grown' in the time between the workshops and the interview ... Some relished their new parenting skills and the knowledge they gained. Many stated how positive the workshop was and remembered certain parts in clear detail. It was positive for me as a student to be part of that. (Social Work Student Reflection 3, 2017)

In supervision there was discussion about the relative benefits, challenges and use of quantitative and qualitative, experimental and non-experimental research methods in the social work context and for the project. There was particular discussion about the possible limitations of the research design of the project, which gave priority and value to the perceptions and views of the participants. The approach was, however, consistent with the underlying values and theories of the education programme delivered at Family Support.

## Conclusion

The student placement was crucial in the development, conduct and completion of the research project. It could not have been completed without the students. At the same time the collaboration was a significant learning experience for them, in terms of both knowledge and skill development in social work research and in theory-to-practice integration. So the project met the needs of both the programme facilitators and the students.

> The main learning points for me as a research student, involved connecting research to the theory principles of social work; I relied on my mentor and other experienced social workers to

talk over my perceptions of theories and practice. I had the opportunity to observe clients in group which was a valued opportunity to again reflect on my personal values and the values of social work ... I found the placement to be beneficial to my learning. At the time I felt it was a long placement. On reflection the time was important to developing my practice skills. (Social Work Student Reflection 1, 2017)

This student is now a qualified and practising social worker in the child protection field.

## Acknowledgements

Orange Health Service (OHS) and Staff of the Social Work Department.

Sue Brown, Family Worker, Elly Haynes, Manager, the Board and other Staff of OFSS.

CSU Social Work Students – Noeline Frances, Katie Burke and Christina Walker.

Dr Julaine Allan PhD, Charles Sturt University Student Academic Liaison.

CSU Field Education Coordination Academics Therese Jones-Mutton and Serena Mathews.

## References

Alston, M. & Bowles, W. (2003). *Research for Social Workers: an introduction to methods,* (2nd edn.). Crows Nest: Allen & Unwin.

Harvey, D., Plummer, D., Pighills, A., & Pain, T. (2013). 'Practitioner Research Capacity: A Survey of Social Workers in Northern Queensland', *Australian Social Work, 66*(4), 540–54.

Joubert, L., & Hocking, A. (2015). 'Academic Practitioner Partnerships: A Model for Collaborative Practice Research in Social Work', *Australian Social Work,* 68(3) July, 352–63.

Lamont, A. (2009). 'Evaluating Child Abuse and Neglect Intervention Programs' Child Protection Clearing House, Australian Institute of Family Studies, Resource Sheet No. 5. Updated November 2009.

Lewis, I., & Bolzan, N. (2007). 'Social Work with a Twist: Interweaving

Practice Knowledge, Student Experience and Academic Theory', *Australian Social Work, 60(2)*, 136–46.

McDermott, F. (1996). 'Social work research: Debating the boundaries', *Australian Social Work*, 49(1) 5–10.

McNeill, T., & Nicholas, D. (2012). 'Strategies for Research Development in Hospital Social Work: A Case Study', *Research on Social Work Practice, 22(6)*, 672–9.

Payne, Malcolm (2005). *Modern Social Work Theory* (3rd edn.). Hampshire: Palgrave Macmillan.

Smith, D., Cleak, H., & Vreugdenhil, A. (2015). 'What Are They Really Doing? An Exploration of Student Learning Activities in Field Placement', *Australian Social Work*, 68(4), 515–31.

Soydan, H. (2015). 'Intervention Research in Social Work', *Australian Social Work*, 68(3), 324–7.

Uniting Institute of Education (2016). *Keeping Children Safe: a step-by-step manual on how to run child protection workshops for parents, Version 3*. Uniting Institute of Education, Parramatta, NSW.

# TEN

# Be the Change You Want to See in the World: The Practice of Nonviolence in Social Work Field Education

*Karen Dempsey*

## Abstract

When mentoring students one's own personal and professional framework becomes an influential part of the learning environment. In this chapter I describe how I came to incorporate the practice of Nonviolence specifically through Marshall Rosenberg's Nonviolent Communication Model (NVC) as my main social work lens and communication tool and illustrate its application to student mentoring.

## Introduction

NVC is a non-pathologising needs based communication skills model. It defines violence as a state of compassionate disconnection and sees violence in our culture as systemic rather than as intrinsic to human nature. This definition expands the notion of 'violence' to include any human endeavour which is not aligned with compassion. This expansive definition of violence would thus extend to include conscious awareness of the practice of social work, from the point of view of our own potential to 'do harm'.

Social workers deal with the impact of violence on individuals and communities on a daily basis. The Nonviolent communication model can provide a powerful and protective lens for Social Work practitioners and students alike with which can assist to align assessment and action with ethical, compassionate, power with stances.

## The Cronulla Riots – My Call to Peace and Nonviolence Work

*It is only because of problems that we grow mentally and spiritually.*
(Peck, n.d.)

Perhaps Scott Peck's reflection here is true socially as well as culturally. There were many positive personal and organizational initiatives that have been sparked by the events of the Cronulla riots. For example the 'On the Same Waves' program at Wanda Beach which began training young people from middle eastern background in surf lifesaving. This program, helped to dispel race related cultural stereotypes and spawned a champion in Ali Najem. Ali came through this program and in ten years after the riots he was competing in the World Life Saving championships (SBS News, 2015).

My life was also transformed by the shock of the Cronulla riots. At the same time that the Cronulla riots broke out, I was reading Scott Pecks book, *In Search of Stones: A Pilgrimage of Faith, Reason, and discovery*, specifically these words in the chapter on Peace:

> Peace is a lot of work ... Preserving the peace is every bit as hard as achieving it in the first place. The plain fact of the matter is that on an intellectual and emotional level war is easier than peace. In waging war we will physically often work around the clock in preference to doing the intellectual work of peace, and will gladly risk our physical lives rather than risk ourselves emotionally ... (Peck, 1996: 253)

The combination of these two events – the riots and the words of Scott Peck, strongly brought home the realisation that although one of my deepest longings was for peace I did very little intentionally to bring it about.

I began to reflect deeply on peace and came to the realisation that peace *underpins* the attainment of a socially just and sustainable world. I began looking for ways in which I could contribute to peace work. I found that most of what people would envision as 'peace work' was carried out overseas and in war zones? And yet I saw so much 'non-peace' all around me: in families, in communities, in staff rooms, in schools, and in our government.

Then a friend mentioned that they were seeing a nonviolence counsellor. In the process of investigating what a nonviolence counsellor offered I discovered Nonviolent Communication.

## The Nonviolent Communication Model – NVC

The Nonviolent Communication model (NVC) was developed by Marshall Rosenberg, a psychologist who in the 1980's left psychology because it did not allow him to see the beauty in human beings in every situation. The conception of NVC draws upon interdisciplinary knowledge as well as from psychology, from areas such as history, theology, sociology, and the study of language. NVC is skills based and is supported by a particular consciousness. NVC links ways of thinking, speaking and acting with particular kind of social structures. It compromises a specific view of human evolution and human nature. Importantly, Rosenberg's model emphasises the enormous power of words. All human endeavour is conceived in the mind and communicated through language. Hence one of Marshall's text book is titled, *Speak Peace in a World of Conflict: What you say next will change your world* (Rosenberg, 2005a).

### *Human Evolution from Domination to Partnership Systems*

Marshall Rosenberg describes human evolution as currently shifting from domination to partnership systems. Domination systems are characterised by hierarchical power-over forms of relating at every level of social organisation.

The evolution from domination to partnership systems involves enormous transformation in the way we relate to other human beings and also to the way we relate to the natural world. Bell Hooks summarises the implications of domination: 'Any society based on domination supports and condones violence' (Hooks, n.d.). Thus violence (a state of compassionate disconnection according to Rosenberg) is seen as systemic in domination systems. Domination systems have been prevalent in Western cultures for around 10,000 years (Rosenberg, 2005a). This connection between domination and violence is described by Judy Atkinson (2002), an Australian indigenous academic, in her book *Trauma Trails*:

> Large scale man-made disasters for Aboriginal people world-wide, occurred as European countries practiced colonisation from the late fifteenth century to the early twentieth century … [colonisation] restructured the social and cultural face of the globe with disastrous outcomes which were unforeseeable at the time. Worldwide European colonisation … [supported by beliefs that some groups had rights to power-over others] … was a brutal period…Colonisers came from patriarchal societies in which the strata of class and hereditary male privilege determined who would be the commandant … a foot soldier … slave ship owner or slave … convict overseer or convict … women were generally the camp followers … the effects are still being felt today … (Atkinson, 2002: 51)

Atkinson (2002: 51) describes the level of violence caused by power over cultural systems as 'no less than catastrophic' for the planet and for human beings. She pinpoints the 1980's as a time when awareness of the devastating impact of widespread multi-generational trauma caused by indigenous colonisations, world wars, events such as Hiroshima and the Vietnam war etc was crystallising. She notes that trauma caused by human beings has much greater impact on people than trauma caused by natural events.

## Communication and Socialisation Processes That Support Domination or Partnership Systems

Rosenberg (2005b) terms the cultural conditioning and language of domination systems as 'Life-alienating'. Broadly such language is characterised by moral judgements and demonising and dehumanising language such as: stereotyping, blaming, shaming and enemy images. Dualistic thinking such as right/wrong, good/bad, male/female, abled/ disabled, etc also characterises this approach. Domination systems are supported by systems of rewards and punishments.

Families are primary units of socialisation and thus parenting under domination systems have been very much engaged in life-alienating forms of interaction. Social workers have played a prominent role in supporting the shift away from Life-alienating parenting styles. Rosenberg maintains that we are currently living in a period of history where Life-alienating and Life-affirming ways of relating co-exist.

Rosenberg terms the cultural conditioning and language of egalitarian or partnership relational systems as 'Life-affirming'. The aim of Life-affirming communication is empathic or compassionate connection. It is non-nondualist and thus able to hold complex and seemingly contradictory elements of human behaviour in the one framework. Governed by compassion, non-dualistic thinking can generate creative and innovative understandings and responses to human dilemmas. Social work values resonate with this approach; see for example AASW (2010) *Code of Ethics* section 1.3.

## NVC – A Needs-Based Communication Model

Identifying needs is a core aspect of compassionate communication. Empathy involves being able to communicate to others that you understand and are willing to support them in meeting their needs. Self-empathy involves connecting with the vital nature of our own needs. Compassionate relationships involve recognition of our fundamental interdependence and thus the aim is to achieve mutuality of needs.

Socialisation under Domination systems involved educating people in a way that they were alienated from their own needs:

> Not only have we never been educated about our needs, we are often exposed to cultural training that actively blocks our consciousness of them ... we have inherited a language that served kings and powerful elites in domination societies. The masses discouraged from recognising their needs, have instead been educated to be docile and subservient to authorities. Our culture implies that needs are negative and destructive; the word needy applied to a person suggests inadequacy or immaturity. (Rosenberg, 2015a: 196)

The consciousness that supports Nonviolence

Nonviolent communication cannot be effective as a technical exercise alone. One can say all the right words but if the words are not aligned with a compassionate *Intention* then they are unlikely to create compassionate connection.

This is the best definition I have found for the evolving consciousness about the nature of human existence which supports partnership or egalitarian systems:

> *Nonviolence is cultivated on the inner level*
> *Deep nonviolence requires a shift in the mechanisms of the mind*
> *Which allows the sense of the self to expand to include all others*
> *And therefore breaks the barrier between self and others*
> *And automatically changes relations to one of natural acceptance and compassion*
> *If nonviolence is not built on this inner foundation*
> *It cannot be sustainable*
> (Barbara Fields, 2010, Coordinator of the annual Season for Nonviolence)

NVC has enormous practical relevance for direct client practice, for supporting respectful and supportive peer relationships, for self-reflection, self-care, for critical reflection and analysis, assessment and planning, conflict resolution, mediation, group work and organisational structure.

The following boxed summary contrasts life-alienating with life-affirming language.

---

**Life – alienating Language is characterised by:**
- Critical, Blaming and shaming,moralistic judgements
- Demands
- Dualistic understandings
- Generalisations and Stereotypes
- Pathologising understandings
- Them versus us thinking
- Creating enemy images
- Systems of rewards and punishments for preferred behaviour
- Dehumanisation strategies

**Compassionate or Life-affirming Communication is humanising and inevitably healing and restorative and is characterised by:**
- Universal Needs understandings rather than diagnoses or judgements
- Requests
- Non-dualistic lens
- Objective Observations
- Non-pathologising language
- Non-critical lenses
- Restorative justice frameworks
- Choice and self determination
- Expression of Appreciation and Gratitude

---

# Applications of NVC Awareness and Skills in Social Work Field Education

## Non-hierarchical Education Forms – The Mentor–Student Relationship

Donoghue (2002) states that the term 'supervision' has been used as a tool in social work to reinforce colonisation processes through the establishment and maintenance of social cohesion through state-sponsored welfare.

Hierarchical structures commonly privilege the voice of those with greater power and status over those with less. Social work ethics (AASW, 2010) guide practice in attempting to mitigate power differences between professional and 'client'. The student – supervisor relationship challenges us to also mitigate power differences. Education in Western cultures still operates largely within hierarchical structures. The challenge for social work is to find ways of socialising students into the profession which model partnership and Life-affirming ways of relating.

I prefer to use the term mentoring rather than supervision. I would describe the mentoring relationship as a circular rather than hierarchical one where in reality student and teacher are engaged in a constant cycle of learning from each other.

The conditions for this mentoring partnership need to be set in the beginning phases of placement. To establish an egalitarian dynamic in the supervisor –student relationship I explain to students that I see my role as supporting professional growth rather than one of scrutinising competence. I also assure them that I try to offer my observations rather than offer 'criticism. Related this is the use of questions aimed at students critiquing their own practice through self-reflection.

I write the evaluation reports together with the student. The student self-evaluates and I make comment on their self-evaluation, adding my observations of their challenges and their strengths. This mentor – student partnership is supported by a consciously built environment of trust, where I consciously share my experiences, challenges and vulnerabilities as a social worker to model openness and unconditional acceptance of all of the student's experience. I find students gradually become more open within this consciously created relationship environment and that this environment can accommodate much learning as well as humour and fun.

I aim to practice and model compassionate relating within the mentor student relationship. One way I do this is to constantly transform any life-alienating judgements which arise in me, into Life-affirming responses.

## Example

In the initial stages for first placements in particular, I find that students may take some time to understand the function of supervision/mentoring and their role within it. Students often can contribute minimally to the dialogue and may arrive at our meeting without prepared items or issues for discussion.

At these times I have found that I have been triggered into some Life-alienating thinking, such as 'this student is not valuing the mentoring relationship' and 'this student is not motivated', etc.

Awareness of this Life-alienating thinking in me alerts me to begin the inner reflection process which is the basis of the practice of nonviolence.

The first step in this inner reflection process if to identify any Life-alienating thinking and translate this into an understanding of one's own unmet needs. Life-alienating thinking such as judgements only ever tell us about our own unmet needs rather than anything accurate about the other person.

The second step is to identify my unmet needs. My unmet needs at this stage might be for partnership, shared expectations and vision, reciprocity, ease etc.

The third step is to hold my judgements separate from this situation and look for strategies based on the needs I have identified. I will often use the strategy of opening up a conversation that might externalise the student's experience of supervision. I might ask about how the student feels about coming to 'supervision' and having to discuss her learning with someone who is 'senior' and in the role of a 'teacher'? I would not ask this question however until all my Life-alienating thinking was addressed and I could ask the question with kindness and openness rather than as a kind of interrogation. I check into the sense of ease in me to know whether all the tension of my Life-alienating thinking has dissipated.

Quite often I find that the student's previous experience of supervision is in a work place where the supervisor approaches the role in a scrutinising and critical way. In putting aside my Life-alienating judgements I can learn more about my students and their needs and create more compassionate connection and understanding with them. We can then use this opportunity to refine expectations for the full gamut of social work supervision functions delivered within a partnership framework.

## Connecting With Needs Rather Than Judgements – Implementing the NVC 4 Step Process

Implementing the NVC involves a 4-step process that repeats itself in a continual feedback loop. Rosenberg terms the 4 steps as: observations, feelings, needs and requests, summarised the following diagram.

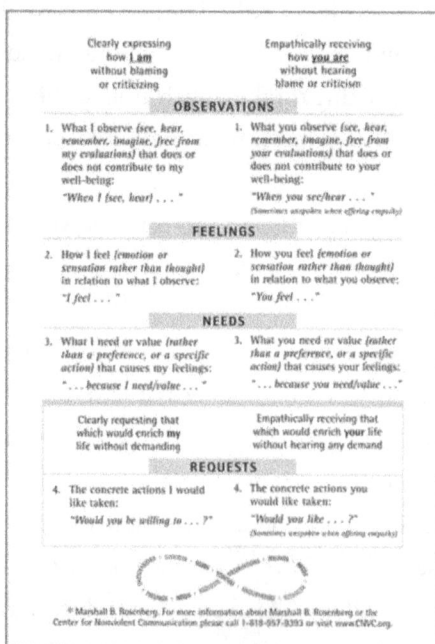

| Clearly expressing how I am without blaming or criticizing | Empathically receiving how you are without hearing blame or criticism |
|---|---|
| **OBSERVATIONS** | |
| 1. What I observe (see, hear, remember, imagine, free from my evaluations) that does or does not contribute to my well-being: "When I (see, hear) . . . " | 1. What you observe (see, hear, remember, imagine, free from your evaluations) that does or does not contribute to your well-being: "When you see/hear . . . " (Sometimes unspoken when offering empathy) |
| **FEELINGS** | |
| 2. How I feel (emotion or sensation rather than thought) in relation to what I observe: "I feel . . . " | 2. How you feel (emotion or sensation rather than thought) in relation to what you observe: "You feel . . . " |
| **NEEDS** | |
| 3. What I need or value (rather than a preference, or a specific action) that causes my feelings: " . . . because I need/value . . . " | 3. What you need or value (rather than a preference, or a specific action) that causes your feelings: " . . . because you need/value . . . " |
| Clearly requesting that which would enrich my life without demanding | Empathically receiving that which would enrich your life without hearing any demand |
| **REQUESTS** | |
| 4. The concrete actions I would like taken: "Would you be willing to . . . ?" | 4. The concrete actions you would like taken: "Would you like . . . ?" (Sometimes unspoken when offering empathy) |

© Marshall B. Rosenberg. For more information about Marshall B. Rosenberg or the Center for Nonviolent Communication please call 1-818-957-9393 or visit www.CNVC.org.

The 4-Part NVC Process – Nonviolent Communication, reproduced with permission from Puddle Dancer Press: Copyright – *Nonviolent Communication: A Language of Life*, 3rd edn. (Rosenberg, 2015b).

The nonviolent communication model gives us the tools to approach seemingly difficult conflicted issues and enhance people's ability to receive our communications non-defensively – this is crucial to effective social work practice which is primarily delivered within complex and contentious human situations and mediated through relationships with others.

## *Example*

A student shared with me that she had judged a worker from a partner agency as 'incompetent' because they had not turned up to several appointments on time. She told me that she had decided she would not interact with this worker anymore.

In the NVC model, emotional responses (such as this student's disappointment) are validated as reliable indicators of important Needs. Using the NVC model of identifying feelings and needs I guessed that the student might have been upset and frustrated as it seemed to her that her needs for partnership and support were not being met.

I helped the student to apply the NVC 4 step process (Observation, Feelings and Needs, Requests) to illustrate a way forward for the student in terms of how she might communicate her needs to the other worker that would not create defensiveness or conflict.

*Observation (without interpretation)* – When you arrived after the time we agreed upon the other day...

*Express Feelings without blame or criticism* – I felt concerned.

Example of Feelings expressed in blaming critical way – 'I felt betrayed and undermined'.

*Express Needs* – because I really value your support and collaboration to assist this family.

*Request* – and I wondering if there is any other way the arrangements can be made that would be make it easier for you in terms of meeting times?

The aim is to create a space in which there might be an openness to hear what was happening for their colleague without preconceived stories or judgement, to allow their partnership to be navigated with more openness and transparency and trust.

The student acknowledged that she would feel comfortable to approach their colleague in this way. She could see some hope that in freeing herself from *the story she was telling herself*, i.e. that the worker was incompetent, she might find other possible understandings which would enable them to mediate this issue in their partnership. The student was surprised that even though the word *nonviolence* was is in the agency's Statement of Purpose, she did not realise there was a body of knowledge and skills available to facilitate the implementation of that principle.

## NVC Life-affirming Assessment Lenses

Marshall Rosenberg left Psychology because he said at that time in the 1980's it did not allow him to see the beauty in people no matter what the situation. In the NVC framework – we are concerned that when we see people through a lens of judgement or diagnosis, this automatically disconnects us from seeing their full humanity and potential. In other words it can put us at risk of being complicit with stories and actions in which we can dehumanise people and not take into account the complexity of their lived experience.

### *Example*

A student spoke to me about being asked by a supervisor to research families from a particular cultural group who have a member with a drug addiction issue, specifically to look for ways that the families 'collude' with and undermine the person with a drug issue by 'helping them too much'.

I asked the student, 'How you would feel if someone came into your family with this kind of intention? Would you be aware of it? How would you feel?' My intention was to invite the student to empathically imagine this situation from the families point of view.

The student reflected that she would not be comfortable with this kind of approach and she would not want to engage.

We then explored what kind of intention and approach the student could take which would align with compassion for these families and keep a vision of the families' 'beauty'? This gave us a different framework to work from. The focus became more about understanding the families' pain, strengths and courage. We became interested rather in what the family had tried in order to help their son or daughter? What had they found worked for their family and what did not. How do they feel we could support them?

## NVC and Social Change

I illustrate to students how NVC can be applied to direct work with clients as well as being a social change framework. Specifically the role that NVC has played in developing Restorative Justice is very useful as a community building method. In *The Heart of Social Change*, a transcript of a NVC workshop given by Marshall Rosenberg (2005b) – he describes the four key dimensions or awarenesses in relation to social change effort and partnership models:

> ... We need to understand our dominant stories, such as ... the cultural myth ... [that] some people are ordained to have Divine rights to rule over others ... the idea that we can divide people into good and bad ... [and] ... stories of virtuous forces crushing the evil forces ... we need to understand the role of cultural conditioning agents such as education, religion, family, media ... The need for structural understanding and the link between Domination systems and violence ... The awareness that our cultural stories and structures engender violence at all levels ... (Rosenberg, 2005b: 14)

## NVC as Protective Factor

It is common for people at all levels of our Domination system derived culture, to disconnect from 'heart based compassionate connection' through dehumanising, blaming judgemental lenses which are widely modelled by our leaders and role models e.g in government, media etc. We are all a product of this society and thus it is possible for any of us to find ourselves engaging in Life-alienating thinking. When we relate to ourselves and others in this way we are relating through our intellect rather than our heart. People exist for us indirectly through the stories we tell ourselves about them.

It is in a state of compassionate disconnection with ourselves or others that we as individuals and as social workers have the potential to do harm. The NVC lens can be a protective factor for social workers and students both in their direct work with people and in their self-care in that its primary aim is for compassionate connection.

As a field educator sharing the practice of nonviolence I try to link students with Social Work literature which advocates for compassionate Power – with approaches such as Sonya Stanford & Sandra Taylor's (2013) article titled 'Welfare Dependence or Enforced Deprivation? A Critical Examination of White Neoliberal Welfare and Risk'. The authors bring our attention to the way that current practices in 'risk assessment', increasingly utilised within neo-liberalist Welfare bureaucracies use language in a way that enables workers to disconnect compassionately from the 'suffering' of recipients of welfare. 'Risk' frames social problems as technical problems that require rational instrumental solutions and this excludes recognition of and responses to the lived experience of 'social suffering'.

## Conclusion

In this chapter I have highlighted some key features of NVC and their application to social work and field education, most importantly the conscious building of non-hierarchical relationships and organisational structures; the awareness of not falling into the trap of perceiving ourselves as the virtuous ones in cultural myths; noticing our own Life-alienating thinking and awareness of the intention underpinning our communications and actions.

I have found it constructive to use the NVC framework to help to contextualise the students' contributions as being within the larger partnership they have with the social work profession. The NVC framework can also be used to demonstrate to students that every word and every action they take matters, and contributes to the combined achievements of social work. This framework can help prevent feelings of powerlessness and hopelessness and can support and maintain hope and optimism thus providing a powerful protection against burnout.

NVC has enormous practical relevance to both social work practitioners and students alike: for direct client practice, for supporting respectful and supportive peer relationships, for self-reflection, self-care, for critical reflection and analysis, assessment and planning, conflict resolution, mediation, group and community work and for social change.

# References

AASW (2010) *Code of Ethics.* Retrieved from: https://www.aasw.asn.au/document/item/1201.

Atkinson, J. (2002). *Trauma trails, recreating song lines: the transgenerational effects of trauma in Indigenous Australia.* North Melbourne: Spinifex Press.

Donoghue, (2002). Research & Program Development and Social Justice Unit, cited in Scerra, N. (ed.). *Research into Models of Supervision for Aboriginal Staff A Review of Literature,* Program Development Social Justice Unit Uniting Uniting Care Children, Young People and Families Parramatta 2011.

Fields, B. (2010). Unity Radio A 13-week series focused on *13th Annual Gandhi King Season for Nonviolence.* Original air date: 29 March.

Hooks, B. Quotes. (n.d.). BrainyQuote.com. Retrieved 24 March 2018, from BrainyQuote.com Web site: https://www.brainyquote.com/quotes/bell_hooks_597911.

Peck, S.M. (1996). *In Search of Stones: A Pilgrimage of Faith, Reason and Discovery.* London: Simon and Shuster.

Peck, S.M. Quotes. (n.d.). BrainyQuote.com. Retrieved 24 March 2018, from BrainyQuote.com Web site: https://www.brainyquote.com/quotes/m_scott_peck_112981.

Rosenberg, M. (2005a). *Speak Peace in a World of Conflict: What you say next will change your world.* California, USA: Puddle Dancer Press.

Rosenberg, M. (2005b). *The Heart of Social Change.* California, USA: Puddle Dancer Press.

Rosenberg. M. (2015a). *Nonviolent Communication: A Language of Life* (3rd edn.). California, USA: Puddle Dancer Press.

Rosenberg, M. (2015b). The 4-Part NVC Process – Nonviolent Communication. Table in *Nonviolent Communication: A Language of Life* (3rd edn.). Retrieved from: www.nonviolentcommunication.com/aboutnvc/4partprocess.htm.

SBS News (2015). *Cronulla Riots anniversary: Calls to focus on 'positive' future.* SBS News, 11 December, Retrieved from: https://www.sbs.com.au/news/cronulla-riots-anniversary-calls-to-focus-on-positive-fut.

Stanford, S. and Taylor, S. (2013). 'Welfare Dependence or Enforced Deprivation? A Critical Examination of White Neoliberal Welfare and Risk', *Australian Social Work*, 66(4), 476–494.

# ELEVEN

# Student Dinners: Engaging and Retaining Online Social Work Students

## Rohena Duncombe

## Abstract

The Charles Sturt University (CSU) social work student body is predominantly enrolled online which can be isolating for students, poses challenges to academics for student engagement and is a student retention challenge for the School. This chapter reports on the evaluation of a strategy referred to as 'student dinners' and explores the potential of this initiative to address these challenges.

The student dinners are offered in association with field education liaison visits and they supplement the face-to-face contact online students experience through residential schools and liaison contacts. The student dinners are sometimes lunches or drinks and snacks, at other times an evening meal.

The evaluation of the student dinners initiative began some years after their inception. De-identified emailed responses from students addressed the open queries in relation to what was useful, and not useful about the dinners and invited suggestions from students about this initiative. The evaluation draws on themes from the student feedback and from literature about online education. The students reported benefits including: the opportunity to meet staff and other students, improved motivation to continue their studies, reduced isolation, a contribution to their developing social work identity and a contribution to developing a community of practice.

## Background

CSU is a major provider of social work education and has one of the largest online enrolments in Australia. In 2017 we had approximately 300 Masters qualifying and 700 Bachelor students, the majority of whom were enrolled both part time and online (CSU, 2017a). Online students come from across urban, regional, rural and remote Australia and a small number are international. The largest cohort is in Sydney and surrounds.

During their course, students attend four residential schools, each of five days duration. In these face-to-face contacts they have intensive practice workshops and lectures from experts and academic staff. The 20 days of face to face contact these intensives provide are an accreditation requirement of the Australian Association of Social Workers (AASW, 2017: 15). The residential schools are typically attended over a period of 8 years for Undergraduates and 5 years for Masters Qualifying students (based on the common part time study mode).

The students' other face to face contact with staff is during their two field education liaison visits, an AASW requirement (AASW, 2017: 27). Social work students undertake 1,000 hours of field education with a CSU social work liaison academic visiting them and their supervisor at their host agency. In my liaison role I had informal lunches with students and field teachers after the formal liaison meeting. When I visited two or more students in a locality this made for a larger sitting. The student dinners developed from these lunches when I began extending invitations to: students who were not on placement, recent graduates and locally based CSU contract staff. Consequently students could engage with a larger cohort in their home district.

For CSU, with students throughout Australia, liaison visits are an expensive component of course delivery. Catching up with students, field educators, recent graduates and local contract staff is an opportunity to 'value add' to formal liaison visits. Student dinners have been hosted between 2000 and 2017 in Adelaide, Tamworth, Port Macquarie, Grafton, Coffs Harbour, Lennox Head, Bangalow, Byron Bay, Cairns, Mackay, Toowoomba, on the Gold Coast, and in Brisbane.

## Literature Review

Online education is associated with student isolation and presents a challenge to engagement and retention (Robinson, 2012). Online and part-time students have higher non-completion rates (Norton, 2017). Their reasons tend to be personal ones, including financial pressures and family responsibilities (Kemp & Norton, 2014) as students typically manage their studies alongside work and family commitments (Kahue, Stephens, Leach & Zepkec, 2013). It is unclear whether being part-time and off-campus are cumulative risk factors, or proxies for students with these other commitments. Distraction from study, family, finances and work commitments, could be the actual main risk factors. Regardless of the exact cause, the ability of an institution to engage their online students is considered of key importance in minimising attrition (Norton, 2017).

### Comparative Performance and Attrition

CSU social work graduates perform highly on starting salaries and employment. We are in the top three universities with a $62,000 median starting salary and 82% full time employment at four months after graduation (Good University Guide, 2017). In comparison to other social work courses, in relation to engagement though, and possibly reflecting our predominantly online enrolments, CSU is in the lower end of rankings (Table 11.1).

Table 11.1. Excerpts from Good University Guide 2017

|  | University | Proportion |
|---|---|---|
| Proportion of students satisfied with overall quality of educational experience | Notre Dame<br>Charles Sturt<br>Monash | 94.4% (highest)<br>79%<br>54.4 (lowest) |
| Learner engagement | Latrobe<br>Charles Sturt<br>Sydney | 78.2 (highest)<br>48.1%<br>37.9% (lowest) |

Universities' attrition rates are calculated after the first year of enrolment and CSU's overall attrition rates are in line with other Universities that are based away from the east coast population centres (Table 11.2).

Table 11.2: Attrition by percentage at end of first year for all students (TESQSA, 2017)

| Institution | Location | % attrition |
|---|---|---|
| Charles Sturt University | Wagga Wagga, Port Macquarie, Dubbo | 28 |
| University of the Sunshine Coast | Mooloolaba | 26 |
| University of New England | Armidale | 27 |
| University of Central Queensland | Rockhampton | 27 |
| Southern Cross University | Lismore, Tweed Heads | 30 |
| Charles Darwin University | Darwin | 31 |
| University of Tasmania | Hobart | 32 |

While comparative attrition rates across Universities for social work students specifically are not available, the attrition rates for CSU online social work students are of concern with the attrition of BSW students at around 40 % and Masters qualifying at 25% depending on the cohort year (CSU, 2017a).

A TESQSA (2017) study based on 2014 data identified common characteristics linked to higher levels of attrition including higher proportions of online enrolments and higher proportions of vocational education and training (VET) based and non-Australian tertiary admission rank (ATAR) admissions by comparison to universities with lower attrition rates (TESQUA, 2017: 19). These high attrition related factors – part time, online, and non ATAR entry – are features of CSU social work enrolments.

## Challenges of Online Study

Family and work commitments inhibit 'on campus' studies, and mature age students, commonly study online and part time (Kahua et al., 2013). This is a typical enrolment pattern for CSU social work students and is reflected in completion rates. Around 25% of the online BSW students complete their studies at Year 8 or 9 (of a 4 year full time course) and around 50% of the Masters qualifying students complete with the slowest progressors achieving this by year 5 or 6 (CSU, 2017a).

Online education tends to be isolating (Robinson, 2012) so students can feel lonely and neglected (Nagel & Kotze, 2010). Social connectedness and belonging are factors that increase student engagement and decrease that isolation. Engaged students tend to complete (Smith, Erlam, Quirke, & Sylvester, 2014; Webster et al., 2016; Yates, Brindley-Richards, & Thistoll, 2014). Generally, strategies to increase connectedness have focussed on more contact through, and better use of, online technology.

Rodriguez-Keyes et al. (2013) argue that social work academics should model the building of rapport and relationships and demonstrate trustworthiness, credibility and caring. This functions as a strategy to facilitate autonomous motivation in learning (and also to model good social work practice). It is argued that students' feeling known to, and by academic staff supports study motivation and student engagement and that connection and engagement are at the heart of successful online learning (Rodriguez-Keyes et al., 2013; Olcott, 2014). Olcott (2014) specifies the importance of student-student, student-teacher and student-life connections.

# Methodology

Evaluation of the student dinners commenced in 2011. Without formal record-keeping for the full period, it is estimated 30 dinners have been held with 80 student attendances (by around 50 students) in 13 locations between 2000–17. The CSU ethics committee approved a more systematic, low-risk, qualitative evaluation. Thirteen responses were collected from students and 3 from CSU contract staff who work as markers, academic liaison and/or field education supervisors. The students emailed their responses to another CSU staff member who then de-identified the information and forwarded it to me. The contract staff provided their thoughts on the dinners experience directly to me by email.

These qualitative, text-based responses (students' comments on their experience of the dinners; positive, negative and suggestions) were stored and initially coded in NVivo. Nineteen early codes were noted and grouped in the four headings of: contemporary social work, networks, the dinners and social work studies. Within these areas, remarks about isolation or connection and local networks were the most frequent. When considered with themes from the literature – retention, engagement, and isolation – the four areas discussed below emerged; professional social work, local networks, the dinner experience and study.

## Results

In general, students enjoyed meeting other students, being party to professional conversations, and discussing their studies. Fortuitous bi-products included contributing to the students' developing professional identity, the development of local professional networks, 'communities of practice', and student engagement around issues in the field. There was also a contribution to engagement with their studies.

An NVivo generated word cloud gives an illustration of the word frequencies from the email text responses and thus common areas of comments from the students (with dominant words: 'social', 'work', 'dinners' and 'placement' omitted).

## Professional Social Work

Three areas of discussion are grouped under this heading; 'contact with experienced professionals', 'social work identity' and 'knowledge of the field'. In relation to dining with experienced social work professionals:

> I felt their support and have more of an understanding of who they are and their connectedness to their profession. (Student 3)
>
> I relished the opportunity to meet and interact with fully fledged social workers in a relaxed, informal way and to regard their opinions on many things and how they conducted themselves. (Student 1)
>
> Listening to conversations between experienced social workers I found this very interesting. (Student 5)

The students valued being accepted by professional social workers in an egalitarian way and being party to their discussions. For some, sharing a meal with qualified social workers, both academics and field educators, contributed to their developing professional identity:

> I felt it was an important building block in creating my social work identity. It added to helping me feel strong in the role. It made it easier to interact with other social workers at work and elsewhere – I felt like one of the crew and gained the sense that I was considered as one of a team. (Student 2)

The students were also able to learn about specialised fields of practice from both the social workers and each other, and to use this in considering upcoming placements and career options.

> Useful information on the justice system and social work. The information given helped me understand which social work fields would be better for me than others. (Student 5)
>
> A student I spoke to at the last dinner works in disability, so it was good to learn a bit more about local programs and initiatives, and her thoughts and concerns regarding the NDIS. (Student 12)

The dinners joined students with local professionals in discussions relevant to the contemporary field and to their understanding of the social work role.

## Networks

Two threads are identified: communities of practice and local support.

> I believe the networks that started to be established due to the vast experiences of other attendees will be really important for me as well. (Student 1)
>
> The highlight for me was the opportunity to network

with other students in the area. At both dinners, I ended up meeting new people, and getting the contact details of other students ... (Student 12)

Last week I had the pleasure of gathering once more with some fellow students and social work members of our community here in Coffs [Harbour]. (Student 9)

These reflections indicate the appreciation of starting to build a network of local social work contacts, effectively, a community of practice. They also valued meeting other people studying in their locality.

## The Dinner

This heading includes both the topics covered and the students' experiences of the dinner. Conversations ranged from the contemporary field, subjects, placements, and theories.

The conversation was general, social work, subjects, and placement. (Student 13)

Talking about theories, challenges, authors, the changing nature of the industry etc. is very useful ... I find a lot of the discussion on the subject specific uni forums are related to the assessment items. The dinners offered an informal way to have more general discussions without the pressure of being assessed. (Student 12)

We talked a lot about our experiences during our placement; how busy it was, the intensity of your placement. (Student 11)

For some, de-briefing about placement and other aspects of their study experiences was important. The most cited positives were getting together, sharing experiences, the informality and being in their home locality.

I really loved the opportunity to have that conversation informally, and face-to-face ... (Student 12)

... even more stories of their lives in the social work field but there is never enough time. (Student 1)

It was really good catching up with fellow students and hearing common concerns plus individual triumphs. (Student 8)

The informal dinner environment appears to have been useful in allowing students to have general conversations that linked their studies with contemporary practice as well as de-briefing and sharing their experiences. The most common negative about the dinners was that the students would have liked more time to talk. The most common suggestion was for more dinner opportunities.

## Overcoming Isolation and Disengagement

The students commented on the isolation of online study and the comfort of meeting. For some this contributed to their motivation and commitment to their studies.

Being a distance student, I have felt very lonely at times... so this was perfect. (Student 5)

I thought the gesture great as we can feel so alone when studying off campus. (Student 6)

I think it is important to maintain contact with other students as distance education can be very isolating. It's comforting to know that the other students are also going through the same process with study. (Student 3)

Meeting some real human bodies that are also doing the course is very reassuring, as the only other chance is at residential school. (Student 7)

I feel more committed to the study – funny I didn't

expect this, however hearing about the completed students experiences, who are now both working in fields they love was a great experience. (Student 1)

This yearly gathering is invaluable to me, and although it is not enough by far to resolve the very real isolation felt during distance education, it is these face to face interactions that I have fallen back on when thinking of giving up. (Student 9)

Another contribution to the students' study experience that emerged as useful was the relationships students felt they were able to build with locally based staff and in an informal setting.

I now know both Ian (contract marker and liaison) and Rohena and feel more comfortable discussing issues even over the phone since I have met them in person. (Student 1)

I do really like the idea of building local networks, and having an opportunity to properly discuss books and subjects with people like Rohena and Greg (contract marker and liaison) in a non-formal capacity – where we are not being assessed! (Student 12)

Rohena was lovely, and took the time to casually chat about my interests, goals, previous experience, and what I wanted to get out of my final placement. (Student 12)

## Social Work Professionals' Comments

Three contract staff employed as markers, external placement supervisors and undertaking placement liaison provided comments.

Given these get-togethers were scheduled well after ... the finalisation of results, most students (I think) were able to provide uncensored and valuable feedback to staff about their practicum/subject experience. (Contract academic 1)

I certainly was always curious to hear from students about the timing, adequacy and appropriateness of my contact with them during their practicums OR as a subject marker – how useful was my feedback on their assignments?' (Contract academic 1)

I have found the experience to be useful and insightful. I applaud ... the tenacity to maintain this activity for over a decade, for the many regional and remote students ... (Contract academic 2)

I really appreciate the dinners. I like the opportunity to meet students, other supervisors and CSU liaison staff in a friendly informal setting. (Contract academic 3)

## Discussion

The student dinners can contribute to reducing isolation and developing social work identity and communities of practice. Despite its modest size and other limitations the evaluation of the student dinners initiative indicates a likely positive contribution to the engagement of online social work students and a useful way to add value to field education liaison visits.

Isolation is a feature of online study (Robinson, 2012; Nagel & Katze, 2010) and was independently commented on by the student dinner respondents. Many CSU social work students are already working in the human services sector. They are mature aged and their non-ATAR entry, part time and online status are a reflection of the value of increased flexibility in making tertiary education accessible. However, those same features are associated with poorer retention and completion rates (Kahu et al., 20113; Kemp & Norton, 2014). These are important issues for CSU social work whose attrition rate is high and completion rates are modest (TESQUA, 2017; Good University Guide, 2017).

The students enjoyed spending informal time with social work professionals and noticed how these social workers conducted themselves and spoke about their profession and roles. Students independently commented on feeling more comfortable to contact staff they had now met in person in their home locality. These reflections are in line with Rodriguez et al.'s (2013) observations about the importance of modelling social work behaviours both for educational and student engagement reasons. While improving engagement for online students has tended to be undertaken via electronic medium (Smith et al., 2014; Webster et al., 2016; Yates et al., 2014) the student dinners are face-to-face and catalyse the value of liaison visits.

The student respondents also valued meeting fellow students, CSU contract staff, recent graduates and other social work professionals in their home locality and developing social work networks there. Some of the recent graduates also find it supportive to maintain contact with the University and their undergraduate peers through the dinners. The dinners contribute to the student-student, student-teacher and student-life connections that Olcott (2014) has demonstrated are useful for addressing the retention and completion challenges CSU social work faces.

The dinners invite students into an environment where they are sharing, informally and equally, in a community of professional social workers giving them the opportunity to converse about the field, agencies and local issues. They discuss their course and progress with peers, make enquiries of academics and share their own experiences. The dinners link students, recent graduates, academics, practitioners and supervisors contributing to communities of practice, and professional identity.

Student feedback indicates that the dinners can improve engagement, at a face to face and local level, supplementing online connection. The respondents appreciated the opportunity for personal contact beyond their residential school and field education liaison visits. They indicated that the opportunity to discuss their course, placement possibilities and career options in an egalitarian and casual environment was a useful supplement to other course related contacts. Some students commented specifically how the dinners re-motivated them in their studies.

Local social workers participating in the CSU social work programme as field educators, contract staff, and as external supervisors, value the dinners as informal professional support and as a link to the University that would otherwise be electronic-only. This supports the development of relationships locally between students and local staff.

The student dinners project was established as a practical and efficient way to utilise regional liaison visits to students on field education placements. It was not established as a research enterprise and the present evaluation comes many years after it began. There are just 13 responses from approximately 80 student attendances. Despite these limitations, the evaluation identifies some useful aspects of the student dinner initiative in relation to the literature on online and distance education. It also addresses areas of challenge for CSU as a rural university whose social work cohort has higher than desirable attrition rates and lower than desirable completion rates.

Despite being limited in size, the findings of the evaluation are in line with the contemporary literature on online education providing encouragement for continuing to value add to liaison visits with informal meal sharing. Given the expense of student liaison in the social work education endeavour, eliciting the most from these visits to support retention, facilitate professional identity and instigate communities of practice, including support for recent graduates, is a valuable opportunity.

There appears to be a confluence of experiences happening within the student dinners milieu that invites further investigation. Because the project was not initiated as a specific research project to address attrition and completion, it is not possible to definitively assess direct or causal impacts of the student dinners on attrition and completion rates. Similarly the degree to which the dinners contribute to communities of practice and social work identity or serve to strengthen the students' engagement with their social work studies would need further study in order to make specific claims. One could reasonably expect a positive relationship, though not necessarily a uni-directional causality.

# Conclusion

CSU's social work students are predominantly enrolled online and this presents the challenges of isolation for students, engagement for staff and of attrition and completion for the School. The student dinners make a positive contribution toward addressing these challenges. They provide extra opportunities for face-to-face contact over periods of 5-9 years of study and they are delivered at negligible expense and without significant inconvenience to the student, being in their home locality. The student dinners ameliorate isolation by linking students with local peers and building closer relationships with staff.

The social work dinners add value to field education liaison visits by taking the opportunity to catch-up with online students, new graduates, workplace learning supervisors and CSU contract staff in the locality of the visit. The dinners provide an informal opportunity for discussions with staff about subjects, placements and their profession outside of the formal assessment environment. The dinners help in initiating a social work community of practice, for them to develop their social work identity and to experience enhanced support from the University.

# References

Australian Association of Social Workers (AASW) (2017). *Australian Social Work Education Accrediation Standards*, North Melbourne: Australian Association of Social Workers.

Charles Sturt University (CSU) (2017a). Unpublished data supplied in-house from Charles Sturt University administration, Wagga Wagga.

Charles Sturt University (CSU) (2017b). *Charles Sturt University Strategic Direction*. Bathurst: CSU.

Good Universities Guide (2017). Retrieved from https://www. gooduniversitiesguide.com.au/.

Kahua, E. Stephens, C., Leach, L. and Zepkec, N. (2013). 'The engagement of mature distance students', *Higher Education Research & Development*, 32(5), 791–804.

Kemp, D. & Norton, A. (2014). *Review of the Demand Driven Funding System Report 2014, Department of Education and Training*. Retrieved from https://

docs.education.gov.au/node/35537.

Nagel, L., & Kotze, T. (2010). 'Supersizing e-learning: What a Community of Inquiry survey reveals about teaching presence in a large online class', *Internet & Higher Education,* 13(1/2), 45–51.

Norton, A. (2017). *Higher education admissions,* Retrieved from: http://andrewnorton.net.au/category/higher-education/higher-education-admissions/

Olcott, D. J. (2014). *An analysis of selected models of online, open and distance learning universities.* Consulting Research Paper conducted for the African Virtual University. Nairobi, Kenya.

Robinson, S. (2012). 'Freedom, aspiration and informed choice in rural higher education: Why they are saying "no"', *Education in Rural Australia,* 22(2), 79–95.

Rodriguez-Keyes, E., Schneider, D. & Keenan, E. (2013). 'Being known in undergraduate Social Work education: The role of instructors in fostering student engagement and motivation', *Social Work Education,* 32(6), 785–99.

Smith, N., Erlam, C., Quirke, N., & Sylvester, G. (2014). 'Establishing a sense of connectedness amongst theology students in distance education', *Journal of Open, Flexible, and Distance Learning,* 18(2), 11–28.

Tertiary Education Standards Quality and Standards Agency (TEQSA) (2017). *Characteristics of Australian higher education providers and their relation to first-year student attrition,* Australian Government, Retrieved from http://www.teqsa.gov.au/media-publications/characteristics-australian-higher-education-providers-and-their-relation-first.

Webster, E., Johnson, C., Kemp, B., Smith, V., Johnson, M., & Townsend, B. (2016). 'Theory that explains an Aboriginal perspective of learning to understand and manage diabetes', *Australian and New Zealan Journal of Public Health,* 41(1), 1–26.

Yates, A., Brindley-Richards, W., & Thistoll, T. (2014). 'Student engagement in distance-based vocational education', *Journal of Open, Flexible, and Distance Learning,* 18(2), 29–44.

# TWELVE

# Insights – Making the Invisible Visible in Education and Practice

*Cate Thomas, Monica Short, Heather Barton*

## Abstract

Challenging social constructs, barriers and blockages to social inclusion, social cohesion, social justice, respect for diversity and human rights experienced by people living with disabilities is essential social work. This chapter presents through an auto-ethnographic investigation a critical reflection into society's norms about deserving or undeserving – using the example of hidden disability. The chapter questions the current societal acknowledgement and perceptions of hidden disability and focuses on the constructs of 'you must see a disability to have it' or 'I walk and talk therefore I must be OK'. Critical thinking, personal experience and theoretically informed social work practice underpin this exploration.

According to Fook (2012), critical thinking is important to the social work profession because it provides a framework for considering the construction and deconstruction of structural norms (and impediments) of society and the nexus with the individual. Critical theory challenges discourses and narratives, is fundamental to knowing, being reflective and interactive with individuals, assists in understanding their connections to society, and conceptualising individual and social change (Fook, 2012: 17). Allan, Briskman and Pease (2009) support Fook's claims of the importance of critical theory for social work and highlight the impact of discourses. They reflect on the social worker's role with a critical theory lens when engaging with people who have a disability (Allan et al., 2009: 198–200). Through this chapter, the authors critically converse with each other and the audience about hidden disabilities and the impact of negative communications and engagement with broader members of the public. It refers to the role that social work practice and education plays. It focuses on the example of accessing priority parking, also known as disability parking or accessible parking.

Challenging the societal perceptions of disability and to examine the construct of 'you must see a disability to have it' or 'I walk and talk therefore I must be OK' we argue is imperative. This chapter aspires through social work informed thinking, to challenge existing myths of what constitutes a disability and also stereotypes about who are and who are not deserving of services. This led to the question does the literature and society acknowledge diagnosed hidden disability? The quote below by Cate demonstrates the importance of researching this question.

> I find it really interesting living with a diagnosed hidden disability – I feel it is really important that society rethinks what constitutes a person who has a disability … the perceptions that are out there. The existing views of appearing to be abled-bodied and utilising resources and services is clearly confronting to broader society, which in turn leads to confrontations by members of society towards people who have hidden disabilities. This has significant impact on the person with a diagnosed hidden disability and needs to be challenged.

The Australian Bureau of Statistics defines disability as any limitation, restriction or impairment which restricts everyday activities and has lasted or is likely to last for at least six months (Australian Bureau of Statistics, 2009: 3). An estimated 4.3 million people in Australia (nearly 1 in 5 people or 18%) reported having a disability in 2015 (Australian Institute of Health and Welfare, 2017: 1; Australian Bureau of Statistics, 2009: 3). In contrast the United Nations (UN) perceive disability as an evolving concept (2006: preamble). According to the UN Convention on the Rights of Persons with Disabilities, disability results from the interaction between persons with impairments and attitudinal and environmental barriers that hinders their full and effective participation in society on an equal basis with others (United Nations, 2006: preamble). The World Health Organisation (WHO) continues the idea of the impact of interactions with people with disabilities in their World Report on Disability, and its associated international classification of functioning framework for disability and health (World Health Organisation, 2014). It defines disability as 'an umbrella term for impairments, activity limitations, and participation restrictions, denoting the negative aspects of the interaction between an individual (with health conditions) and that individual's contextual factors (environmental and personal factors)' (World Health Organisation & The World Bank, 2011: 303).

In these three high level definitions, unseen, invisible or hidden disability are not explicitly stated. What is omitted in all of these definitions is the recognition that a disability does not have to be visible or the person 'classified' as having a disability in order to be 'acknowledged'. The World Report on Disability does examine the diversity of disability by conveying '... Disability encompasses the child born with a congenital condition such as cerebral palsy or the young soldier who loses his leg to a land-mine, or the middle-aged woman with severe arthritis, or the older person with dementia, among many others. Health conditions can be visible or invisible; temporary or long term; static, episodic, or degenerating; painful or inconsequential' (World Health Organisation & The World Bank, 2011: 7–8). Invisible disability is valid and the conditions identified as hidden or invisible disabilities are large and diverse (Davis, 2005: 157; World Health Organisation & The World Bank, 2011).

It is known that regardless of Acts, Statements, Codes, Legislation and Rights, people living with disabilities regularly experience barriers (Hearn, Short, & Healy, 2014: 1344–5). That this group of people remains one of the most marginalised and oppressed groups in society, at risk of experiencing poverty and/or exclusion (Healy, Tillotson, Short, & Hearn, 2015; Stainton, Chenowth, & Bigby, 2010). They can have limited access to services including social work based services (case management, counselling, advocacy for example) and opportunities (World Health Organisation & The World Bank, 2011). They are also at risk of being negatively stereotyped and morally judged as deserving or undeserving of services (Garthwaite, Bambra, & Warren, 2013: 1104). Struggles to be seen as equal, and as valued citizens, can characterise lives of people living with disabilities (Healy et al., 2015; Kim, 2010; Stainton et al., 2010).

The Social Model of Disability challenges structures, such as the lack of accessibility, that oppress or socially exclude people living with disabilities (for example, Oliver, 2009; Oliver & Barnes, 2012). This model argues that society imposes disability on top of peoples' impairments, causing people to be isolated, oppressed and socially excluded (Oliver, 2009: 42). Disability is not the impairment but rather the restriction or disadvantage of activity caused by social organisations and it hence excludes people from mainstream activities (Oliver, 2009: 42). WHO, the UN and other key international organisations are attempting to raise the political and policy impacts of such restrictions; for example, raise the failure to address access to resources and services of people with disability and their associated fundamental human rights issues (United Nations, 2006; World Health Organisation & The World Bank, 2011).

Additionally disability advocates like Oliver and Barnes (2012) also discuss and action debate surrounding disability, the politicisation of issues, and the role of government and society in enabling positive life discourses for people living with disability as well as the construction of positive identities. They argue that people living with disabilities need to resist discrimination and oppression and work towards creating a better society for all (Oliver & Barnes, 2012: 175–6).

People living with hidden or invisible disabilities can face unique struggles because their impairments are not always acknowledged by society. They experience the impact of impairments that they are living with, as well as being subject to rejection, humiliation and social disapproval (Davis, 2005: 154–5). Some argue that the facial invisibility of impairment does influence how society treats people. They posit facial invisibility or hidden disability enables a person to escape the stigmatisation attached to visible disability (Davis, 2005: 155). Davis refutes this arguing people living with invisible disabilities are bearing the burden of securing the assistance they need to function effectively and they suffer the discomfort of strangers' interrogations (Davis, 2005: 155–6). For example, a study undertaken by Stone of 22 women living with a hidden disability, haemorrhage stroke, found that most experienced the need to continually explain their hidden disabilities to others (Stone, 2005: 300). Furthermore, many were frustrated that their apparent 'able-bodies' led others to have unrealistic expectations they could not meet (Stone, 2005: 300). These tensions of the seen and unseen, the hidden and unhidden, deserving and undeserving experienced by people living with disabilities are not always visible to society or expressed in extant literature.

According to Oliver and Barnes, socialisation teaches people social norms, cultural expectations and shared standards (Oliver & Barnes, 2012: 110). Personal and social perceptions about who are disabled or not disabled and who are deserving or undeserving are derived from interactions with other people and social institutions (Oliver & Barnes, 2012: 110). Critically understanding the lack of acknowledgement of people living with hidden disabilities by society and the consequential perceptions and interactions can help inform social work practice and education.

Additionally, social workers can critically contemplate how societal perceptions about hidden disability can impact on their being, thinking and doing of social work (Pawar & Anscombe, 2015). According to these authors, being is 'the dynamic and developing total state of a social worker, who consciously learns to continually reflect on self and others with a view to raising critical self and social awareness' (Pawar & Anscombe, 2015:

33). Thinking is how social workers 'apply theory and knowledge in what they do' and includes critical, creative or lateral, systemic, divergent and convergent elements of thinking' (Pawar & Anscombe, 2015: 24–7). Doing is the 'roles undertaken by social workers and the skills they employ in their roles' (Pawar & Anscombe, 2015: 27).

In relation to disability, social workers are encouraged to 'think' about and understand the political dimensions of impairment and disability and the barriers that society's perceptions can place upon people living with disabilities (Milner, Myers, & O'Byrne, 2015: 234). Social workers can recognise that through 'being', they are intentionally or unintentionally members of the political system impacting on others and their political views are shaped by their own knowledge and standpoints (Australian Association of Social Workers, 2010: 14). In response social workers can promote and 'do' social justice and advocate for the full inclusion of people living with disabilities within society (International Federation of Social Workers, 2014, 2015). Such foundational ideas about being, thinking and doing and disability can also inform elements of teaching social work and practicing it.

The Australian Association of Social Workers (2010) values reflective self-awareness. Social workers are expected to be reflexive in their practice (White, 2001). Reflexivity is a process of looking *inward* and *outward*, to the social and cultural artefacts and forms of thought which saturate our practices (White, 2001). As 'thinking, doing and being' professionals, social workers through their practice and teaching can be catalysts for social change, cohesion, inclusion and justice. This awareness creates a challenge for educators and practitioners, for example, that their advocacy includes empowering individuals, students and colleagues living with invisible disabilities and their carers. This challenge inspired us as authors and social workers to undertake a research project.

This inductive research project (Alston & Bowles, 2012: 12) is based on careful observations by the co-authors about the social world of disability. All authors are female, over 45 years, immersed in this topic, have experience in industry and academia and each has more than 25 years of professional experience in the welfare sector. Cate Thomas is a social worker, academic/lecturer and social researcher at Charles Sturt University and identifies as living with connective tissue and associated autoimmune diseases. Monica Short is a social worker, lecturer and social researcher with Charles Sturt University. Monica's father has passed away and he lived with numerous disabilities from birth. Heather Barton is a social worker, and an adjunct lecturer with Charles Sturt University. Cate, Monica and Heather's intimate connections with the topic led to an auto-ethnographic exploration, critical reflection and conversation about this social field of hidden disability. This research undertook to reduce the gaps in literature and public dialogue about hidden disability.

Auto-ethnography is a known methodology within disability studies. Denshire argues it is used to challenge dominant techno-rational discourses in health and other settings about illness, well-ness, self and other (Denshire, 2014: 838). It brings new visibilities to power relations and raises ethical issues (Denshire, 2014: 838–9).

Ethnography can be defined as social scientific writing about particular people (Silverman, 2006: 67). It involves studying the people in their (or our) natural settings or fields and in doing so valuing the human-ness of the situation (Denshire, 2014; Silverman, 2006: 67). The researcher participates directly in the setting and collects data in a systematic way (Silverman, 2006: 67). Auto-ethnography examines the relationships between the self and others within culture (Tomaselli, 2013: 167; White, 2001).

A particular form of 'participant observation', informs this methodology and this project, in that, living with a hidden physical disability gives a unique understanding into it (Hallahan, 2010; Silverman, 2006: 68). The authors are convinced that careful reflection on our own lived experience of disability provides very different insights into this social field than those observed by social work practitioners or social researchers from a distance (Silverman, 2006: 68). We also agree with the premise that an author, social researcher and/or social worker cannot escape the subjectivity of their own biography and cultural assumptions (Shaw & Gould, 2001).

This auto-ethnographic investigation contains the following features: a strong emphasis on exploring the nature of hidden disability rather than testing hypotheses about it; working with three social workers' autobiographical stories and hence unstructured data; investigation, comparison and analysis of three people's experiences; and the interpreting of meanings and functions of actions associated with this social field (Silverman, 2006: 79). A strength of this methodology is also its limitation. In auto-ethnographic ventures, a small number of people are involved. In this project, there were three participants. This makes the research vulnerable to a blurring of boundaries between fact and fiction, and could allow people to re-write their self within their social world (Denshire, 2014: 381). We navigated this risk by presenting the facts of our experiences and then we provided our interpretations. We contracted at the beginning of the project to question and challenge each other's analysis and critique. This allowed us to reflect on western society's constructs about hidden disability as well as our own (Denshire, 2014: 834).

Western society can attribute importance to being able-bodied, privileging one group of peoples' achievements and abilities over another's (Davis, 2005: 163). Society can chose not to acknowledge hidden disability. This creates barriers for people living with disabilities such as, when someone morally judges another as deserving or undeserving of services and resources. This is seen in the example below about accessible parking.

> [Cate:] Because my disability is not obvious to the everyday person, according to some I therefore do not have a disability. This construct is very 'wearing' and impacts personally ... My last confrontation was by a woman in her 60s who aggressively walked over to my car as I got into it after doing grocery shopping at the local supermarket, putting her hand on my car door stopping me from closing it. She proceeded to berate me as an able bodied person parking illegally in a disability parking space.

This narrative by Cate in conjunction with the social model of disability's view about how barriers (Oliver, 2009) reinforce the existence of obstacles that people living with invisible or hidden disabilities experience. One obstacle is the social notion about people's inability and their lack of independence that results in disempowering people living with disabilities so that they do not fight to maintain their independence. Another is the negative social notion associated with people living with invisible disabilities and this impacts on people who are trying to maintain their independence but are requiring others to acknowledge their need to access resources. Cate's narrative above identified for us, that society imposes a definition on a person about their body, needs and resources.

Concepts of deserving or undeserving of assistance are not descriptors of the author's experience of impairment. This auto-ethnographic venture confirmed for the authors the social model's view that disability is not the impairment experienced by people living with disabilities, but rather that disability is the disadvantage or restriction that one faces when accessing resources and services (Oliver, 2009) such as disability parking. What is the consequence of this confirmation for us as three social workers? We argue it involves integrating our thinking and reflections about this field into our being or identity as social workers and into our doing of social work – which for us is our practice and teaching. That is it impels the three of us to move from reflecting on to promoting social change and development, social cohesion, and the empowerment and liberation of people, as seen by the comments below.

> [Cate:] This culminated in the decision that it is actually necessary to challenge the existing societal identification formation and perception of constructs of what constitutes a disability. More importantly, it reminds me of the role that social workers have under critical social work theory [Allan et al., 2009; Fook, 2012] to both advocate for new constructs, and agitate against the existing constructs, to ensure that people with hidden disabilities are not confronted with unjust

societal behaviours. Social workers also have a challenge on a client or service delivery level to ensure that their personal construct of disability incorporates hidden disability to effectively respond to the individual, their family/carers, community and environment.

[Monica:] I am aware that people living with disabilities can feel oppressed by others, even if this is unintentional. For me, as a social worker I affiliate with people living with disabilities who are oppressed. I stand in solidarity with those experiencing exclusion and try to empower others and create opportunities for social inclusion and belonging, a sense of connection and welcome, full participation and justice. As a result of this project I am now contemplating how I am going in incorporating my aspirations into my lecturing, research and personal life.

[Heather:] The convenience and choice I have as a person without a hidden physical disability, is often an unconscious source of capacity and power that I carry with me. It is only at the times I am temporarily constrained in my ability or when I observe that constraint in others that I am truly challenged to think about the added difficulty of life without this particular privilege. As a social worker, it embarrasses me to realise I am mostly so unaware of how I take this position of power for granted. Yet the power is not completely out of my consciousness and I am still learning how to negotiate the tricky terrain of offering assistance where it might be welcomed or staying that offer where it represents potential disempowerment.

Advocacy, power and empowerment, as indicated by these three quotes above, are key to this research about acknowledging hidden disability. Our reflective conversations revealed that it is in the small every day acts and in our relationships with others, that social workers can replicate or change or share the power relations that we and others experience. This project presents the idea that change needs to start with the consciousness of awareness (thinking) about hidden disability, and that this becomes a conscious action (doing) over time until it becomes an unconscious way of life (being). The author's recommend that social workers aim to also influence, where we can, the larger structures and arrangements of society. This is so as to effect societal change for those who may not have the skills, resources or opportunities to do so and who experience disadvantage as a result.

To conclude, disability is an evolving concept and currently the literature does not always acknowledge hidden disability (United Nations, 2006: preamble; World Health Organisation, 2014; World Health Organisation & The World Bank, 2011). Furthermore, according to the authors' experiences, examples exist indicating that western society does not always readily acknowledge hidden disability. Social workers as thinking, doing and being educators, practitioners and political agents can challenge the existing constructs about people living with hidden disability. Individually and collectively, they can shape and mould their own and advocate for change in societal concepts in a way that translates to a more equal and positive life experience for all people who live with a disability, hidden or not.

## References

Allan, J., Briskman, L., & Pease, B. (eds.). (2009). *Critical social work: theories and practices for a socially just world*. Crows Nest, NSW: Allen & Unwin.

Alston, M., & Bowles, W. (2012). *Research for social workers*. (3rd edn.). Oxon: Routledge.

Australian Association of Social Workers. (2010). *Code of Ethics*. Canberra: AASW.

Australian Bureau of Statistics. (2009). *Disability, Aging and Carers, Australia: Consolidated set of tables. Main condition causing disability by age*. Retrieved 29 April 2015, from http://www.abs.gov.au/AUSSTATS/abs@.nsf/DetailsPage/4430.02009?OpenDocument.

Australian Institute of Health and Welfare. (2017). *Australia's welfare 2017.* Australia's welfare series no. 13. AUS 214. Canberra: AIHW.

Davis, N. A. (2005). 'Invisible disability', *Ethics,* 116(1), 153–213.

Denshire, S. (2014). 'On auto-ethnography', *Current Sociology Review,* 62(6), 831–50.

Fook, J. (2012). *Social work: a critical approach to practice* (2nd edn.). London: SAGE.

Garthwaite, K., Bambra, C., & Warren, J. (2013). 'The unwilling and the unwell? Exploring stakeholders perceptions of working with long term sickness benefits recipients', *Disability and Society,* 28(8), 1104–17.

Hallahan, L. (2010). 'Legitimising Social Work Disability Policy Practice: Pain or Praxis?', *Australian Social Work,* 63(1), 117–32.

Healy, J., Tillotson, N., Short, M., & Hearn, C. (2015). 'Social work field education: Believing in supervisors who are living with disabilities', *Disability and Society,* 30(7), 1087–102.

Hearn, C., Short, M., & Healy, J. (2014). 'Social Work Field Education: Believing in students living who are living with disabilities', *Disability and Society,* 29(9), 1343–55.

International Federation of Social Workers. (2014). Global definition of social work. Retrieved 3 November 2014, from http://ifsw.org/get-involved/global-definition-of-social-work/.

International Federation of Social Workers. (2015). People with disabilities. Retrieved 28 December 2015, from http://ifsw.org/policies/people-with-disabilities/.

Kim, H. S. (2010). 'UN Disability Rights Convention and Implications for Social Work Practice', *Australian Social Work,* 63(1), 103–16.

Milner, J., Myers, S., & O'Byrne, P. (2015). *Assessment in social work* (4th edn.). London: Palgrave.

Oliver, M. (2009). *Understanding disability: From theory to practice.* Hampshire: Palgrave Macmillan.

Oliver, M., & Barnes, C. (2012). *The New Politics of Disablement.* Great Britain: Palgrave Macmillan.

Pawar, M., & Anscombe, B. (2015). *Reflective social work practice: Thinking, doing and being.* Melbourne: Cambridge University Press.

Shaw, I., & Gould, N. (2001). 'A review of qualitative research in Social Work'. In I. Shaw & N. Gould (eds.), *Qualitative Research in Social Work* (pp. 32–47). London: SAGE Publications Ltd.

Silverman, D. (2006). *Interpreting qualitative data* (3rd edn.). London: Sage

Publication Ltd.

Stainton, T., Chenowth, L., & Bigby, C. (2010). 'Social Work and Disability: An Uneasy Relationship', *Australian Social Work, 63*(1), 1–3.

Stone, S. D. (2005). 'Reactions to invisible disability: The experiences of young women survivors of hemorrhage stroke', *Disability and Rehabilitation, 27*(6), 293–024.

Tomaselli, K. (2013). 'Visualizing different kinds of writing: Auto-ethnography, Social Science', *Visual Anthropology, 26*(2), 165–80.

United Nations. (2006). *Convention on the Rights of Persons with Disabilities.* Retrieved from: https://www.un.org/development/desa/disabilities/convention-on-the-rights-of-persons-with-disabilities.html.

White, S. (2001). 'Auto-Ethnography as reflexive inquiry: The research act as self-surveillance'. In I. Shaw & N. Gould (eds.), *Qualitative research in Social Work* (pp. 100–16). London: Sage Publications Ltd.

World Health Organisation (2014). *International Classification of Functioning, Disability and Health (ICF) framework to facilitate Interprofessional education and collaborative practice*: World Health Organisation.

World Health Organisation, & The World Bank (2011). World Report on Disability: World Health Organisation.

# THIRTEEN

# Recognition of Prior Learning in Practice

*Bruce Valentine and Wendy Bowles*

## Abstract

This chapter critiques the Australian Association of Social Workers' (AASW) credentialist model of Recognition of Prior Learning (RPL) at CSU and reimagines it as a reflective professional development process, known as Professional Practice Assessment (PPA). In discussing the PPA model the limitations of the credentialist model and the advantages of the PPA process are examined, particularly in relation to students developing social work identity.

## Introduction

Ever since the CSU social work program by distance education began, the student body has been characterised by a majority of mature-aged students, many of whom are experienced workers in their own right. These students enter the program with backgrounds as welfare practitioners, managers, counsellors and community development workers to name a few, with experience in fields such as child protection, sexual assault, drug and alcohol, disability, Indigenous workers, youth, aged care and multicultural settings. Most have family, caring and financial responsibilities and must juggle work, and family responsibilities together with study requirements if they are to successfully complete their degree.

Field education is an important, and many would claim central, part of accredited social work courses across the globe. Indeed since 2008 the US Council of Social Work Education has designated field education as the 'signature pedagogy' of social work education (Wayne, Bogo & Raskin, 2010). This claim has been debated ever since (see for example Holden et al. (2011) exploring the evidence for this claim, Lyter's (2012) discussion of implications arising and Ledger, Hillman, Harreveld & de Warren's, (2017) recent examination of it in the Australian context.

However it is designated, field education has always been important and valued in Australian social work education, notwithstanding increasing concern about a 'crisis' in field education, especially in relation to the shortage of placements available (for example Gursansky & Le Sueur, 2012; Egan, Waugh, Giles & Bowles, 2017; and in Canada Ayala et al., 2018). Crisis or not, the professional body the Australian Association of Social Workers (AASW) currently requires social work students to complete 2 long unpaid placements totalling 1,000 hours in all (AASW, 2012a, 2017). This can be a heavy burden for the mature aged students that apply to CSU and other universities where distance education is offered (Valentine, Bowles & McKinnon, 2016; Maidment & Crisp, 2011).

Since 2008 in Australia, the same year as field education was announced as the signature pedagogy in US social work education, the AASW has introduced the concept of recognition of prior learning or RPL as it is termed, for the first field education subject in its revised *Education and Accreditation Standards*, termed ASWEAS in the profession's jargon (AASW, 2008). Since the 2008 ASWEAS was introduced there has been the potential for eligible students to be exempted from up to 500 hours of the first placement or part thereof (AASW, 2008, 2012a, 2017). Perhaps this initiative was in response to the field education crisis mentioned above, and perhaps it was also one way to recognise the changing student profile following the spread of distance education courses and the professional entry level Masters of Social Work (qualifying) across Australia.

# Recognition of Prior Learning in Social Work Education

Recognition of prior learning, or RPL as it is known, is relatively new in Australian higher education, having been introduced in the early 1990s (Cameron, 2011). The AASW's application of RPL derives from the definition adopted by the Australian Qualifications Framework (AQF) Advisory Board (AQF, 2007: 91), which states:

> Recognition of Prior Learning (RPL) may be defined in a number of ways ... All definitions, however, include the key notion that RPL involves the assessment of previously unrecognised skills and knowledge that an individual has achieved outside the formal education and training system. RPL assesses this unrecognised learning against the requirements of the qualification, in respect of both entry requirements and the outcomes to be achieved.

Cameron (2011) argues that this definition favours an outcomes and market-based assessment of professional competences, termed 'credentialism'. This approach assumes that professional behaviours displayed in one context translate directly to another and that applicants simply provide 'proof', judged against external standards, that they have met the required competencies and thus gain credit for the corresponding part of a course.

The AASW's approach to RPL is very much in line with this, requiring eligible students to provide evidence 'that they have met the standards and performance outcomes for the first placement' (AASW, 2012b: 5). In order to be eligible to apply for an RPL assessment of these performance outcomes, the AASW specifies that social work students must have a minimum of three years full-time equivalent practice experience in a relevant context of which at least one-year full-time equivalent has to have been during the last three years (AASW, 2012b: 5).

Several questions arise in relation to a credentialist or outcomes-focused approach to RPL for social work field education. First, is it reasonable to assume that skills demonstrated in one area, such as youth work, directly translate into another such as social work? This question has been asked by social work field education academics (Valentine et al., 2016) as well as teaching academics (Down, 2008) on the basis that specific skills are meaningless unless taught within the social context of the profession in which they will be practised.

A related question is what happens to professional socialisation, one of the main values of the process of field education, if a credentialist approach to RPL is adopted? Giles, Irwin Lynch & Waugh (2010) argue that achieving the outcomes for field education involves a transformative process in which course work is related to practice and social work identity is promoted (see also Cleak & Wilson, 2013). Developing a social work identity is a challenging experience for some students who may have had years of experience in the workforce with only limited exposure to working with social work practitioners. Field education placements can be key to developing professional identity (Moorhead, 2017; Zuchowskil, 2016) which is becoming an increasingly important issue for social work more generally (Webb, 2017). For the purposes of this chapter we adopt the definition of professional identity proposed by Webb (2017: 2–3) who argues that professional identity is a complex, unstable and contested concept closely aligned to professional socialisation. It includes both the notions of *identity* which is relational and contextual, and *identification*, which is more about the process of aligning with the profession. Under a credentialist model of RPL, the complex notion of professional identity development is at best ignored and at worst dismissed as irrelevant. With the implicit assumption that skills acquired and demonstrated in one context will simply translate to the next, the whole notion of professional socialisation disappears.

While ASEAS rhetoric concurs with the Giles et al. (2010) and Cleak & Wilson (2013) when it asserts that field education is a developmental process (AASW, 2012b: 3), there is no recognition of the need for this development under the AASW's current credentialist approach deriving from the AQF framework (Cameron, 2011: 17). Yet Cameron (2011) argues that pockets of a developmental approach to RPL can still be found in higher education in Australia. It is the contention of this chapter that a developmental approach is needed in RPL for social work field education.

## The Developmental Model of RPL at CSU

The developmental approach to RPL identified by Cameron (2006) lies at the opposite end of the RPL spectrum to the credentialist model. Instead of focusing simply on credit, this humanistic developmental approach focuses on process as much as outcome. The RPL 'assessor' becomes more of an educator and mentor, taking the applicant on a reflective and transformational learning journey through their previous work and life experiences. In harmony with social work values, social justice and social inclusion underpin this approach. Researchers into RPL such as Hamer (2013) support the argument that developmental approaches to RPL offer the opportunity for more fluid, transformational educational roles and promote social inclusion of non-traditional learners.

After a few years of attempting to implement the credentialist approach to RPL for eligible students at CSU, staff, some students and field educators were expressing dissatisfaction. In summary our experience suggested that most students entering the social work course with prior work experience in the sector were good technicians, able to explain how they practice, but not why they practice as they do, beyond describing how they adhere to their agency's policies and procedures. We also found that some students given a credit for their first field education placement came to their second placement assuming they have nothing to learn from field education. Finally our experience suggested that some students in receipt of RPL for their first field education placement were not meeting the expected milestones of readiness and preparedness for their second field education placement.

In response to this experience, CSU staff devised a developmental, process-based model of RPL called Professional Practice Assessment or PPA. Rather than applying for a credit, eligible students were required to enrol in their first field education subject and undertake a series of assessments.

Central to this process is the refining of the RPL eligibility criteria through defining 'relevant context' (AWEAS, 2012b, p 5). This we defined as being:

> as a position that either manages, or directly provides, what social workers consider to be social work or social welfare services to clients of the agency involving activities that the University regards as suitable for a field education placement, including familiarity with and use of a range of social work practice skills and methods, such as assessment, counselling, casework, group work and community work (Valentine et al., 2016: 499).

Particular emphasis is placed on whether the students' role(s), documented in their formal position descriptions, would be suitable for a social work field education placement, either direct or indirect, but for the presence of a social worker. This has led to roles such as direct care workers, employment consultants and human resources staff, which are not considered suitable for a field education placement, being excluded from PPA eligibility.

Having met the eligibility criteria students undertake developmental assessments that introduce them to social work values, ethics, theory and identity by which they are assisted to reframe and interrogate their practice history in the light of social work practice discourse.

The first assessment involves students completing essays on the social work theories that inform their practice along with describing how their values align with those of the profession. These essays are complemented by each student reframing how their practice accords with the AASW Practice Standards (AASW, 2013).

This enables a determination of each student's understanding of what it means to be a professional social worker, of their ability to relate course work to practice and the extent to which they have internalised social work values, ethics, practices and theories. Once an initial benchmark is achieved each student is taken on a learning journey that parallels the field education experience, progressively developing their social work profile. They are given specific feedback on their assessment and allowed to resubmit until it is apparent that no further development of their thinking is occurring, usually on their second or third attempt.

If the first assessment commences the journey of transformation (Whittaker, Whittaker and Cleary, 2006), the second assessment, which consists of the student presenting to two academics, involves their reflecting on the journey thus far. During the presentation students have the opportunity to articulate the extent to which they have internalised social work values, ethics and theories along with mapping out their expectations for the second field education subject.

Acquiring a social work identity does not occur by osmosis, but rather is a transformative process (Whittaker, Whittaker and Cleary, 2006; Moorhead, 2017) during which students are socialised to think like social workers, by internalising and merging their understanding of social work theory, values and ethics with their experience. The PPA process seeks to achieve this by working with students to reframe their work experience and consider it from within a social work context. It can be the most difficult part of the PPA journey for some students if they have been well socialised into their employment roles. It can mean revising what it means to be a professional social worker and involves the acquisition of new values. This requires time for the students to work through issues and to work with the academic mentor, exploring the difference between social work and non-social work concepts. As they undertake this journey a transition occurs as they commence seeing the world through social work eyes.

It has been observed that students who work(ed) with social workers, particularly if the social worker was a supervisor, undertook the transition journey far more readily than those who did not. Building on this observation we now suggest to students that they obtain social work supervision to facilitate the journey of transition during the PPA process.

Another significant aspect of the socialisation process is the acquisition of the language of social work; language defines who we are (Beatty, Collins and Buckingham, 2014). In the context of social work, language includes or excludes individuals from the profession. While this is initially acquired through course work, using it for the first time is part of the field education experience, something not acknowledged in the AASW model of RPL. Again the developmental nature of the PPA process seeks to mirror this retrospectively. Language reflects and shapes values. However, language used in different contexts has different meanings which students often do not recognise. Terms like social justice, professional integrity and respect for persons, may have one meaning as referred to in the Code of Ethics (AASW, 2010) but take on different meanings when referred to in agency codes of conduct. Similarly, it is not uncommon for students to use the terms casework and case management interchangeably and not appreciate the difference in the two concepts. Likewise, students may conflate the AASW Code of Ethics with their agency's Code of Conduct, reflecting a lack of understanding as to what a profession's code of ethics represents and how it differs from an agency code of conduct. Other examples include confusing professional supervision with task supervision or line management, and similarly, ethical dilemmas and conflicts of interest.

A further element of the PPA process is the use of reflection, of thinking, doing and being (Pawar and Anscombe, 2015). Students are encouraged to reflect on their practice experience through the lens of the Practice Standards (AASW, 2013) and so reframe their practice as social work practice. This is often a skill that has to be developed as some students find it difficult to step back from their practice in order to conceptualise and reflect, to explore their practice methods and the informing theories rather than their pre-social work approach of seeing their practice as a series of actions informed by agency policies and procedures.

Inherent in this process is the question of to what extent social work practice differs from other practices? In discussing the PPA process with them, most students start off with the belief that they are already practicing as social workers. However, by the time they complete the PPA journey and associated assessments they have shifted position, realising that their initial expectations were wrong and that they are only now starting to think 'like social workers'.

Central to this process is the role of the academic mentor who, concurrently with assessing students against the learning outcomes for the first field education subject and AASW Practice Standards, works alongside them in a mentoring capacity as they develop a social work identity. The academic mentor assists students to work on reframing their experience to fit in the social work construct; developing their social work identity and preparing for the second assessment – the presentation. The role is both pragmatic (to what extent can individual students change in the time available) and pedantic (insistence on the use of social work language). Anecdotal reports from staff and students suggest that using this reflective developmental approach to reconsider previous experience using social work language, assists students to develop their professional identities. Whether this impression will be substantiated once the results of the planned evaluation are known, remains to be seen.

## Evaluating Outcomes for the Developmental Model

While the PPA model of RPL draws on both research and practice wisdom, after five years of operation and refinement a formal evaluation is needed. We wish to explore whether through PPA we are achieving the same student learning outcomes as those attained by students undertaking a conventional social work first placement. We also want to establish whether those students undertaking PPA have the same or different experiences in undertaking their second field education subject compared with those who undertook placements for both field education subjects. To this end we have commenced interviewing students who undertook a placement and those who went through the PPA process to enable a comparative analysis to be made. This will include discussing their developing professional identity with both groups. We will also approach field educators and academic liaison staff involved with the participating students.

## Summary and Conclusion

We argue that, just as field education should be transformative, relating course work to practice and promoting a social work identity, so should RPL. This is not possible under the current credentialist outcomes-based model of RPL which dominates the AASW approach. However, there is an innovative alternative which CSU social work is trialling.

Instead of being given a credit for the first field education subject, based on their qualifying work history, social work students at CSU are required to enrol in the first placement subject and undertake a series of social work based assessments directed at developing their social work identity. These assessments mimic the placement experience by progressively reframing each student's work experience within a social work construct using social work language. In demonstrating how they meet the AASW Practice Standards (2013) students complete an assessment that parallels the placement learning plan; two short essays on social work values and practice theories that reflect the learning and development essay for the first CSU placement; and finally, students give a presentation that mirrors the mid placement presentation which CSU placement students complete. Key to this process is the academic mentor who combines the roles of field educator and academic liaison.

Thus the developmental PPA model advocated here is both process and outcomes based, taking students on a learning journey with the potential to transform their practice, values, ethics, and theory to align with those of social work. This reflective process also aims to support students to develop a professional social work identity.

It is an exciting time to be in social work education. At the time of writing AASW's 2017 revised ASWEAS standards (AASW, 2017) are under review. Changes to RPL are one of the contested areas. In this context the results from the evaluation PPA are likely to be significant for the future of social work education.

# References

AASW (2008). *Australian Social Work Education and Accreditation Standards (ASWEAS) 2017.* Canberra, ACT: AASW.

AASW (2010). *Code of Ethics.* Retrieved from: https://www.aasw.asn.au/document/item/1201.

AASW (2012a). *Australian Social Work Education and Accreditation Standards (ASWEAS) ASWEAS 2012 V1.3 – Revised May 2014.* Retrieved from: http://www.aasw.asn.au/document/item/3550.

AASW (2012b). *ASWEAS Guideline 1.2: Guideline on field education programs.* Retrieved from: http://www.aasw.asn.au/document/item/3553.

AAAW (2013) *Practice Standards.* Retrieved from: https://www.aasw.asn.au/document/item/4551.

AASW (2017). *Australian Social Work Education and Accreditation Standards (ASWEAS) 2017.* Melbourne: AASW.

Australian Qualifications Framework Advisory Board. (2007). *Australian Qualifications Framework, Implementation Handbook* (4th edn.). Carlton South: Author.

Ayala, J., Drolet, J., Fulton, A., Hewson, J., Letkemann, L., Baynton, M., Elliott, G., Judge-Stasiak, A., Blaug, C., Gérard Tétreault, A., Schweizer, E. (2018). 'Field education in crisis: experiences of field education coordinators in Canada', *Social Work Education*, 37(3), 281–93.

Cameron, R. (2006). 'RPL and the disengaged learner: The need for new starting points'. In P. Andersson & J. Harris (eds.), *Re-theorising the recognition of prior learning* (pp. 117–39). Leicester: National Institute of Adult Continuing Education (NIACE).

Beatty, S., Collins, A. and Buckingham, M (2014). 'Embedding academic socialisation within a language support program. An Australian case study', *International Journal of the First Year in Higher Education* 5(1) 9–18.

Cameron, R. (2011). 'Australia: An overview of 20 years of research into the recognition of prior learning (RPL)'. In J. Harris, M. Breier and C. Wihak (eds.). Researching the recognition of prior learning.

Cleak, H. & Wilson, J. (2013). *Making the most of field placement* (3rd edn.). Australia: Cengage.

Down, C. M. (2008). 'Understanding the role of context in lifelong learning'. In D. Orr, G. Danaher, & R. E. Harreveld (eds.), *Lifelong learning: Reflecting on the successes and framing futures. 5th International Lifelong Learning Conference* (pp. 147–52). Rockhampton: Central Queensland University: Retrieved from EBook Library.

Egan, S., Waugh, F., Giles, R., Bowles, W. (2017). 'Authentic Assessment:

Partners in Developing a Web-based Guide', *Social Work Education*, *36*(6), 731–44.

Giles, R., Irwin, J., Lynch, D. & Waugh, F. (2010). *In the field. From learning to practice*. Oxford, Australia.

Gursansky, G., & Le Sueur, E. (2012). 'Conceptualising field education in the twenty first century: Contradictions, challenges and opportunities', *Social Work Education*, 31(7), 914–31.

Hamer, J. (2013). 'Love, rights and solidarity in the recognition of prior learning (RPL)', *International journal of lifelong education*, 32(4), 481–500.

Holden, G., Barker, K., Rosenberg, G., Kuppens, S., Ferrell, L. W. (2011). 'The Signature Pedagogy of Social Work? An Investigation of the Evidence', *Research on Social Work Practice*, 21(3), 363–72.

Ledger, S., Hillman, W., Harreveld, B., de Warren, D. (2017). 'Field education as signature pedagogy – insights for Australian social work', *Advances in Social Work and Welfare Education*, 19(1), 62–70.

Lyter, S.C. (2012). 'Potential of Field Education as Signature Pedagogy: The Field Director Role', *Journal of Social Work Education*, 48(1), 179–88.

Maidment, J., & Crisp, B. R. (2011). 'The impact of emotions on practicum learning', *Social Work Education*, 30(4), 408–21.

Moorhead, B. (2017). *The Lived Experience of Professional Identity: A Year-Long Study with Newly Qualified Social Workers*. PhD thesis published online. Retrieved from: https://researchoutput.csu.edu.au/ws/portalfiles/portal/13512079.

Pawar, M. and Anscombe, W. (2015). *Reflective social work practice*. Cambridge, Port Melbourne.

Valentine, B., Bowles, W. and McKinnon, J. (2016). 'A developmental approach to the recognition of prior learning in social work field Education', *Australian Social Work,* 69(4), 495–502.

Wayne, J., Bogo, M., Raskin, M. (2010). 'Field Education as the Signature Pedagogy of Field Education', *Journal of Social Work Education*, 46(3), 327–39.

Webb, S.A. (2017). Matters of Professional Identity and Social Work. In S.A. Webb (ed.). *Professional Identity and Social Work* (pp. 1–18) London: Routledge. Retrieved from ProQuest Ebook Central.

Whittaker, S., Whittaker, R., and Cleary, P. (2006). Understanding the transformative dimension of RPL. In P. Anderson and J. Harris (eds.). *Re-theorising the recognition of prior Learning* (pp. 301–19). NIACE, Leicester.

Zuchowski, I. (2016). Getting to Know the Context: The Complexities of Providing Off-Site Supervision in Social Work Practice Learning. *The British Journal of Social Work,* 46(2), 409–26.

# FOURTEEN

# Wellbeing and Social Work – Is It Possible?

*Fredrik Velander*

## Abstract

Since the beginning of time work has been a vital part of our lives. It is an important part of how we identify ourselves; it puts food on the table and provides a social environment where we engage with other people. Therefore, work is an activity that provides us with a range of positive and valuable outcomes to ourselves and the community at large. That said, we also know that work can be highly hazardous to our health and wellbeing, in the past mainly due to the physical risks associated with it, but these days the risks are more insidious, less visible but equally harmful.

## Introduction and Background

Working life has transformed significantly over the last 300 years and each transition has seen its unique challenges. During the first industrial revolution when people began urbanising to seek employment in the cotton mills, mining or saw mills, work was associated with poor physical work environments and it was not uncommon that severe physical injuries such as amputation of limbs and cancer due to high levels of dust occurred. The influx of people into urban centres also led to poor sanitation and unclean water which in turn led to the proliferation of a range of illnesses such as typhoid, cholera and smallpox.

The second industrial revolution was characterised by new technologies such as the telegraph and telephones (Roy, 2008), electrification (Constable & Somerville, 2003) and production lines. During this time we also saw the introduction of industries such as the petrochemical industry (Russel, 2003; Vassiliou, 2009), high-capacity paper making (Zabawski, 2017) and automotive industry (Hounshell, 1984). Greater effort was placed on minimising the harms of the physical work environment and experiments on the linkage between work environment and productivity were done, for example Elton Mayo's experiment at Western Electric's factory in Hawthorne.

We have now moved into what is known as the third industrial revolution which to a great extent was caused by the birth of computerised information and communication technology (ICT), globalisation and change of preferences in consumption patterns with more individualised preferences driven by consumerism and capitalism (Magnusson & Ottosson, 2003). Another phenomenon that is part of the third industrial revolution is greater flexibility in working life, a topic discussed at length by Leadbeater (2000) and Castells (1996), including a variety of employment situations, e.g., part-time work, and time-limited contract employments.

## Transition from Physical Danger to Psychological Danger

In most industrialised nations, including Australia, we now see a working life that could not be much further from what was experienced 300 years ago. Most of the physical threats to our wellbeing have been eliminated, or reduced to a minimum, and the physical work environment has improved significantly through new ways of production. Great effort has gone into minimising the potential harms of the physical work environment. This was accompanied by workplace policies and government legislation to minimise the risk for employees and employers.

While most physical dangers have been eradicated or controlled, a new type of danger has arisen. Over the last 10-15 years there has been a growing concern about the psychological work environment. The new working life is characterised by a service oriented production system that provides individualised services to customers, where the concept of who is a customer has taken a much broader perspective than previously. Another aspect of the new working life and in alignment with neoliberal philosophy is the growth of casualised employment contracts where more and more people find themselves in time-limited, project or part-time employment. The trend in Australia has been fairly consistent since 1967 with part-time employment rising from 9.9% in 1967 to more than 36% in 2017 (Reserve Bank of Australia, 2016).

## Part-time Employment Shares*

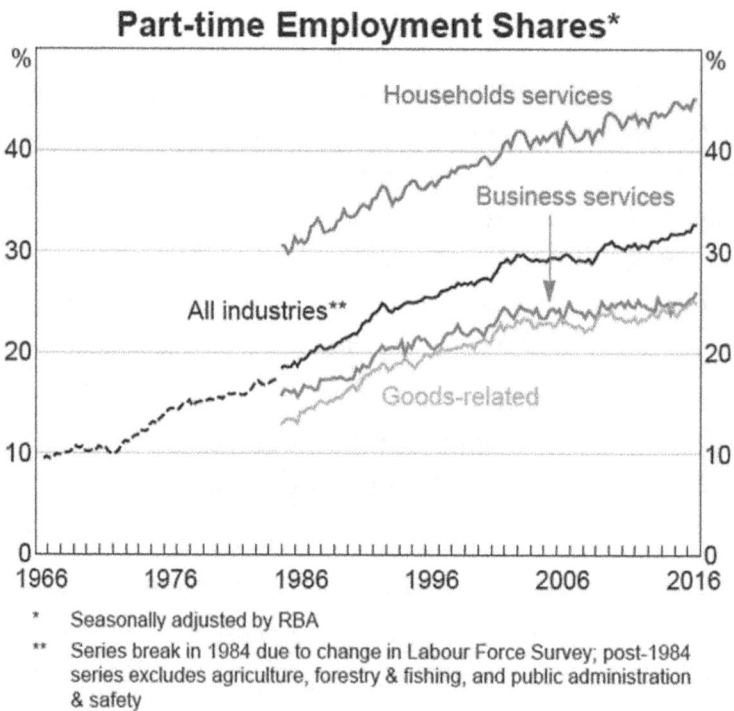

\*   Seasonally adjusted by RBA

\*\*   Series break in 1984 due to change in Labour Force Survey; post-1984 series excludes agriculture, forestry & fishing, and public administration & safety

This rise in part-time employment is not unique for Australia but what sets Australia apart from other OECD countries is that we have one of the highest proportions of part-time employment (Cassidy & Parsons, 2017). The cause of this trend can be found in long-term changes to working life in general through increased globalisation, changes in consumer consumption patterns, just-in-time production, and a number of other factors (Marklund & Härenstam, 2010; Lundberg & Cooper, 2011).

## Impact of Stress and Anxiety in Australia

Between 2000/01 and 2011/12 a dramatic increase in negative outcomes associated with increased levels of stress and anxiety among the Australian workforce was observed. Figures from Safe Work Australia (2014) indicate that there was:

- a 22 percent increase in serious claims for mental disorders

- a 17 percent increase in the numbers of serious claims arising from mental stress

- an increase in median time lost from work by 27 percent, from 11.2 weeks (2000/1) to 14.2 weeks (2011/12)

In terms of monetary costs associated with stress and over-work for Australia the picture is rather dire and the cost from lost productivity, workplace claims and sickness absence, to mention a few, looks as follows:

| Cost generator | Annual Cost |
|---|---|
| Workers compensation claims for stress-related mental disorders | $200 million |
| Depression (cost to employers caused by sickness absence & Presenteeism) | $8 billion |
| Job strain and bullying (total cost) | $693 million |
| Lost productivity (total cost) | $10 billion |
| Job strain-related depression (total cost) | $11.8 billion |
| Presenteeism and absenteeism due to stress and overwork (total cost) | $14.81 billion |
| Work-injury claims for mental disorders | $480 million |

Source: Econtech (2008); Safe Work Australia (2013); Safe Work Australia (2015a).

By contrast, the 'ice' or methamphetamine epidemic which receives more media attention, is estimated to cost the Australian economy approximately $3.7 billion (Allsop et al., 2015).

One has to wonder as to how an issue that costs the Australian economy in excess of $34 billion can go unnoticed in media, public debate, and politics. In addition to this, mental stress claims are the most expensive form of workers' compensation due to the lengthy period of absence from work (Safe Work Australia, 2013).

# Emerging Psychosocial Risks to Occupational Health and Safety

## Excessive Working Hours

Across the industrialised world there is a growing trend of people that work themselves to death. For example, in Japan some 2,310 deaths were categorised as 'death by overwork' but some believe the figure is grossly underreported and the actual deaths directly linked to overwork is around 10,000 (Gorvett, 2016). Australia is one of few nations where paid and unpaid overtime is increasing, currently employers are estimated to get free overtime to the value of approximately $116 billion annually (Swann & Stanford, 2016).

## Burnout

In 1974 the German-American psychologist Herbert Freudenberger created the term 'burnout' in relation to the following symptoms, a *physical or mental collapse caused by overwork or stress.*

Physical signs include:

- Feelings of exhaustion and fatigue
- Frequent colds that stay longer and longer
- Frequent headaches
- Gastrointestinal disturbances
- Problems sleeping
- Shortness of breath

Behavioural signs include:

- Short fuse
- Difficulties controlling feelings (anger or sadness)
- Raised voice
- Suspicion and paranoia
- Increasing risk-taking behaviour
- Rigidity in thinking, stubbornness and inflexibility.
  (Freudenberger, 1974)

In Australia the estimated cost associated with work-related mental stress, based on figures from 2008–9, was approximately $5.3 billion per year, a figure that includes costs for reduced productivity and medical costs (Safe Work Australia, 2012).

Price Waterhouse Coopers (PwC) found health care and social assistance in the private sector had by far the highest number of compensation claims for mental health disorders, with 1,705 claims per year, with an average compensation payment of $16,200 (PwC, 2014). In addition to this there are costs for absenteeism, presentism as well as cost associated with employee turnover, collateral damage costs from colleagues and other employees, management costs, incident costs, and income insurance payments for organisations (PwC: 10). Beyond this, there are other costs that will spread out into the wider society relating to, for example, health care costs, reduction in income tax, and a reduction in disposable household income.

In terms of who is carrying the burden of this financial cost it is estimated that 5 percent is carried by employers, 74 percent by workers and 21 percent by the community at large (Safe Work Australia, 2015b).

## Technology Advancements and Greater Flexibility

Part of the new working life is also a greater flexibility. Through the use of computer technology we can work almost anywhere at any time. There are numerous positive aspects of this flexibility and a study conducted by

Garner et al., (2016) found that flexible work arrangements led to increased productivity linked to the ability to adjust individual work hours to the requirements of private life, and greater work satisfaction.

Greater flexibility was also associated with improved employee wellbeing and a decrease in sickness absence. This goes against the general trend where long commutes and long hours have been associated with deteriorating health. One of the reasons proposed as to why this study shows a contradictory result was a shift of power to the employee as to when and where they work; and when it occurs with the support of management it can become a positive feature.

In addition to this, there is evidence that indicates that it is easier to attract talented workers and improve staff retention if an organisation offers more flexible work arrangements. This is particularly true among those that were born into the digital age and are accustomed to using technology, as well as perceiving organisational restraints, For example Reale (2015) who studied millennials found the following:

- 51 percent planned to look for a job in a flexible organisation within the next 36 months.

- 69 percent believed that regular office attendance is unnecessary.

- Millennials place greater importance on flexible working conditions than previous generations.

- 77 percent said that flexibility is a vital criterion when looking for a job.

- 89 percent prefer individualised work hours so that they can choose when and where to work.

At the same time there are employees that believe this growing flexibility has a negative impact. When the decision on flexible arrangements is taken out of the employee's hands it becomes a negative feature as it creates uncertainty and anxiety, which then leads to increased levels of workplace stress.

Therefore organisations need to be aware and sensitive to individual needs as well as the needs of the organisation; and Garner et al. (2016) recommend enabling employees rather than enforcing flexible work conditions.

## The Social Work Profession

Turning our lens towards social work specifically, there is little doubt that the social work profession is highly stressful, dealing with a range of stressful situations and working with people who tend to be in difficult situations in life. In addition to this, the social work profession is also affected by limited resources, the expectation to do more with existing resources, uncertain funding conditions and ongoing critique in media (Beer & Asthana, 2016; Lloyd et al., 2002).

In a study by Schraer (2015) on social workers in the UK, 80 percent of social workers responded that their current stress levels impacted negatively on their performance. Compared to other professions, social work and human services professions more often than not rank among the top 5 professions when it comes to high stress levels, mental health conditions, workplace injury claims and as a result is a priority area of the *Australian Work Health and Safety Strategy 2012–2022* (Safe Work Australia, 2017). This becomes particularly alarming when the Australian Association of Social Workers (AASW) Code of Ethics clearly state that 'Social workers will take appropriate action if ill-health, impairment or any other factor is likely to interfere with their professional judgement or performance of duty' (AASW, 2010: 21). In short, social workers have an obligation to address factors in working life that impacts on professional performance.

## Workplace Bullying

Social work, as part of health and community services, regularly comes up as one of the professions where workplace bullying is highly prevalent. In an Australian study by Potter et al. (2016) the industries with the highest levels of workplace bullying were electricity, gas and water supply; health and community services; government administration and defence; transport and storage; mining; and education. The underlying drivers of these levels of bullying were attributed to job design and job demands. As psychological demands increased so did levels of bullying.

Longitudinal analysis confirmed that a low interest in the psychosocial safety climate within organisations was directly correlated to increased levels of bullying. What could explain the lack of interest in the psychosocial work environment is the neoliberal climate that is driven by globalisation and profit management leads managers to prioritise productivity at the expense of workers' psychological health and wellbeing. We currently see numerous organisations downsizing, seeking leaner production, restructuring, and outsourcing non-core work, both in the public and private sector as a result of more market driven models (Cooper, Dewe, & O'Driscoll, 2001; Potter et al., 2016).

Furthermore, this also creates an environment where employees are viewed as commodities that are disposable and replaceable if they do not conform to increasing demands of higher productivity. As managers are expected to meet certain goals they may turn to bullying tactics and poor performance management systems to achieve greater productivity (Potter et al., 2016).

A practical implication of current trends in the Australian workplace is that changes need to occur as current practice is neither economically, socially or ethically acceptable (Potter et al., 2016). Additionally, women in the workplace experience higher levels of bullying than men, with greater frequency and longer duration, factors that have direct correlation to increased levels of depressive symptoms and double the risk of suicidal thoughts. Poor organisational culture where there is little or no support from colleagues and/or management is fertile soil for workplace bullying and as such bullying needs to be treated as an organisational issue rather than individual (Potter et al., 2016; Butterworth et al., 2013).

# Can We Turn This Trend Around?

The first step to turn this current trend around is to acknowledge that stress and wellbeing are not only the responsibility of the individual employee; they are issues that affect the entire workplace and society as a whole and as such require a systemic response. The second step is an understanding that healthy people are productive people. In fact, countries and organisations around the globe are already addressing this, so, yes, it is possible.

## Cost-Benefit of a Healthy Working Life

The goal of any organisation is to survive, and to survive they need to cover the cost of production by generating an income. What is often overlooked is the organisational factors that lead to an unhealthy workplace. A helpful vehicle to change organisational culture is to place monetary values on costs and benefits as this tends to create an interest at managerial levels. It is therefore pleasing to note that for every $1 invested in tailored, evidence based, interventions aimed at creating a mentally healthy Australian workplace the average return for the organisation is $2.30 (PwC, 2014). These financial gains are generated by increased productivity, reduced levels of absenteeism and presentism (i.e., people who are at work while sick and therefore not performing at their normal level) and reduction in workplace compensation claims. If we add data for reduction in recruitment, induction and training costs the gain would be even greater than $2.30.

## An Organisational Approach

Organisations do not only have a responsibility to respond to the current levels of work-related stress and overwork, but they also have a strong financial incentive as empirical evidence shows it is possible to create a win-win situation for employers and employees alike. From the above discussion, it is clear that it would make good 'business sense' to retain workers within organisations for the long haul, and make sure that the work environment promotes positive mental health and wellbeing.

## An Individual Approach

For far too long, workplace stress has been treated as an individual issue where workers were sent to stress management training. In most cases this training was a poor investment for the organisation as the causes of workplace stress were left unchallenged. This model can be compared to putting a band aid on a melanoma rather than carrying out the more invasive surgery to remove the source of the cancer.

But as individuals we cannot lay blame completely on the organisations. There are many cases where we are our worst enemy. One such example is the common practice of working unpaid overtime just in order to get case notes written up or prepare a report. This practice leads to giving the impression that we are able to complete all the necessary tasks with the existing resources rather than demonstrating that we can only do so much with the resources that are currently at our disposal. Of course this can be driven by management bullying tactics or a perception that in order to be a good social worker we need to manage everything, even it means working extra. However if we do not acknowledge out limits within the existing resources, the resulting harm not only affects us but may impact on clients or co-workers.

## The Vital Importance of Self-Care – Mindfulness

In social work education we tend to discuss the importance of self-care with students rather than equipping them with the necessary tools to survive in the high pressure environment of social work. Among social workers in general there is a need to change the way we approach our obligation and responsibilities. Jackson (2014) stated that social worker self-care is an overlooked core competency and when it is mentioned it is rather tokenistic. One pathway to self-care that has received growing attention is the concept of mindfulness. The fundamental principle of mindfulness is to *'pay attention, in a particular way, on purpose and non-judgementally, in the present moment.'* (Kabat-Zinn, 1994). Mindfulness-based stress reduction has proven highly effective in reducing stress and anxiety (Chiesa &

Serretti, 2009) and is an evidence based avenue for a healthier and happier life for social workers.

## Conclusion

The situation for Australian social workers is rather dire with work stress, anxiety and bullying at epidemic levels, costing the Australian government, the not-for-profit, and private sector billions of dollars annually. Even though there are sufficient data to demonstrate this very little has been done so far to change this downward trajectory. There are numerous examples from other countries that we can implement a range of measures to change this, that interventions have been successful and produce positive outcomes for both employers and employees. In fact, with minimal investments employers can reap great benefits if they are willing to invest and create healthy organisations; it is more a change of attitude than anything else. We also need to get away from individualising stress, anxiety and overwork because as long as we do not get to the root of the problem we are wasting valuable funds on stress and anger management programs while the cause remains the same.

Health and wellbeing at work should be a collective effort, involving both employers and employees so that we can create a working life that is sustainable, where people are happy, productive and willing to invest physically and emotionally in their work. This is also why social workers have a vital role to play in Australian working life, both in their own workplace as well as others, to fulfil the aim of AASW Code of Ethics (2010) where social workers are working with and supporting people to achieve the best possible levels of personal and social wellbeing. After all, as social workers we have dedicated our commitment to providing assistance to improve wellbeing. Some of the information included in this chapter clearly place social workers themselves in a very vulnerable position and the data provided further cement this conclusion.

# References

AASW (2010). *Code of Ethics*. Canberra, ACT: Australian Association of Social Workers.

Allsop, S., Chikritzhs, T., Lenton, S., Gray, D., Wilkes, T., Liang, W., Tait, R., Shanahan, M., Farrell, M, Degenhardt, L., Ritter, A., Burns, L., & Kaye, S. (2015). *What is the economic impact of methamphetamine us on Australia?* National Drug Research Institute (NDRI), National Drug and Alcohol Research Centre (NDARC), University of Adelaide / Flinders University, the Australian National University and Curtin University.

Beer, O. & Asthana, S. (2016). *How stress impacts social workers – and how they are trying to cope*. Accessed 19 February 2018 from http://www.communitycare.co.uk/2016/09/28/stress-impacts-social-workers-theyre-trying-cope/.

Butterworth, P., Leach, L. S. & Kiely, K.M. (2013). *The relationship between work characteristics, wellbeing, depression and workplace bullying: summary report*. Canberra, ACT: Safe Work Australia.

Cassidy, N. & Parsons, S. (2017). *The rising share of part-time employment*. Bulletin, Reserve Bank of Australia, September Quarter, 19–26.

Castells, M. (1996). *The information age: economy, society and culture*. Blackwell (Vols. 1–3), Malden, Mass.

Chiesa, A. & Serretti, A. (2009). 'Mindfulness-based stress reduction for stress management in healthy people: a review and meta-analysis', *Journal of Alternative and Complementary Medicine*, 15(5), 593–600.

Constable, G. & Somerville, B. (2003). *A century of innovation: twenty engineering achievements that transformed our lives*. Washington, DC: Joseph Henry Press.

Cooper, C. L., Dewe, P. J. & O'Driscoll, M. P. (2001). *Organisational stress. A review and critique of theory, research, and application*. California, SAGE.

Econtech (2008). *The cost of workplace stress in Australia*. Medibank Private.

Freudenberger, H. J. (1974). 'Staff burn-out', *Journal of Social Issues*, 30(1), 159–65.

Garner, C., Forbes, P., Sheldon, H., Shoesmith, D. & Ternouth, P. (2016). *Working anywhere – a winning formula for good work?* London: The Work Foundation Alliance Limited.

Gorvett, Z. (2016). *Can you work yourself to death?* Capital, London: BBC. Accessed 16/02/2018 from http://www.bbc.com/capital/story/20160912-is-there-such-thing-as-death-from-overwork.

Hounshell, D. A. (1984). *From the American system to mass production,*

*1800-1932: the development of manufacturing technology in the United States.*
Baltimore, Maryland: Johns Hopkins University Press.

Jackson, K. (2014). 'Social worker self-care – the overlooked core competency', *Social Work Today*, 14(3): 14.

Kabat-Zinn, J. (1994). *Wherever you go, there you are: mindfulness meditation in everyday life.* New York: Hyperion Books.

Leadbeater, C. (2000). *Living on thin air: the new economy.* London: Penguin.

Lloyd, C., King, R. & Chenoweth, L. (2002). 'Social work, stress and burnout: a review', *Journal of Mental Health*, 11(3), 255–65.

Lundberg, U., & Cooper, C. L. (2011). *The science of occupational health: stress, psychobiology, and the new world of work.* Chichester: Wiley-Blackwell.

Magnusson, L. & Ottosson, J. (2003). The third industrial revolution and 'the new economy' – between appearance and reality. (Den tredje industriella revolutionen och 'den nya ekonomin' – mellan sken och verklighet). In von Otter, C. (ed.), *Ute och inne i svenskt arbetsliv – forskare analyserar och spekulerar om trender i framtidens arbete*, Working Life in Transition, Stockholm, National Institute for Working Life, 2003: 8, 57–76.

Marklund, S., & Härenstam, A. (eds.) (2010). *The dynamics of organizations and healthy work.* Växjö: Linnéuniversitetet, Institutionen för samhällsvetenskaper.

Potter, R. E., Dollard, M. F. & Tuckey, M.R. (2016). *Bullying and harassment in the Australian workplaces: results from the Australian workplace barometer project 2014/2015.* Canberra, ACT: Safe Work Australia.

PwC (2014). *Creating a mentally healthy workplace – return on investment analysis.* The Mentally Healthy Workplace Alliance, Canberra, ACT: Beyondblue.

Reserve Bank of Australia, (2016) Statement on Monetary Policy – November 2016, Box B: Trends in Part-time and Full-time Employment. Canberra, Reserve Bank of Australia.

Reale, A. (2015). *11 stats about flexible work in the U.S.* Accessed 19 February 2018 from https://www.flexjobs.com/blog/post/stats-about-flexible-work-in-us/.

Roy, A. (2008). *Cambridge 'pioneer' honour for Bose.* The Telegraph, Kolkota.

Russell, Loris S. (2003). *A Heritage of Light: Lamps and Lighting in the Early Canadian Home.* University of Toronto Press.

Safe Work Australia (2017). *The mid-term review of the Australian work health and safety strategy 2012–2022.* Canberra: Safe Work Australia.

Safe Work Australia (2015a). *Work-related mental disorder profile.* Canberra: Safe Work Australia.

Safe Work Australia (2015b). *The cost of work-related injury and illness for Australian employers, workers and the community: 2012–2013*. Canberra: Safe Work Australia.

Safe Work Australia (2014). *Australian Workers' Compensation Statistics 2012–2013*. Canberra: Safe Work Australia.

Safe Work Australia (2013). *The incidence of accepted workers' compensation claims for mental stress in Australia*. Canberra: Safe Work Australia.

Safe Work Australia (2012). *Cost of work related injury and disease for Australian employers, workers and the community: 2008–09*. Canberra: Safe Work Australia.

Schraer, R. (2015). *Social workers too stressed to do their job according to survey*. London: Community Care. Accessed 19 February 2018 from http://www.communitycare.co.uk/2015/01/07/stress-stopping-job-social-workers-say/.

Swann, T. & Stanford, J. (2016). *Excessive hours and unpaid overtime: an update*. Canberra: Centre for Future Work, The Australian Institute.

Vassiliou, M. S. (2009). *Historical dictionary of the petroleum industry*. Lanham, MD: Scarecrow Press.

Zabawski, E. (2017). 'Pulp friction', *Tribology & Lubrication Technology, Park Ridge,* 73(4), 6.

PART III

# INNOVATIONS IN APPLIED
# SOCIAL WORK RESEARCH

# FIFTEEN

# The Lived Experience of Acute Mental Health Inpatient Care: What's Social Work Research Got to Do with It?

*Bronwyn Hyde*

## Abstract

This chapter is an example of how a social work practitioner can contribute to social work research. It examines the meaning of recovery and recovery-focused practice within an acute mental health inpatient setting. By employing the hermeneutic phenomenology method interviews of consumers, workers and managers have been analysed. The analysis suggests that when two types of lived experience evident in an episode of acute mental health inpatient care are aligned, recovery is optimized. More importantly it highlights the significant contribution social work research can make to the transition to recovery-focused practice and consequently to mental health reform.

## Introduction

The field of mental health has undergone significant changes over recent decades precipitated by a strong consumer movement that has challenged the biomedical-based foundation of traditional mental health care and service delivery. Consumer voices grounded in lived experience have redefined the meaning of recovery as it pertains to mental health, generating a rethink and repositioning of knowledge and practice. The notion of recovery in mental health has moved from a scientific, decontextualized and deficit perspective to one now embedded with personal meaning, strengths and empowerment. This language of recovery should automatically grab the attention and interest of social workers whose professional principles are in such close alignment. Social workers, it appears, are reluctant researchers and may not realise their potential as significant contributors to the development of knowledge and practice change in the mental health field. This chapter briefly describes an example of social work research that examines the meaning of recovery and recovery-focused practice within an acute mental health inpatient setting. More importantly it highlights the significant contribution social work research can make to the transition to recovery-focused practice and consequently to mental health reform.

## The Notion of Recovery in Mental Health

Bloom (2005) takes a historical perspective as he traces the interweaving paths between medicine and sociology across the 19th and 20th centuries. Bloom notes the close alignment between sociology and medicine particularly psychiatry from the 1920s, in understanding 'the functional dynamic of human behavior' described by both (Bloom, 2005: 82). He laments the displacement of Engel's biopsychosocial model by a neurophysiological view in the 1980s that resulted in a preference for psychopharmacological treatment modes. Engel (1977) had earlier asserted that psychiatry was aligning itself with a reductionist biomedical model in order to reclaim its status within the field of medicine. In doing so the profession of psychiatry was moving away from its central purpose of dealing with human distress, an essential component of which is the ability to analyse the person's own account of their condition. Engel's biopsychosocial model requires acknowledgement of both the personal narrative as well as the wider social context to more fully understand the determinants of disease and to provide relevant treatment.

Engel's writings closely preceded the emergence of a strong consumer movement in mental health. This movement, propelled by the writings of Deegan (1988 & 1995) and Anthony (1993) reclaimed consumer lived experience as an integral component of the epistemological foundation of mental health and a determinant of care and treatment. Recovery in mental health began to be recognised as much more than the resolution of symptoms. Instead recovery is now considered to be a uniquely individual experience defying attempts to narrow the concept down to one conclusive definition. The complexities inherent in the concept of recovery can be seen in the most quoted definition of recovery in mental health by Anthony:

> Recovery is described as a deeply personal, unique process of changing one's attitudes, values, feelings, goals, skills, and/or roles. It is a way of living a satisfying, hopeful, and contributing life even with limitations caused by illness. Recovery involves the development of new meaning and purpose in one's life as one grows beyond the catastrophic effects of mental illness. (Anthony, 1993: 527)

Slade, Amering & Oades (2008) propose a two-part definition of recovery in order to provide a degree of conceptual clarity to the discussions of recovery in mental health. They distinguish between clinical recovery described as an absence of symptoms and functional impairment, and personal recovery that, taking from Anthony's definition above, is uniquely individual and involves gaining new meaning and purpose in life even in the presence of ongoing symptoms. While survivor movements had been around since the 1930s, Ramon, Healy & Renouf (2007) note that mental health literature only began to incorporate the concept of recovery in the early 1990s.

Definitions of recovery continue to be contested, however, the principles of recovery practice are now embedded internationally in mental health policy and practice guidelines. Despite this ongoing contention there are a number of agreed components of recovery that provide meaning and substance to the concept and a guide for practice. Slade et al. (2008) outline ten elements of recovery-focused practice identified through a consensus based approach in the United States. These include, self-direction; individualized and person-centred; empowerment; holistic; nonlinear; strengths-based; peer support; respect; responsibility; hope. What social worker could resist the attraction of these words?

## Social Work and the Concept of Recovery in Mental Health

The profession of social work is based on internationally agreed principles including the inherent worth and dignity of human beings, doing no harm, respect for diversity and upholding human rights and justice (Global Definition of Social Work IFSW 2016). These are reflected in the principles of social work outlined in the Australian Association of Social Workers (AASW) Code of Ethics (2010) that include acceptance of the uniqueness of individuals, belief in collaboration and individual choice, valuing diversity and difference and engagement in participative and empowering processes to enable clients. The parallels between recovery principles and those of the social work profession are striking and held sufficient attraction to this social worker to consider embarking on a research path from within my position as a senior social worker in an acute mental health inpatient facility.

One of the observations made while initially conducting a literature review for the research was that few documents sourced using search terms 'recovery' and 'mental health' yielded articles authored by social workers. This absence of social work as a voice in mental health research was also noted by Ramon (2009) who comments on the invisibility of social work in the move to recovery-focused practice in the UK. This is despite the acknowledgement that some of the changes in mental health practice such as the introduction of a strengths approach and the inclusion of service users in policy making are credited to social work. Ramon also notes social work's reluctance to engage in research as a weakness of the profession and in a further publication (Ramon, Shera, Healy, Lachman & Renouf 2009) asserts that social work perceives itself as being less powerful than other professions in the mental health field. Probst (2012) comments on social work's subordinate role to psychiatry despite being the largest group of mental health professionals in the USA and Morley (2003) is critical of mental health social work for not taking a critical approach in deconstructing the biomedical model, instead aligning itself to medical constructions of mental illness. There appears to be a parallel here between psychiatry's pull towards biomedical explanations as an attempt to overcome a perceived position of inferiority in the world of medicine and social work's alignment with psychiatry driven by its feelings of powerlessness in the mental health world.

As a social worker of 10 years in a mental health inpatient facility at the time of the research, I had often pondered the incongruity between the person-centred, anti-oppressive calls to practice generated by the recovery approach and the observed realities of my day-to-day work. This is explained in an excerpt from my reflective journal at the time as I considered my motivation for undertaking the research:

> There is constant tension between preserving and respecting an individual's personhood and rights while at the same time providing protection for them when there is very evident danger of risk of harm to themselves or those around them. The system of care errs on the side of risk reduction, often sacrificing the personhood of the individual...On the one hand I felt the injustices that were perpetrated on those requiring help and the effects on those around them – loss of decision-making, heavy-handed treatment in the pursuit of protection, the isolation and evident distress of family members. On the other hand I felt empathy for the staff often having to bear the brunt of both physical and verbal abuse that was difficult to not take personally and making decisions that were often time-pressured and contrary to the person's wishes.

I wanted to make sense of this situation that pulled me in a number of directions – was I, at times, compromising my social work values working in a system so wedded to a biomedical discourse that drove the care response to presentations of acute mental ill health and could these very values provide a new way forward in a context that was so risk averse; or was the biomedical discourse the best and only way to provide an acute mental health inpatient service; did consumers and staff in this setting view recovery in the same way? Mental health care is being mandated to work from a recovery-focused stance. Social work as a profession is aligned with recovery principles. What contribution could social work research make in bringing acute mental health inpatient care closer to a recovery approach?

## The Research Begins

Social workers, as noted earlier, are reluctant researchers (Ramon 2009; Harvey, Plummer, Pighills & Pain 2013). There are a number of possible reasons for this as outlined by Harvey et al. (2013). Traditionally the foundation of evidence-based practice has been randomized controlled trials (RCTs). This methodology is based in a positivist paradigm that seeks to decontextualize human experience and places the clinician or practitioner as the expert decision maker. This does not sit comfortably with social work values where context or person-in-environment, lived experience and practice wisdom are of paramount importance. Other factors such as time constraints, limited research knowledge and skills along with lack of confidence are also cited by Harvey et al. as the barriers for social workers in undertaking research. Yet, these authors also view practitioner research as a significant source of new knowledge and service innovation (Harvey et al., 2013: 54). It is therefore crucial that the choice of methodology satisfies not only standards of research rigour but are also compatible with social work values.

## The Position of Practitioner-Researcher

Fook (2002) talks of 'contextual practice' asserting that social workers have the ability to work with and within several different contexts thus affording us the opportunity to create more powerful discourses in our organisational context that can lead to change. This is a critical approach, one that can be realized by taking on a position of practitioner-researcher moving in and across the domains of both positions (researcher and practitioner) within a specific organisational context. Drake & Heath (2010) coin the phrase 'inhabiting the hyphen' to explain the unique positionality inherent in the practitioner-researcher role. They encourage researchers to actively take charge of the hyphen through a process of reflective and reflexive writing to clarify their identity. Practice wisdom, reflective and reflexive processes, critical approach – this is the language of social work that fits perfectly with a research mindset. With a vast choice of research methodologies that are compatible with social work values and that contribute to a strong empirical evidence base, social workers need no longer worry about compromising their professional integrity.

## Methodology

It was important that the choice of methodology for this study honoured the principles inherent in the recovery movement such as meaning-making, empowerment and the recognition of the uniqueness of each individual's experience. The human experience is complex and ambiguous and therefore cannot be easily reduced to generalised explanations with claims of proof. In this study the choice of methodology was supported by a structure or 'scaffold' (Crotty, 1998) that included an epistemological position of constructionism and a theoretical perspective of interpretivism. Both elements are a good fit with recovery principles. Constructionism is based on the premise that knowledge production is generated through the exploration of experience of a particular phenomenon rather than the discovery of an objective truth. Interpretivism holds that interpretations of the world are culturally derived and historically situated, rendering researcher objectivity unattainable as the researcher is an intrinsic part of the world being studied. This study was designed to look at the lived experience of a particular phenomenon – acute mental health inpatient care. The choice of a qualitative methodology structured on an epistemological stance of constructionism and a theoretical perspective of interpretivism appeared most appropriate. It was compatible with the complexities of lived experience, the reflective needs of a practitioner-researcher perspective and it aligned with social work values by giving voice to individual experience. There are a number of qualitative methodologies available that are congruent with these requirements and in the case of this research I chose hermeneutic phenomenology. Hermeneutics is the theory of interpretation while phenomenology seeks to understand a phenomenon through the way in which it is experienced (Vagle, 2014).

## Research Questions

Two core research questions were formulated to address the curiosity I felt in reconciling the recovery approach with the reality of my daily work observations and experiences:

> 1. How is an episode of acute mental health inpatient care experienced by consumers, workers and managers in the chosen facility?
>
> 2. Do consumers, workers and managers in an acute mental health inpatient setting share a common understanding of the meaning of recovery from mental illness?
>
> Additional questions were then posed:
>
> 3. What are the challenges for an acute mental health inpatient facility in changing to recovery-focused practice?
>
> 4. What are the implications for social work practice?

The technique of purposive sampling was used to identify participants from three distinct groups chosen for their common experience of the phenomenon of mental health inpatient care. These included:

1. Consumers who were current inpatients of the acute facility

2. Workers of various professional backgrounds who worked on a daily basis in the acute facility

3. Managers who were responsible for the delivery of care in the facility specifically those who had a responsibility for the acute inpatient services.

The selection of these groups meant that the concept of 'lived experience' was expanded from how it is generally used in the mental health literature. The term 'lived experience' in the context of recovery in mental health is usually confined to consumers who have experienced an episode of mental illness. An innovative aspect of this research was the reconfiguring of this term to embrace all those who experienced the phenomenon of acute mental health inpatient care – consumers as well as those workers providing care.

## Methods

Recruitment was undertaken in a number of ways depending on the group in question. The consumers were recruited using an 'arms-length' approach, that is, the Allied Health Assistant on the selected unit advertised the research at each morning meeting. Those who were interested initially approached this worker who then passed on the details to me. The invitation to participate was extended to all consumers regardless of their status under the Mental Health Act. Those who were involuntary were informed that participation needed to be discussed with their treating psychiatrist to reduce any possible exposure to risk of further harm and to ensure their wellbeing. Recruitment of workers was undertaken through attendance at staff handovers and staff meetings while managers were recruited through a personal approach requesting participation. Information sheets were developed and designed for each participant group and all participants were required to sign a consent form. Those who agreed to participate could change their mind at any time without consequences. Of all the groups only one person (consumer) pulled out before proceeding to interview. This process resulted in the recruitment of 24 participants. A brief overview of participant characteristics is included in Table 15.1

Table 15.1: Participant Characteristics

|  | Number | Average Age | Male | Female |
|---|---|---|---|---|
| **Consumers** | 8 | 40 | 5 | 3 |
| **Workers** | 10 | 43 | 5 | 5 |
| **Managers** | 6 | 47 | 4 | 2 |

The self-selection of worker participants resulted in a mix of professional backgrounds and an absence of others. Those who participated included nurses, doctors, allied health assistants and one social worker. The manager participants represented only one professional background, that of nursing, and reflected the dominance of this profession at the management level of the organisation.

Data gathering was undertaken through the use of semi-structured interviews. This strategy is the most commonly used in phenomenological research as it is the most dialogic, open and conversational. A skill set including the establishment of rapport, careful listening, the use of open and non-directive questions and the maintenance of a responsive and empathic stance are crucial to facilitating the narrative account of a phenomenon. This is also part of the core skill set of social work.

Ethics approval for the study was sought through the local Human Research Ethics Committee. Conditional approval was given initially after concerns were raised about the ability of people who were involuntary under the Mental Health Act to provide consent. With a supportive letter from the Medical Superintendent of the hospital the Ethics Committee agreed to approve the inclusion of people who were under an involuntary status as long as their consent form was co-signed by their treating psychiatrist. It was argued that their inclusion was essential to provide this often silenced group with a voice. Two of the eight participating consumers were involuntary at the time of interview.

## Data Analysis and the Main Argument

The process of analysis in hermeneutic phenomenology is not one that follows a strict progression of steps or stages. While this is daunting for the novice researcher it also invites discovery, unearthing new meanings and interpretations and facilitating innovative practice. It requires the researcher to develop an engagement with the data, in this case the interviews, and to look *through* the data rather than just *at* it. I was guided and encouraged in this process by authors such as Dahlberg, Dahlberg & Nystrom (2008), Finlay (2011), Vagle (2014) and Willig (2012). I chose to transcribe the interviews as part of this process allowing me to engage with the data at a slower pace, to consciously note the silences, the laughter, the hesitations. It requires 'taking many passes' at the data (Finlay, 2011) through listening and re-listening, reading and re-reading. It also involves active reflection. In my case, I kept a reflective journal and was able to take advantage of my supervision sessions to talk through my ideas and thoughts. Even the actual writing up of the emerging interpretations became a filter that allowed me to test out the interpretations against the data. Any social worker reading this should automatically connect with the skills this task called on.

Tentative interpretations that are grounded in and validated by the data are formulated and compared with each other to seek out similarities and differences. Small segments of meaning are put together in order to see larger structures and patterns of meaning – the phenomenological process of continually moving between the whole and the parts. The work of Dahlberg et al. (2008) was used to arrive at one major interpretation. They assert that an empirical hermeneutic study should not end simply with a particular phenomenon being revealed in a new light. Instead there should be one further step – the production of an interpretation that brings all these perspectives together. Two main interpretations were arrived at using each of the two core research questions. These were then considered together to arrive at the one major interpretation of the study. The process of data analysis is captured in Figure 15.1.

Figure 15.1: Process of data analysis

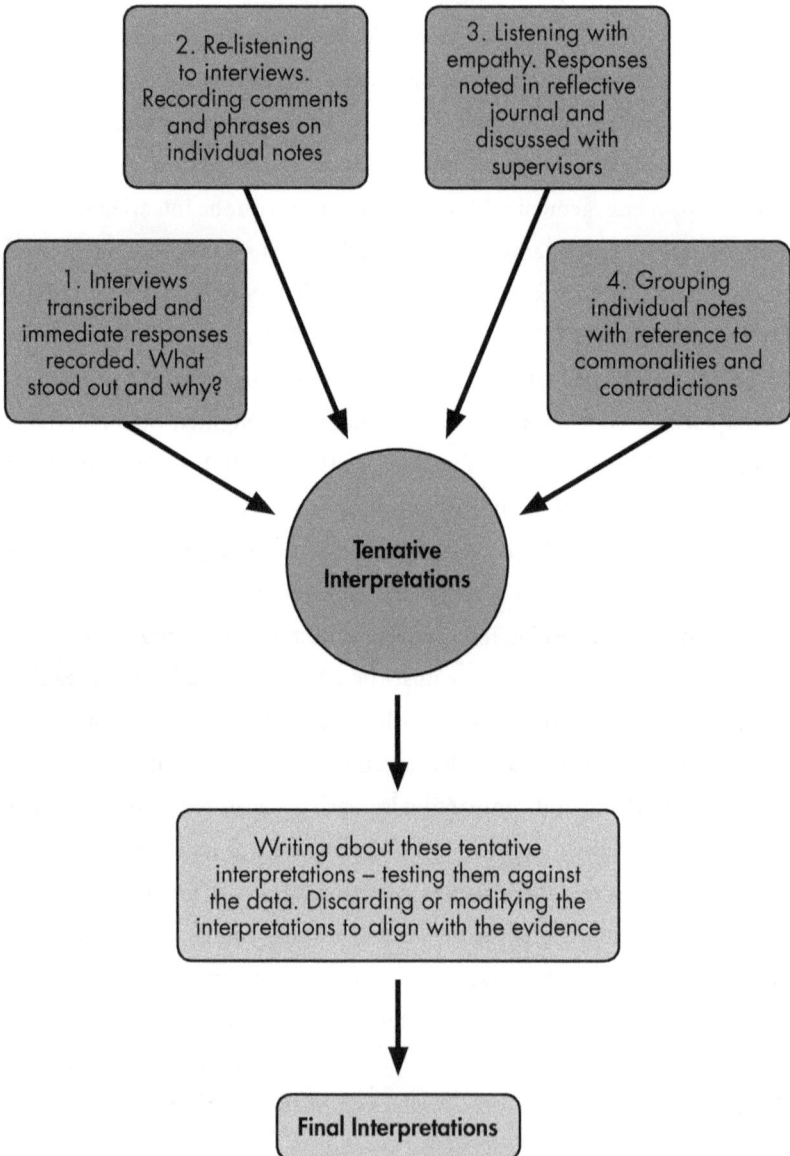

When the two main interpretations were considered alongside each other the following major interpretation was arrived at:

Two types of lived experience are evident in an episode of acute mental health inpatient care. When these are aligned recovery is optimised.

With this major interpretation it was possible to consider the inpatient experience in a new light. The research inadvertently took on a strengths approach of its own despite my initial expectations that the inpatient setting would be exposed as a negative environment adverse to a recovery focus. Instead the findings revealed a scenario where deficits and differences took a back seat giving way to the positivity of emerging strengths and opportunities. With my social work brain engaged with a research brain my own perceptions of the forces at play within my mental health workplace took on a new level of understanding. The two most prominent elements of practice change that shouted at me from the research findings included the significance of the facilitation of mutual or peer support and the skill of deep listening as a way of acknowledging and respecting consumer lived experience. Here is another point of this story where social work ears should be burning.

## Conclusion: Social Work Research – So What?

I commenced this research from a position of negativity and disillusionment; indeed, this is what formed my motivation. Instead of a person-centred, strengths-based system of care I saw custodial and restrictive measures that were repressive and affronting. How did I arrive at findings that identified recovery experiences and pointed to opportunities and hope? Certainly the deficits and negatives were present. Consumers were critical of many aspects of care and workers expressed frustration at systemic limitations that prevented them from fulfilling their work roles in a way they would like. Despite this, some consumers had experienced an extraordinary transformation from an unwell state to one in which they felt control and agency. Workers, to my surprise, demonstrated a strong emotional attachment to their work and to the consumers for whose care they were responsible. It was the positives, the strengths that kept calling to me as I moved through the process of data analysis. This experience of research was totally and utterly a social work experience. From the anti-oppressive values that motivated the research, the principles that guided my choice of methodology, the skill set required to undertake the interviews, the process of reflection and reflexive writing and the bringing together and giving meaning to diverse and complex experiences – all of it drew on the skills and knowledge of the social worker I had become over the forty years since my graduation. The field of mental health needs social work research, research that inherently understands the requirements of recovery-focused care. It can challenge the dominance of the biomedical discourse, but more importantly it can model how recovery-focused practice can be done alongside and in collaboration with the traditional biomedical focus. It can give voice to those most silenced and it can unearth strengths and opportunities that lead to innovative practice. Research can be a tool of reform – another social work mantra – and is a way in which social work can contribute to a more responsive and effective system of mental health care.

## References

AASW. (2010). *Code of Ethics.* Canberra: Australian Association of Social Workers.

Anthony, W. A. (1993). 'Recovery from Mental Illness: The guiding vision of the mental health service system in the 1990s', *Psychosocial Rehabilitation Journal,* 16(4), 11–23.

Bloom, S. (2005). 'The relevance of medical sociology to psychiatry: A historical view', *Journal of Nervous and Mental Disease,* 193(2), 77–84.

Crotty, M. (1998). *The Foundations of Social Research. Meaning and Perspective in the research process.* St Leonards: Allen & Unwin.

Dahlberg, K., Dahlberg, H., & Nystrom, M. (2008). *Reflective Lifeworld Research* (2nd edn.) Sweden: Studentlitteratur.

Deegan, P. (1988). Recovery: 'The lived experience of rehabilitation', *Psychosocial Rehabilitation Journal,* 11(4), 11–19.

Deegan, P. (1995). Recovery as a journey of the heart. Presented at: 'Recovery from Psychiatric Disability: Implications for the training of mental health professionals', Massachusetts State House Gardner Auditorium, 10 May.

Drake, P., & Heath, L. (2010). *Practitioner research at doctoral level: Developing coherent research methodologies.* Milton Park: Routledge.

Engel, G. (1977). 'The need for a new medical model: A challenge for biomedicine', *Science,* 196(4286), 129–36.

Finlay, L. (2011). *Phenomenology for Therapists. Researching the Lived World.* West Sussex: Wiley-Blackwell.

Fook, J. (2002). *Social Work, Critical Theory and Practice.* London: Sage Publications.

Harvey, D., Plummer, D., Pighills, A., & Pain, T. (2013). 'Practitioner research capacity: A survey of social workers in Northern Queensland', *Australian Social Work,* 66(4), 540–54.

IFSW (2016). *Statement of Ethical Principles,.* Retrieved from http://ifsw.org/policies/statement-of-ethical-principles/.

Morley, C. (2003). 'Towards critical social work practice in mental health: A review', *Journal of Progressive Human Services,* 14(1), 61–84.

Probst, B. (2012). 'Not quite colleagues: Issues of power and purview between social work and psychiatry', *Social Work in Mental Health,* 10, 367–83.

Ramon, S., Shera W., Healy, B., Lachman, M., & Renouf, N. (2009). 'The Rediscovered Concept of Recovery in Mental Illness', *International Journal of Mental Health,* 38(2), 106–26.

Ramon, S. (2009). 'Adult Mental Health in a Changing International Context: The Relevance to Social Work', *British Journal of Social Work,* 39(8), 1615–22.

Slade, M., Amering, M., & Oades, L. (2008). 'Recovery: an international perspective', *Epidemiologia e Psichiatria Sociale,* 17(2), 128–37.

Vagle, M.D. (2014). *Crafting Phenomenological Research.* Walnut Creek CA: Left Coast Press.

Willig, K. (2012). *Qualitative interpretation and analysis in psychology.* Berkshire, England: McGraw-Hill.

# SIXTEEN

# The Co-Operative Inquiry Research Method: A Personal Story

*Monica Short*

## Abstract

Co-operative inquiry is accessible participatory research, which can enable the collection of knowledge, experience and the practice wisdom of research inquirers. The method facilitates mutually supportive relationships and conversations with colleagues and the field. This chapter introduces the co-operative inquiry method and narrates my experience of being a co-researcher, co-inquirer, co-author and co-subject in six co-operative inquiries. The inquiries have allowed me to develop my social work knowledge and assisted my critical reflexivity and reflections around field education, disability, supervision, faith, the Anglican Church, people from culturally and linguistically diverse backgrounds, and personhood. The six published inquiries evidence the usefulness of this method across different social work fields of practice.

## Introduction

The purpose of this chapter is to introduce the co-operative inquiry method and to narrate my experiences of being a co-operative inquiry co-researcher, co-inquirer, co-author and co-subject in six published co-operative inquiries. This paper aims to demonstrate the accessibility, functionality and flexibility of this method. For me, an innovative aspect of the co-operative inquiry method is its potential to generate knowledge by integrating social work practice wisdom and experience with theoretical concepts. I also appreciate how it demystifies research and shares power.

## A Research Story: My First Experience of a Co-Operative Inquiry

About five years ago, John Healy, a colleague, and I decided to investigate the field education experience of students who are living with disabilities. We invited Cass Hearn, who had the lived experience, to join the research team. Cass was a graduate from Charles Sturt University in social work who was studying a master's degree and had an interest in research. Together we began looking for a method with particular strengths, one which was: easily accessible; highly flexible; free; functional across multiple research sites; promoted dialogic exchanges; and engaged with traditional and non-traditional research epistemologies. We were also looking for a method that integrated professional and personal knowledge; honoured emic (insider) and etic (outsider) perspectives (Buckley, Chapman, Clegg, & Mattos, 2014); was consistent with the Australian Association of Social Workers' Code of Ethics (2010); valued relationships, inclusion and diversity; shared power; upheld egalitarian principles; and was in accord with the mantra 'nothing about us without us' (Charlton, 2000). We had lofty expectations. John recommended the co-operative inquiry method because of its research principle of writing with people rather than about or on people (Reason & Bradbury, 2006). We realised through this first inquiry that the co-operative inquiry method contained all the above listed strengths and that it also naturally generated future research projects. This first inquiry led to further research and associated publications, and the formation of the Believing in People Living with Disabilities Research Community (BPLD).

# What Is a Co-Operative Inquiry?

A co-operative inquiry can be action focused. Alston and Bowles argue that action research approaches are based on 'a commitment to research as an empowerment activity for all' (Alston & Bowles, 2012: 201). They explain this action research commitment can be observed in collaborations like the authoring of 'A guide to supervision in social work education' (Agllias et al., 2010; Alston & Bowles, 2012: 203).

Co-operative inquiry is a collaborative and participatory research method because it brings together like-minded people to explore areas of mutual concern and interest (Reason & Heron, 2016). Pioneered by Heron and later Reason, this approach differs from research approaches which expect the researcher to have all the ideas, ask the questions, conduct observations, run activities and apply purely theoretical approaches (Reason & Heron, 2016). It considers that people are not passive, are capable of generating knowledge about their world and able to develop creative actions that address real life matters (Reason & Heron, 2016).

Co-operative inquiry considers theory and practice to be related and is also an experiential and reflective approach to exploring practice or social phenomena (Jones-Mutton, Short, Bidgood, & Jones, 2015: 86; Reason, 2002: 169). Every person involved agrees to be part of an inquiry and is equally a co-researcher, co-inquirer, co-subject and co-author (Reason & Heron, 2016). Collectively the co-researchers determine such things as the research questions, generate ideas, participate in the research activities (Reason & Heron, 2016). Each co-researcher has a say in the conclusions reached (Reason & Heron, 2016). I found this method accessible because it provides an opportunity for all, including students, people who receive services, activists, field educators and/or social work practitioners, to be researchers and/or published authors. I consider it to be a highly functional method due to it being naturally suited to a range of research projects, for example, both multi-disciplinary or social work focused investigations. Currently co-operative inquiry topics explored by CSU social worker colleagues and myself include off-site supervision, field education, (dis)ability, working with difference on placement, personhood, faith and religion, learning music in community (see the chapter by John Healy), case management, gender and the value of the case study for teaching and research.

## The Breadth of the Co-Operative Inquiry Method

Further to my first inquiry mentioned above, I have had the good fortune to participate in five other co-operative inquiries as a co-researcher, co-inquirer, co-subject and co-author. These are listed below.

1.  Four social workers, two from the field and two from university, conducted an inquiry into *'Field Education: Off-site Social Work Supervision in Rural, Regional and Remote Australia'* (Jones-Mutton et al., 2015). Without breaching the privacy and confidentiality of supervisees, this inquiry narrated historical experiences of supervision and shared current off-site supervision encounters.

2.  Three social workers and two theologians inquired into *'Rural Australian Anglican Church engagements with people from culturally and linguistically diverse backgrounds'* (Short, Broughton, Short, Ochala, & Anscombe, 2017). This research recognised the need to converse across disciplines so as to allow a more complete picture to emerge about the church and migration (Short et al., 2017: 119, 125).

3.  Three social work field educators from the human services sector requested training in research (Short et al., 2017). Other field educators were invited to join in the professional development activity about research. This led to five field educators and one academic conducting a co-operative inquiry titled *'The power of the case study*

*within practice, education and research'* (Short et al., 2017).

4.  Four social workers, as part of the BPLD, inquired into *'Social work field education: Believing in supervisors who are living with disabilities'* (Healy, Tillotson, Short, & Hearn, 2015). This article partially extended the literature about being an Australian social work field educator by including a conversation about ability, and it valued the practice wisdom of a current student supervisor and a social worker aspiring to become a supervisor, both who are living with disabilities (Healy et al., 2015: 1087).

5.  The current membership of BPLD of three social workers, a sociologist and a scientist – four co-inquirers from Charles Sturt University and one from the University of British Columbia – inquired into the focus area *'Faith matters: From a disability lens'* (Tillotson, Short, Ollerton, Hearn, & Sawatzky, 2017). This paper explored two clashes between the medical model of disability and people's faith. It discussed reasons why faith matters, such as it has the ability to empower and build people's resilience (Tillotson et al., 2017: 335).

These inquiries evidence the utility of this method. I believe co-operative inquiry is able to adapt to a wide range of investigations or fields because it follows a reflection-action-reflection process until key themes about the research topic emerge (Short & Healy, 2017). Please see Figure 16.1 which charts a co-operative inquiry process (Short & Healy, 2017: 217). Figure 16.1 is an adaption of Heron and Reason's description of the co-operative inquiry cycle phases (Reason & Heron, 2016; Short & Healy, 2017).

Figure 16.1: Co-operative Inquiry Phases

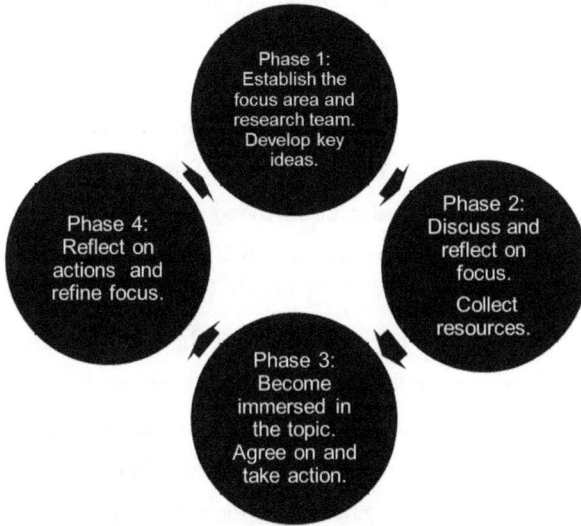

## Introducing the Inquiry Phases

I personally have found these cycles helpful because they provide structure to investigations. In phase one a research team comes together and collectively and consciously decides to undertake an inquiry. (The decision to undertake an inquiry tends not to be made retrospectively about a nearly finalised or finalised project because a retroactive approach could be inconsistent with the egalitarian and democratic nature of this method.) The team establishes the focus area and associated key ideas are developed. In this phase a group of like-minded people who are willing to work co-operatively comes together as co-researchers (co-inquirers) and form a focus group to investigate a topic known as the focus area (Short & Healy, 2017: 195). Democratically they decide such elements of the research as the aim and purpose of the project; author order; the research question or theme; how often and where the group will meet; what literature and key ideas to engage with; the timeline; how the inquiry data will be generated, kept, collected, cleaned and analysed; and how the research will be presented.

In the above six inquiries in which I have participated, we started each inquiry with a reflexivity exercise where we introduced ourselves to each other and outlined our connection to the topic. Such activities help an inquiry group build rapport and trust, which in turn facilitates the sharing of perceptions. Furthermore, each member of each of the six inquiries agreed to meet weekly for an hour via telephone, for conversations to be minuted, for the minutes to become the data for the projects (Short et al., 2017) and that the data would be analysed both manually and/or with assistance from a computer program – NVIVO 10 (QSR International, 2010).

Once the focus area is established and the key ideas are identified, the inquiry transitions or cycles into the next phase. In phase two the inquiry group discusses and reflects on the focus area, and starts collecting resources. In this phase each member of the research team (inquiry group) becomes a co-subject investigating the inquiry (research) theme. Each inquirer begins to observe their environment, collect traditional and non-traditional literature about the field and share practice wisdom (Short & Healy, 2017: 196). The inquiry group starts to identify research tasks or activities and allocates them (Short & Healy, 2017: 196). Observations and conversations about the topic are recorded and kept secure. This leads to phase three.

In phase three the co-subjects become fully immersed in the topic (Heron & Reason, 2001: 180) and agree upon actions and begin implementing them. Reason and Heron (2016) states, 'this phase is in some ways the touchstone of the inquiry method, and is what makes it so very different from conventional research, because here people are deeply involved in their own experience so any practical skills or new understandings will grow out of this experience'. Critical reflexive and reflective thinking are essential elements of this stage. People's beliefs, values, norms, ethics and even faith can be explored (Short & Healy, 2017: 197; Tillotson et al., 2017). If trust exists between members within the inquiry group, then this phase can be empowering of the co-subjects, allowing people to gain new insights into the focus area and to develop a profound self-awareness of their connections to the field and of their actions and thoughts. They may even change or expand their thinking about the topic. The data collected in this phase is rich and engaging. It is so rich it can appear to be thriving because it is speaking into the thinking of all co-subjects and is rapidly growing. The data is constantly being reviewed, discussed and analysed and consequently key themes start to emerge. This leads the inquiry to transitions or cycles into phase four.

Phase four involves reflecting on actions and refining the focus area. The co-subjects resume being co-researchers and begin to identify the emerging key themes (Short & Healy, 2017: 199). If a document is produced, then the co-researchers also become co-authors. In this phase, data collection slows and the co-researchers focus on reviewing, cleaning, organising and presenting the data. This can be time consuming as the data has been allowed to flourish and has not been collected systematically such as through a questionnaire. In other words the data has not been pruned, encrypted, filtered or controlled. Computer programs like NVIVO (QSR International, 2010) can assist with analysing the data by drawing out key words and themes. In reviewing the data, a particular inquiry theme may appear under-developed. The inquiry group can choose to return to phase one and recycle over the theme and in doing so generate more data. The group may recycle over themes multiple times until there is consensus in the group that there is enough material to begin writing up the inquiry and presenting it.

## An Opportunity to Wonder

The Australian Association of Social Workers Code of Ethics (2010: 14–15) requires social workers to examine their personal and professional values, prejudices and preferences and to critically reflect on their practice and ethical dilemmas. As a result social workers engage in critical reflexivity and reflection about their work.

Additionally, Anscombe (2001) and Pawar and Anscombe (2015) posit social workers need to 'think', that is apply knowledge, 'do', that is practice and 'be', that means recognise people are both shape and are shaped by their environment. These arguments encourage me to wonder about my engagement as a social worker with social phenomena.

Each co-operative inquiry provided me with opportunities in community to critically look at premises on which thinking, actions and emotions are based (Fook & Gardener, 2007: 14). As a result I have critically wondered about my practice, observations, personal troubles or social and public issues. The inquiries provided me, and others, with the opportunity to turn personal troubles into public issues and to consider what Mills calls the connection between milieu and social structures (Mills, 1959: 130).

The inquiries also provided me with the opportunity to respectfully share my insights with others and to hear others perspectives. My fellow inquirers, who were applying egalitarian principles, helped direct my explorations of the topics such as by recommending literature and resources for me to engage with and to critique. At times this meant engaging with non-traditional epistemologies and ontologies. For example, in our first inquiry (Hearn, Short, & Healy, 2014) we engaged with poetry and artwork by colleagues Burningham and Pipe (2011) titled – *I am a Person First*. Discussing the artwork allowed me to examine and challenge my ideas of disability in a safe environment with people I trusted.

All the inquiries have had a profound impact on me. My co-researchers who are also my colleagues have gifted me with the dignity to grow as a social worker and the privilege of co-authoring with people who inspired me. I believe (and hope) this has been a reciprocal experience for all involved.

## Limitations and Issues with This Method

Not everyone finds collaborative research such as a co-operative inquiry attractive. This may be because a co-operative inquiry as a research method has a number of limitations and issues.

With regards to the limitations, inquiries are often small research projects, vulnerable to subjectivity and hence not a representative sample of the field or spectrum of thinking about the focus area (Jones-Mutton et al.,

2015: 93). The co-subjects/researchers tend to be like-minded because they share an interest in the inquiry's focus area (Jones-Mutton et al., 2015: 93). This can make an inquiry vulnerable to groupthink (Short & Healy, 2017: 227). Some blind-reviewers of journals have rejected our journal articles for publication because of these reasons. For example, one of the reasons a paper was rejected by a journal was that the inquiry group contained a small number of like-minded people. This did not dissuade us from submitting the paper to another journal because we felt there was a place in current discourses for the lived experience, narratives and conversations about social phenomena (Short et al., 2017: 129).

With regards to issues, three common ones which may impact an inquiry are:

1. The co-inquirers often have busy jobs and can miss inquiry meetings because they are consumed by their workloads.

2. The commitment of co-researchers can vary and some may not have time to complete tasks between sessions, and,

3. An inquiry struggles with transitioning from immersion in a topic to finalising the inquiry such as by writing a journal paper.

When these issues occur, an inquiry can risk becoming confused or aimless and end prematurely.

It is possible to navigate all of these above limitations and issues. The first step is for the inquiry group to respectfully acknowledge what is happening and then they can develop together a solution that empowers all members. It may mean the inquiry group needs to revisit the focus area, review the research question or theme, develop new timeframes, create a writing environment and/or be reminded of the greater purpose of the project (Short, 2017).

## Tips for Identifying a Journal for Submission and Creating a Writing Environment

When writing a paper for publication, I find it helpful as a co-author if possible journals for submission are identified by the inquiry group during phase one. Together we read the author instructions on the journal's webpage and view a sample of articles published in the journal. We include articles from the chosen journal in our reference lists. If there is uncertainty as to which journal to submit a paper, what worked for one of our inquiries was to look at the articles we read and consider where they had been published. In another inquiry we perused the reference lists at the end of journal articles and observe which journals published articles in our field.

I have noticed that when an inquiry enters phase four, writing an article occurred relatively quickly when as a group we divided up the writing tasks between each of us and regularly set dates to review pieces of writing. For example, one person volunteers to write the first rough draft of the literature review, one person scripts the first rough draft of the method and so on. This was one way to create an empowering writing environment which respects each person's contribution and writing experience.

I have also found regularly blocking time in my diary for both writing individually and as a group helpful, disciplined use of time. For example, as an individual putting aside one hour for writing first thing every Wednesday morning before reading emails or attending to other work activities and, meeting as a writing group one hour every Thursday afternoon. Personally, I find the experience of drafting a paper exciting.

## Conclusion

This chapter has outlined my co-operative inquiry narrative and provided insights into the utility of this accessible research method which advocates for writing with people rather than about people (Reason & Bradbury, 2006). I personally have found this approach to research to be innovative in many respects. First, it demonstrates how cooperation can be nurtured when undertaking research. Second, it shows how academics and practitioners can work together to generate new ideas and publications. Third, it provides in an empowering way a prime place for the researched or participants, who can be often ignored in conventional research.

Note: Please feel free to email me at mshort@csu.edu.au for details about workshops on how to run a co-operative inquiry or for a copy of a handout about writing co-operative inquiry journal articles.

## Acknowledgements

Thanks to all those who have helped me to undertake research by employing the co-operative inquiry method and write for publications.

## References

Agllias, K., Bowles, W., B Cassano, Collingridge, M., Dawood, A., Irwin, J., Zubrzycki., J. (2010). *A guide to supervision in social work field education.* Strawberry Hills: Australian Learning and Teaching Council.

Alston, M., & Bowles, W. (2012). *Research for social workers* (3rd edn.). Oxon, UK: Routledge.

Anscombe, B. (2001). 'Not either/or but both/and: An academic/field partnership in practice', *Australian Social Work,* 54(4), 19–27.

Australian Assocation of Social Workers. (2010). *Code of Ethics.* Canberra: AASW.

Buckley, P. J., Chapman, M., Clegg, J., & Mattos, H. G.-D. (2014). 'A linguistic and philosophical analysis of emic and etic and their use in international business research', *Management international review,* (54), 307–24.

Burningham, G., & Pipe, J. (2011). Montage: I'm a Person First: Displayed by Belconnen Art Centre.

Charlton, J. (2000). *Nothing about Us without Us: Disability Oppression and Empowerment.* California: University of California Press.

Fook, J., & Gardener, F. (2007). *Practicing critical reflection: A resource handbook.* Berkshire, England: Open University Press.

Healy, J., Tillotson, N., Short, M., & Hearn, C. (2015). 'Social work field education: Believing in supervisors who are living with disabilities', *Disability and Society,* 30(7), 1087–102.

Hearn, C., Short, M., & Healy, J. (2014). 'Social work field education: Believing in students who are living with a disability', *Disability and Society, 29*(9), 1343–55.

Heron, J., & Reason, P. (2001). 'The practice of co-operative inquiry: Research "with" rather than "on" people'. In P. Reason & H. Bradbury (eds.), *Handbook of Action Research: Participative Inquiry and Practice* (pp. 179–88). London, UK: Sage.

Jones-Mutton, T., Short, M., Bidgood, T., & Jones, T. (2015). 'Field education: Off-site social work supervision in rural, regional and remote Australia', *Advances in Social Work & Welfare Education, 17*(1), 83–97.

Mills, C. W. (1959). *The sociological imagination.* New York New York: Oxford University Press.

Pawar, M., & Anscombe, B. (2015). *Reflective social work practice: Thinking, doing and being.* Melbourne, Vic: Cambridge University Press.

QSR International. (2010). Introducing Nvivo. Retrieved 28 September 2013 from http://www.youtube.com/watch?v=x_UYavbr8g8&list=PL98A557D234 27B3BC.

Reason, P. (2002). 'Editorial introduction: The practice of co-operative inquiry', *Systemic Practice and Action Research, 13*(3), 169–76.

Reason, P., & Bradbury, H. (2006). *Handbook of Action Research.* London: Sage.

Reason, P., & Heron, J. (2016). A short guide to co-operative inquiry. Retrieved 18/9/17, 2017, from www.human-inquiry.com/cishortg.htm

Short, M. (2017). *Workshop for the AASW NSW Branch Field Education Practice Group – Co-operative inquiry: A student and worker friendly research method.* Retrieved from https://www.aasw.asn.au/events/event/aasw-nsw-branch-field-education-practice-group-meeting-25-May-2017.

Short, M., Barton, H., Cooper, B., Woolven, M., Loos, M., & Devos, J. (2017). 'The power of the case study within practice, education and research', *Advances in Social Work & Welfare Education, 19*(1), 92–106.

Short, M., Broughton, G., Short, M., Ochala, Y., & Anscombe, B. (2017). 'Connecting to belonging: A cross-disciplinary inquiry into rural Australian Anglican Church engagements with people from culturally and linguistically diverse backgrounds', *Journal of Contemporary Religion, 32*(1), 119–33.

Short, M., & Healy, J. (2017). 'Writing "with" not "about": Examples in Co-operative Inquiry'. In S. Gair & A. V. Luyun (eds.), *Sharing Qualitative Research: Showing Lived Experience and Community Narratives* (pp. 188–203). London: Routledge.

Tillotson, N., Short, M., Ollerton, J., Hearn, C., & Sawatzky, B. (2017). 'Faith matters: From a disability lens', *Journal of Disability and Religion, 21*(3), 319–37.

# SEVENTEEN

# Older People and Music Participation: Community Aspects of Learning

*John Paul Healy*

## Abstract

This chapter explores my own participation and that of other older people in Bluegrass and Old Time music and festivals from a personal and experiential perspective and considers some of the social aspects of learning in community. Music festivals are mostly thought of as the domain of younger people; however there are some musical styles and events that are more attractive to a broader age group. In particular, Bluegrass and Old Time music has major involvement from older people as audience, performers and casual musical participants. For older people, Bluegrass and Old Time music festivals can be a place for informal learning of their chosen instrument. Bluegrass and Old Time music associations and festivals present the opportunity for a lifelong learning experience within a shared community. It is often regarded that adult learning is aided by experience, and within this musical community and festival spaces there are ample opportunity for participation. Social workers already use innovative practices such as music and art therapy to help to enhance the lives of older people in aged care settings; what I am attempting to bring out within this chapter is how the learning of music for these older people in community seems to enhance aspects of social inclusion without pathologising or ageist attitudes. Of course, the members of the this musical community presented here are very much able to continue independent lives and have the opportunity to mix with younger people, and this is true of many older people in our society. An innovative aspect of this chapter is to explore this example of older people, and reflect on the learning styles and opportunities to inform and enhance my own teaching of adult learners.

The chapter is informed by an auto-ethnographic approach that tells a particular story of my own experience, learning and participating within this musical community. 'Auto-ethnography particularly offers a way to situate the self within the research process and its written product, by making the self the object of research (Burnier, 2006: 410). This form of writing is purposefully self-conscious and introspective ...' (Ellis, 2004: 30). As a style of writing 'it is setting a scene by telling a story, weaving intricate connections between life and art' (Jones, 2005: 765). 'Autoethnography shows struggle, passion, embodied life, and the collaborative creation of sense-making ...' (Ellis & Bochner, 2006: 434). Using this type of unobtrusive method, which included, participating in this community based music, observing and reflecting on the festivals and other activities – or as Whyte (1973) famously put it, just 'hanging out', I present my reflections on learning within this community and in the final part of the chapter I reflect on what I have learned from this experience that I can take as innovative practice to my role as a social work educator.

The first part of the chapter sets the scene of my own introduction within the Old Time and Bluegrass community and then I reflect on what I have seen by the way of learning for myself and others in community and especially at music festivals and other gatherings. I was first introduced to the idea of Bluegrass and Old Time music and their festivals when I began to become a regular at The Bluegrass & Traditional Country Music Society of Australia (BTCMSA) in Sydney.

It's mid-winter but the room is humid; 20 to 30 people packed into the front room of the old neighborhood centre in Annandale, Sydney. Large bay windows facing out on to the street, and the whole room, except for the worn bare beige carpet, a brilliant white. Many hands going through the motions, plucking, strumming, hammering, such a cacophony, and the sound doesn't seem to be coming from any one individual. I started to join in by playing my mandolin and any self-consciousness I had planned to feel, fell away as I realised I couldn't even hear myself. The person immediately to my left, bashing his guitar, nudges me with his elbow; a big smile, 'First time here'. He must have noticed the bewilderment in my face as I attempted to make sense of this ragged group of musical practitioners. I reflected that the last time I encountered such a mixed bag of ages, gender and social class, was passing by an Alcoholic Anonymous meeting in Kings Cross during the smoko break when they would stream out of their meeting onto the street to enjoy one of the only addictive pleasures not frowned upon by Bill. There was also an evangelical feel to the experience in the room, and much like Alcoholic Anonymous, the group I had entered considered themselves sinners; however, in this case, sinners was a type of acronym for Safety in Numbers. And yes, it was certainly a comfortable way to turn up and play a relatively new instrument; I'd learnt some chords to sing along too, but I was certainly no mandolin player, however, I was here to learn something about Bluegrass; was this it?

What stuck me when I first entered the world of Bluegrass and Old Time music, was the amount of Older people engaged in playing and learning instruments. And I can't exclude myself from this; when I first turned up, to the above scenario, I was not far from 50, and had thought my musical life was over. I'd played drums in bands throughout my life and as that fell away I dabble with guitar; but as youth moved further away from me, and fame had not found me, engaging in music had gained a futility. It was in my depth of musical depression, playing at songwriter nights to other songwriters when somebody, thinking I was playing country music, said that I should check out the Bluegrass Association. He looked at me knowingly, and smiled, 'you'll like it'; and I did.

Sinners (safety in numbers) is a common introduction to the Bluegrass and Old Time Music Association in Sydney. Yes, we play both types of music, Bluegrass and Old time. And there are some quite specific musical practices that differentiates these the two forms of American traditional country music.

The types of music I am concerned with are in the tradition of stringbands, that is, Old time and Bluegrass, which focus on stringed instruments such as fiddle, banjo, mandolin, guitar; this type of music came out of America and is commonly know as, Old Time, Old Time country, mountain music, Bluegrass, or even just country music, or mockingly as hillbilly music. It originated in and around the Appalachian Mountains on the East coast of the United States from Virginia to Tennessee around the 1800's (Malone, 1994; Price, 2011). Culturally the music is considered a blend of Irish, Scottish, African (Perryman, 2013: 27). Bluegrass would be the most recent incarnation of this tradition, stemming from the late 1930's (Price, 2011; Stetson, 2006). The popularity of this Mountain music for those outside the mountains came towards the end of the 1920's after Victor records and others began to travel into the regions and recorded the music (Langrall, 1986; Olson, 2016). Those early recordings spread around the world influencing the popular music of its day. A further wave of popularity came as the young people of the late 1950's, early 1960's rediscovered the music; and the musicians that were still alive began to perform at colleges, folk clubs and festivals to this younger audience (Perryman, 2013). These Oldtime, Bluegrass and Early Blues musicians influenced many of the 60's musicians and continue to have influence today (Turino, 2008: 155).

Many festivals where established out of the 60's revival, although organized Fiddle meet-ups and competitions had been going on in the mountains continuously since the 1920's (such as Fiddlers Grove NC) and of course informal gatherings have a much longer history. In Australia, these types of meet-ups and festivals have been going since the early 1970s; although the music of American String bands, through the introduction of the radio in 1920s, have become part of Australia's own history of country music (Jones, 2017). I've been attending these events and festivals for the past 4 years and during that time have also been part of The Bluegrass & Traditional Country Music Society of Australia (BTCMSA) in Sydney, and began my own learning through the association in their Sinners group. The BTCMSA has been going continuously since 1975 with regular concerts and musical events. Over the years I have taken an interest in the way people take up, often an unfamiliar instrument, and over time, learn how to play this type of music. My interest, I feel, is connected to my own learning in community and my teaching at university. As a lecturer, I often wonder how do students learn best, what do they need, and especially older learners. The next section presents some of my observations from my own time learning and participating and my observations of others in the community.

## How to Begin to Learn

There seems very little formal teaching for beginners; occasionally someone from the BTCMSA will advertise that they are running some lessons, however, over the years I've been involved, this has been very rare. The closest the BTCMSA come to any type of formal learning is in the Sinners group, and this only involves sending out chords, lyrics and a video of the 3 songs the group will learn to play at the monthly get-together, although, learning is not what happens on the night. On the night the group runs through the songs several times and allocates lead opportunities for those who are ready to try. Much of the learning of the songs happens independently before the night. You can learn on the night if you are quick enough, but there is no instruction beyond and discussion of the chord progression and running through the songs several times with the large group. I guess this might suggest interested and individually motivated learners, however, it seems the Sinners group is fairly open and does not insist on everybody learning the songs before hand, and people can join in as much or as little as they feel or have the ability to do so; some people may just sit and listen.

However it is not unusual to ask somebody in the community to show you how to play a song or tune. As long as you're not taking up too much of their own playing time; everybody is looking out for something new to learn. Also it is not unusual for people to come up to you suggest corrections to your playing, some subtly, and others rather abruptly; however, never formally, always in the throws of a jam or other type of communal musical sharing. Festivals are possibly the best opportunity to learn from others because of the close proximity and the extended time people can spend together over the festival weekend, or festival week. Also, festivals offer some workshops with some tips on playing (many of these are more suited to advanced player). Playing casually with other campers seems to be one of the best ways to learn new music, or particular ways to play and improve on your instrument.

Generosity is a real quality around Bluegrass and Old Time musicians, and if you are willing to learn, they are willing to put up with beginners. That is, as long as you don't play too loud, and focus more on listening and learning the tunes. Because there is limited formal teaching going on, listening, watching and just being in the musical space is where much of the experiential learning takes place. The learning is not easy or quick, but over time it seems to get in. One thing I often reflect on is the difficulty of learning new tunes, however this sits along side the pure joy of being able to participate with other musicians far beyond my own skill level. It seems that no matter where you are musically, there is space to participate, something to reach for and a real joy in the journey.

Playing at the campsite with other campers is a real informal affair. One afternoon I wanted to make some tea but I couldn't find our lighter or matches, so I walked over to the campers next to us and asked if they had any matches. Sure they had matches, but they were also starting up a jam and asked if I'd like to join them, they also had some good looking cheese and crackers laid out on the table, so I just forgot about making tea and sat down to play some music. I hadn't met any of the people before but we played for the rest of the afternoon. In the group there was one man who was in his late eighties and still playing a mean fiddle; I watched his style and tried to follow some of what he was doing. During our session, I learned a little about each person and new ways to play my own instrument. When I finally got up to leave one of the older men said, 'Amazing what a box of matches can do'. Highlighting how some simple introductions and interactions can lead to meaningful music sharing and learning around the campsites at festivals.

When I got to know people over time and had an idea of their abilities and my own, such as their level of playing, beginner, intermediate or advanced, I could see how people, for the most part, gravitate towards each other at their own skill level. It seems to be comfortable to play with those who are similar to you. However, it is also clear that to advance musical learning, people have to begin to reach beyond their skill level and try to enter more advanced groups. For instance, early on I was a good strummer and singer, so I hung out with other strummers and singers and could enjoy my musical participation that way without any real challenges; however, when I began to take up the Fiddle as a second instrument I had to learn melody on the instrument which led me to hang around more advanced players and move beyond my comfort zone into some very challenging learning. Fiddle players rarely sing and seem to spend all their time and energy learning new tunes, instrumentals. The same could be said of banjo players. These are both melody-oriented instruments.

The first festival I went to was a real eye-opener. I arrived very late, set up my tent and thought I'd get some sleep after the long drive so I'd be good for the rest of the weekend. Well first, I couldn't get to sleep too easily as I set up a little close to what became an all-night jam. I woke up sporadically during the night to a different song; and couple of hours after they finished, I thought I'd get up early, or what I thought was early, 7am, to get to the showers without much competition. But as I walked over to the shower there was already a steady stream of people heading to and from the shower blocks; a some were quite old, I noticed a few with walking frames. As I stood in the urinal next to this very old man who didn't seem to be passing anything, just waiting, he turned and said 'It's coming; always takes a while in the morning'. I started to wonder where I was; it was like nursing home residents on a holiday break. It's amazing how young 50 can seem in comparison to 80 something. However, it was a very friendly bunch, chatty, good-mornings all-round. Because I came to the festival on my own it was nice to be around such welcoming campers. As the day went on, I realised it was mainly the older people who got up early, including myself, and the youngers ones who were keeping me up most the night that got up around mid-day. As the weekend rolled on I would find myself in one of those all night jams keeping people awake.

Many of the people I had met at the (BTCMSA) in Sydney were also at my first festival and we got to know each other better and played a lot of music together. This really enhanced the sense of a musical community that existed beyond the initial scene I found in Sydney. Years latter I was at a Bluegrass festival in Sweden, and it was just so familiar, I passed a bunch of people playing a tune that I knew and then joined them for the rest of the night. We didn't speak much, and we didn't need to, the music was our common language.

After a festival, there is much learning to take home, but much of it is not solidified. I often go away with a new tune or two, maybe a couple of songs. However even these need to be worked on, and that seems to be done in several ways. One important way to consolidate the learning is too look up the tunes and songs on YouTube when back home or other online resources, such as mandolin, fiddle or banjo hangout; music sharing and discussion sites target specifically to each instrument. Ironically the Internet is a surprising resource for learning and sharing music; especially this early form of American acoustic music. The tunes and songs seem much easier to learn from these online resources after the festival, or other gathering, when you have a working knowledge and experience of the music. Getting together at people's houses to go over some new tunes is also a good way to keep up the learning. It's insatiable, the desire to constantly learn reflects the notion of lifelong learning. And for older people, the old saying, 'you can't teach an old dog new tricks' doesn't hold for these learners; it certainly seems they can keep learning new tricks in this community setting. From my own experience and what I see from those older than me, leaves me with a perception that growing older, with all its changes and adjustments, can still be a good time; older people can be keen learners and participators in the musical community.

# So What Have I Learned Towards My Own Teaching in Social Work

I guess the main thing I reflect on is, no formal teaching and no formal curriculum. And what has to be stressed here is the notion of formal. So instead of overly structured expectation of teaching and learning, much of what is learned and taught is incidental in a community and experiential setting. This informal musical learning seems self-directed in line with adult theories of learning such as Heutagogy (Dyer, 2016). The musical participants, including myself, seemed to be learning how to learn. People can work from where they are at, and progress when they are ready; a self-determined form of learning (Blaschke, 2012). People work hard when they are interested in something, and the feedback on progress is quick – whether from personal evaluation or feedback from other musician.

How do I try to inform my own teaching with what I have experienced in my musical community; I think I do it in small ways. First I consider all those who attend my subjects as people rather than students; I also refrain from calling or thinking about them as 'my students' but consider them as individuals who have entered our degree for their own reasons and possible advancement. It's not my wish to shape the students into a particular type of social worker, this I feel they will do themselves, and they will become the sort of social worker they want to be, just as I have become. I recognise they are adult learners. I guess that's my standpoint, that's were I start from. This is what I see in my musical community; people becoming the type of musician they want to be, they eventually follow their own interests and their interest is what keeps them engaged.

I am fortunate, as I coordinate a research subject in the social work degree, so I have some freedom in what I do. I shape the assessments so that students get to follow their own interests. They can choose to research an established passion or research a new one; just like the musical learners. Therefore, although the curriculum looks to be very formal, people can also use it as a jumping off point to pursue their own research journey and I am there on the sidelines to give support and guidance. This is something

I see in my musical learning, although there is no formal curriculum, there is a body of knowledge out there, including, even if only in a limited way, musical theory, that over time you can begin to become familiar with. This is also how I see one of the main aspects of research practice, that is, learning how to find information, and once you know how to find it, then learn how to find the information that truly interests you. For research practice, it's the large body of literature out there in journals and library data bases that informs us, and with music, it is the vast growing library of songs and tunes on recordings, and more so of late, on the Internet and YouTube. For me, both research and music present a community of knowledge and learning. I always feel that when we engage with research we are entering into the large ongoing conversation, and the same with music, when we engage with music and learning there is a similar ongoing conversation, and both seem to be embedded in the notion of community.

At Charles Sturt University we have many bricks and mortar campuses but my teaching is predominantly online, so creating a sense of shared community such as the Bluegrass and Oldtime is a real challenge and a constant work in progress. We have forums, which are helpful, and real time online seminars. With both these types of learning platforms I have tried to be as non-directive as possible. We do have core content, however, I encourage the people in the subject to lead by asking questions or sharing there own learning and experience; now I see as a key component of Heutagogy (Snowden, Halsall, Huang, 2016). This creates a conversation and helps to build new avenues of knowledge that I as the coordinator could not have done on my own through building curriculum. I also record videos of people I know doing research projects and have interview conversation with them that I then share with the people from the subject. These video conversations of real world researchers doing real research helps to extend our learning community out from the confines of the course structure, and then, feeds back into the conversation on the forum and our real time online seminars. I feel together we are building some sense of a learning community. Learning in community, we definitely see and experience different ways of learning. The community is therefore an important place of learning; so to think of the university as a community of learning is helpful for me as a lecturer. And further engaging older people in life long learning could really be an addition to our university community. Some innovations from the chapter I feel include, 'you can teach old dogs new tricks'. Adult learners learn best when they are engaged and imbedded in a community of learners; and, the importance of the different types of informal learning happening outside the universities that may help to inform our own teaching practices.

# References

Burnier, D. L. (2006). 'Encounters With the Self in Social Science Research', *Journal of Contemporary Ethnography*, 35(4), 410.

Blaschke, L. (2012). 'Heutagogy and lifelong learning: A review of heutagogical practice and self-determined learning', *International Review of Research in Open and Distributed Learning*, 13(1), 56–71.

Dyer, W. L. (2016). *Development and maintenance of identity in aging community music participants* (Order No. 10135048). Available from ProQuest Dissertations & Theses Global. (1802533260). Retrieved from https://search-proquest-com.ezproxy.csu.edu.au/docview/1802533260?accountid=10344.

Ellis, C. (2004). *The ethnographic I: A methodological novel about autoethnography*. Walnut Creek, CA AltaMira Press.

Ellis, C. S., & Bochner, A. P. (2006). 'Analyzing analytic autoethnography: An autopsy', *Journal of Contemporary Ethnography*, 35(4), 429–49.

Jones, M. A. (2017). 'Playing bluegrass in Australia across country and folk scenes', *Perfect Beat*, 18(2), 131–53.

Jones, S. H. (2005). Autoethnography: Making the personal political. In *Handbook of Qualitative Research*, 3rd edn., (eds.) N. K. Denzin and Y. S. Lincoln (763–92). Thousand Oaks, CA: Sage.

Malone, B. C. (1994). 'Appalachian Music and American Popular Culture: The Romance That Will Not Die', *Appalachian Heritage*, 22(5), 68–76. The University of North Carolina Press. Retrieved 31 August 2017, from Project MUSE database.

Price, L. B. (2011). 'Bluegrass Nation: A Historical and Cultural Analysis of America's Truest Music'. University of Tennessee Honors Thesis Projects, http://trace.tennessee.edu/utk_chanhonoproj/1465.

Perryman, C. W. (2013). *Africa, appalachia, and acculturation: The history of bluegrass music* (Order No. 3605866). Available from ProQuest Dissertations & Theses Global. (1491167243). Retrieved from https://search-proquest-com.ezproxy.csu.edu.au/docview/1491167243?accountid=10344.

Turino, T. (2008). *Music as Social Life: The Politics of Participation.* Chicago: University of Chicago Press.

Snowden, M., Halsall, J. P., Huang, Y. X. (2016). *Self-determined approach to learning: A social science perspective.* Cogent Education 3:1.

Stetson, A. (2006). Expressing Identity in Colorado Bluegrass Music Sub-Culture:

Negotiating Modernity in the American West through Music, Humor and Shared Experience. University of Colorado; Honors Department.

Whyte, W. F. (1973). *Street Corner Society.* Chicago: The University of Chigago Press.

Olson, T. (2016). 'The 1927 Bristol Sessions and Ralf Peer: A Myth and A Legend Losing Luster'. In 'The Cold Light of Recent Scholarship', *Old-Time Herald,* 14(3), 6–8.

Langrall, P. (1986). 'Appalachian Folk Music: From Foothills to Footlights', *Music Educators Journal,* 72(7), 37–9. Retrieved from http://www.jstor.org/stable/3396598.

# EIGHTEEN

# Emerging Ageing and Age-Related Issues Amongst Migrant Population in Regional Australia

*Sabine Wardle and Ndungi wa Mungai*

This chapter aims to explore the migrant communities' perceptions of age related issues by interrogating the needs of these communities and the preparedness of service providers to respond to the needs of the changing demographics. Drawing on focus group discussions and interviews, this chapter highlights specific challenges associated with the concept of 'aged' and ageing' among service providers in regional areas like Wagga Wagga in the Riverina region of rural New South Wales (NSW). It looks at what new aged care services, if any, are needed to accommodate culturally and linguistically diverse groups' (CALD) needs and perceptions of 'aged' and 'ageing'. Further, it discusses implications for designing more flexible and needs-based services for CALD communities.

## Introduction

Australia is one of the most culturally diverse populations in the world (Hiruy & Mwanri, 2013) and the Australian Bureau of Statistics (ABS, 2013b) census data show that 32% of families in Australia have both parents born overseas and 11% for one parent. In Wagga Wagga, these numbers are smaller with 9.9% and 7.5% respectively (ABS, 2013b). The trend in Australian population shows the proportion of those born overseas increasing in the years 2005–2015, with those born in India and China doubling over that period (ABS, 2017a).

Some migrants choose to settle in rural and regional areas as a lifestyle choice and also for opportunities such as employment. The government has also been settling migrants with a refugee background to ease congestion in metropolitan areas and stimulate economic growth in rural towns and regions (Mungai, 2014). For successful settlement to occur and to meet the needs of migrants without burdening the host community, careful planning and appropriate resourcing of services by the government is critical (Mungai, 2014).

A growing migrant population in rural and regional Australia is posing a greater challenge to these communities than those in metropolitan areas. Services for the ageing members of the community are relatively more developed and well established, with umbers providing them with an economy of scale (Mungai, 2014). A small number of migrants, particularly from minority cultural groups present challenges to regional towns that need to be researched. This is to understand their views, concerns, needs and issues on ageing. Capital cities have a greater population density, public transport and the financial ability for agencies to support an ageing population, where regional towns (like Wagga Wagga) have limited resources to facilitate cultural specific needs.

To define a retirement age in Australia, the pension eligibility age (PEA) is one guide to understanding old age. To try and save more money in the budget, the government announced in the 2009/10 budget that the pension eligibility age would gradually rise to 67 years (Kudrna & Woodland, 2011). The rise in age of pension eligibility reflects concerns with the age pension budget as well as the rising life expectancy and changing attitudes towards old age. This demonstrates that using chronological age to mark old age could be problematic. Thus the definition of old age constitutes three elements:

1) chronology; 2) change in social role (i.e. change in work patterns, adult status of children and menopause); and 3) change in capabilities (i.e. invalid status, senility and change in physical characteristics). Results from this cultural analysis of old age suggested that change in social role is the predominant means of defining old age. (WHO, 2017: par. 10).

Given the limitations of using either chronological or social/cultural/ functional markers, it is best to use a combination when dealing with non-Western communities. But, there is no determination on what the migrant population from CALD backgrounds regard as 'old', 'aged' or 'aging'. Within each CALD group there are individuals with diverse experiences and cultural backgrounds with varying requirements and expectations. Australia being a multicultural nation, such information on the concept of age and ageing is foundational to determining what issues various cultural groups will experience and at what age.

Finding out this information and relating the age difference between the migrant population and the age at which age related services are usually provided will allow for improved delivery by the service providers to cater for the growing needs at the right time and in a culturally acceptable manner in various regional locations of Australia in the future. With the current services including personal care, domestic tasks, as well as home modifications, there are a lot of provisions for age related services that may not be accessed or understood by the migrant populations, cultural groups or family units. With the increasing cultural diversity in regional Australia, a greater understanding and innovative design and delivery of services are needed.

The review of the literature shows no evidence at present that research has been conducted into what constitutes old age or ageing amongst the migrant population from CALD backgrounds. Thus this pilot study aims at exploring the meanings and perceptions and needs of 'aged' amongst the migrant populations, as well as issues and gaps experienced by service providers.

# Research Methods

A qualitative phenomenological research approach (Liamputtong, 2013) was used to engage migrant community from CALD backgrounds and service providers in Wagga Wagga. Research participants were purposeful selected (Silverman, 2000). With the help of Multicultural Council of Wagga Wagga (MCWW) four focus groups were conducted as an ideal way to engage CALD community groups. All participants had to be migrants from CALD backgrounds. Participants had to be adults, 18 years and over, and residing in Wagga Wagga.

The focus group participants came from diverse cultural and linguistic backgrounds, for example Burmese, African, Afghani, Chinese, Malaysian, Persian, Sri Lankan and Polish. Each focus group had 2–8 participants. Where it was necessary, professional interpreters were employed to ensure participants understood the information in the general information sheet, consent forms and the focus group questions. To protect their identity in a close knit community, additional demographic and other potentially identifying information is not provided.

Three individual interviews were undertaken with three service providers involved in direct or indirect services to people from CALD background aged 18–100 years residing in Wagga Wagga. All focus groups and individual interviews were audio recorded with the consent of the participants, which were later professionally transcribed. The resultant data were then analysed manually using a thematic analysis (Braun & Clarke, 2006).

# Findings and Discussion

## Perceptions of 'Old Age'

Participants acknowledged it is rather problematic to determine what age is considered 'old age'. Traditional communities do not necessarily have records of birth or celebrate birthdays as it is done in Western countries. Retirement age for civil servants was mentioned and even that one was noted to be increasing from 50s to about 60. Traditionally then it is social role of becoming a grandparent that designated you as 'old' or elder. That position conferred some level of respect in the community. Complications could arise if one had no children as the African focus group noted:

> Because if you are a girl you are still expected to live with your parents, and you are very much treated as if you are still a young person. You're not going to get the respect of a grandmother, when you've never had children. And the other thing that I was forgetting, is about rituals. There are also some rituals that take you to a different level. Say for instance, in my culture, for you to be considered an Elder, and be able to sit in the Council of Elders and pass judgement you have to go through some rituals. You have to give some goats and things like that ... then you are formally accepted into that sort of category. [These elders] are the only ones who can be consulted and can give their wisdom.

Old age is then not regarded as a problem. The older people have the wisdom and can guide the younger ones. They may not be able to do some task requiring muscles but they have other roles that are equally important, such as minding and teaching children. As indicated in the quote above they also have to conduct themselves in a manner that earns them that respect. You look after the family and the family looks after you. This observation on the importance of the social role in defining old age is consistent with WHO (2017) observation on the importance of social roles in understanding ageing.

## Limited Services Rural and Regional Areas of Australia

The general complaint in rural and regional areas is the lack of services, which includes but is not limited to translating and interpreting services to combat the language problem, compared to metropolitan areas. It was suggested that this is one reason people prefer to live in the cities but this could change if services were improved:

> I think in the cities – and that's why I think maybe a lot of people prefer to live in the city too, because there's more, so they get more services. Here it's very difficult in Wagga to provide all that sort of thing. But they could think laterally … with the services. (Agency 1)

Correa-Velez, Barnett, Gifford and Sackey (2011) argue that challenges for providing services to the migrant community includes language problem and a poor understanding of their cultural and religious needs. In terms of services such as health facilities, major cities have wide range of specialist health services and a larger financial base to support a more diverse cultural population.

In small towns with little experience in dealing with CALD migrants there is need for training to improve cross-cultural awareness. However, it was noted that this is sometimes either poorly done or there is considerable resistance and an assumption that it is the migrant who need to change and assimilate:

> If you go in knowing what culture they come from, and showing the respect. We do a bit of research sometimes before we go in, say, 'Oh okay, that's – it's that religion from that country.' I'm interested in all that sort of stuff anyway. … We don't have many people from other cultural backgrounds, except for the older Europeans that came here 50–60 years ago. … There's still an amount of, I guess, ignorance and distrust and that sort of thing. Which they did display toward the European people when they first came out, by calling them 'Wogs'.
>
> But the cultural training you don't really have to pass any kind of a test. You just have to read it and press the

buttons and say, 'Yes, I've read that,' and kind of do case scenarios and things. ... We need to have access to people from different cultural backgrounds that may work or be some sort of liaison person, something like that, yeah. ... My employer needs to give us time or resources to be able to access these communities and build a rapport. (Service Provider 1)

Family and community service providers offer a variety of aged care services across Australia but in regional communities there is insufficient understanding on what services the growing migrant population needs. Populations in regional Australia continue to experience a relative disadvantage compared to the metropolitan cities (Massey & Parr, 2012: 15). Government spending on education, roads, public transport and health are centralised around large population centres for faster economic returns while the regional location have smaller funding allocated. With smaller funding, limited resources would be made available for the growing migrant populations in regional Australia.

## Preparedness of Service Providers

Considering the above mentioned issues, it is fair to ask how the service providers in regional locations are prepared for meeting the emerging ageing needs. Language services are noted as one major obstacle as services cannot be provided optimally if communication is hampered. Small ethnic groups face special problems as a focus group participant noted:

And I guess here in Australia for people who came from other countries – non English speaking countries to Australia in the old age – there's another level of difficulty. Because obviously you're putting them in the centres where English is the language spoken and so obviously there has to be translating services and these services need to be culturally sensitive because it's no point – it's like sticking someone in a prison where they have no say pretty much. If they can't communicate and if their needs cannot be communicated to those who take care of them and ... the issue becomes even more complex when there is people that are suffering from dementia. (Polish community)

Languages can present their own challenges to service providers. For example, with a growing number of migrants coming to regional locations from India which alone has 22 official languages means it is a big challenge for all of them to be supported by the service providers. However, the common language which is Hindi could be supported with interpreters and translation of information packages. Even though there is a common language for most of India that does not mean that religious beliefs and traditions are common for everyone with Indian background. Different regions of India have different religious beliefs as well, and similar diversity applies to migrants from Africa and wider Asia.

The aged and frail migrants who are at the end of life are an increasing share of migrants living in Australia (Hiruy & Mwanri, 2013). For the service providers in regional locations to provide for an ageing migrant population, they need to be prepared for emerging issues and needs that an increasingly multicultural society brings. One of these issues is how the linguistic and cultural differences will impact on access to health-care services (Hiruy & Mwanri, 2013). With an increasing number of migrants settling in regional locations of Australia rather than the five major cities, there is no central area where a particular cultural group is settling. The current perspectives on services for older people being designed as culturally neutral or servicing specific cultural groups (Skinner et al., 2014) does not assist in addressing the needs of CALD older people or their families.

## Preparedness – Funding Growth in Ageing Population Support

Aged services are expensive and with ageing society this is a major concern for the government. People from the CALD communities indicated that their preference is to grow old at home. Sometimes though, this is not possible where the needs are high and their offspring are busy with their lives. The Burmese community noted this desire but also the new challenges in Australia:

> We strongly believe that if we take care of our parents, we will be blessed. So it is considered inappropriate to send your parent to an aged care facility. Even if an old person is fully qualified to go to an aged care facility, children are reluctant to send them to the facility. They do not want them to go there. With everyone having to go out to work, it will be difficult to observe the same thing we do at home. (Burmese focus group)

There is therefore resistance to use the services on one hand and the pressures to change to the new circumstances on the other. On top of this, the service providers noted that providing residential aged care is expensive, even before the cultural factors were considered:

> Our ability to provide that [residential care] in a cost effective way ... [for] elderly people on pensions or disability pensions without the finances – the ability to provide it is difficult. Nursing homes are expensive businesses to run. ... How we still pursue the reverence of caring for an individual and their needs, under an individual that wants to dumb down everybody to the same level to save money, is one of our challenges for the future. (Service Provider 1)

Wanting to enjoy old age with the family and not in an institution is consistent with the sentiments of other Australians. The preferred model would be ageing in the familiar setting as 'community-based, primary-health care approaches emphasise health, education, prevention and chronic disease management, and reduce the need for and reliance upon high-cost acute care' (Giles, Irwin, Lynch & Waugh, 2010, cited Bell, 2015). Supporting families to care for their ageing members is therefore considered much more cost-effective than institutionalised care. The Partners in Culturally Appropriate Community Care Program (PICAP) is the network that is supposed to facilitate this (Martin, 2014). However no one mentioned being aware of it in Wagga.

## Preparedness for Religious Beliefs and Rituals

The challenge for a multicultural country like Australia is how to honour and respect all the cultures from more than 300 ancestries in a country where nearly half (49%) of all Australians were born overseas or have at least one parent who was (ABS, 2017a). The special challenge for rural and regional areas is the small numbers which mean the lack of economy of scale. One service provider noted that it was easy to overlook the needs of these small numbers:

> If they're going into care there is a question on our assessment
> of when they go into care what sort of food would they need
> – do they like it, and I don't know, I don't – I think they're
> pretty much not very well catered for in rural and remote
> areas as much as in the city. (Service Provider 2)

Failure to consult the residents and their families mean even what may seem a routine activity may turn out to be culturally offensive as pointed by a Burmese participant:

> Food is different for them. In aged care facilities, we have

seen that older people are provided with time to play and do activities. But for elderly people in our country we believe that they are too dignified to do such things and it is considered disrespectful. (Burmese focus group participant)

Maintaining religious traditions and observing cultural practises in nursing homes and life transition stages presents a major challenge. Providing support for grief and funeral services is one such aspect where misunderstanding can be traumatic as noted by participants:

We don't think that we are allowed to keep the dead body in the house here which we did at home. With rules and regulations here I will have to deal with not bringing the body back home. And when we see the body at home, we feel connected and feel free to cry and express our sadness.

The African group noted that it is time for them to start discussing about end of life because death is inevitable and people needed to be helped to deal with it when it comes. They said, they had to overcome the cultural inhibition on discussing death:

J: And I think Africans don't really think much about things like death, things like ageing. Again, it is because of the kind of communities that we come from. But now that we are here, it's different. And things have changed. We have to change according to the environment.

F: And when J. told me that this focus group was going to be here today I was so excited, because this is something that I really struggle with all the time. I wish that we could come together and begin talking. We [should] begin talking about the aged care issues. We [should] begin talking about death, that we always don't want to mention. Well, whether we like it or not, it's coming. (African community focus group)

With a variety of religious beliefs and various customs each cultural group presents, having a non-denomination-specific set of rules and procedures may not work with the majority of the ageing migrant population in the regional areas with strong allegiance to specific faiths. Because of this it is important and necessary for systems to learn about the religious beliefs of each patient or resident in a nursing home and how these religious belief come into play in the process of dying and after death (Hiruy & Mwanri, 2013). When the health system is more dynamic and can be adapted to new cultural beliefs and customs, the staff will be better prepared through training to provide better and more appropriate support for the ageing migrants and their families, either in a hospital, hospice or through in-home care.

## Conclusion and Recommendations

This research assists in establishing the baseline of what aged, ageing issues for the CALD groups currently are. It also provides a guide for future research to build on when more resources are available to carry out a more comprehensive research. As the demographics change, the needs and issues are also bound to change, so further regular research should be conducted. Defining what 'aged' means is quite complicated and it needs to take into account both actual age and individual circumstances. It was also established that most people with a CALD background would prefer to be with their families as long as possible but they may need support for that depending on the level of care required. This is consistent with the government plans for the sector. It is important to emphasise that extra support is needed due to language, financial, cultural and religious needs on top of the normal ageing needs. These needs would be particularly acute in nursing homes where food, culture and language could be challenging for the more recent ethnic communities. The growing refugee communities could present extra mental health needs in future due to traumatic backgrounds.

The service providers acknowledged that CALD groups from non-European backgrounds may have issues that are vastly different in terms of health, linguistic, cultural, and religious and cuisine needs that they have not dealt with before. They noted that they need further training and support to prepare for this.

This study is innovative and ground-breaking for the Riverina region of New South Wales and highlights the issues and needs that services need to prepare for, however, it is very limited in scale. Larger area and sample size studies may be needed to build on the findings. Despite these limitations, the study recommends the health system to be more dynamic and adapt to new cultural beliefs and customs, better prepare staff through training so as to provide appropriate support for the ageing migrants and their families, either in a hospital, hospice or through in-home care. Developing effective research approaches, and generating the knowledge that contributes to meeting the needs of older persons and their ageing societies into the future is paramount in order for the service providers to meet the existing and future needs of the increasing ageing migrant population in regional Australia.

## References

Australian Bureau of Statistics (ABS) (2017). Australia Demographic Statistics December 2016. Retrieved from: http://www.abs.gov.au/AUSSTATS/abs@.nsf/mf/3101.0.

Australian Bureau of Statistics (ABS) (2017a). Migration, Australia, 2015–16. Retrieved from: http://www.abs.gov.au/AUSSTATS/abs@.nsf/mf/3412.0.

Australian Bureau of Statistics (ABS) (2016). Census. Retrieved from: http://www.abs.gov.au/websitedbs/D3310114.nsf/Home/Census?OpenDocument&ref=topBar.

Braun, V., & Clarke, V. (2006). 'Using thematic analysis in psychology', *Qualitative research in psychology*, 3, 77–101.

Copeland, L. (2014). Good news, America: we are living longer! *USA Today*, 8 October. Retrieved from: https://www.usatoday.com/story/news/nation/2014/10/08/us-life-expectancy-hits-record-high/16874039/.

Correa-Velez, I., Barnett, A., Gifford, S., & Sackey, D. (2011). 'Health status and use of health services among recently arrived men with refugee backgrounds: a comparative analysis of urban and regional settlement in South-east Queensland', *Australian Journal of Primary Health*, 17(1), 66.

Hiruy, K., & Mwanri, L. (2013). 'End-of-life experiences and expectations of Africans', in 'Australia: Cultural implications for palliative and hospice care', *Nursing Ethics*, 21(2), 187–97.

Kudrna, G., & Woodland, A.D. (2011). 'Implications for the 2009 age pension reform' in 'Australia: a dynamic general equilibrium analysis', *Economic Record*, 87 (277), 183–201.

Liamputtong, P. (2013). *Qualitative research methods*. Melbourne: Oxford University Press.

Martin, J. (2014). 'Building a culturally diverse and responsive aged-care health workforce'. In L.H. Kee, J. Martin & R. Ow (eds.), *Cross-Cultural Social Work: Local and Global* (pp. 197–212). Melbourne: Palgrave Macmillan.

Mungai, N. (2014). 'Resettling refugees in rural Areas: Africans, Burmese, Bhutanese and Afghans in the Riverina NSW, Australia'. In A. T. Ragusa (ed.), *Rural Lifestyles, Community Well-being and Social Change* (pp. 145–205). Sharjah, UAE: Bentham Science Publishers.

Silverman, D. (2000). *Doing qualitative research: A practical handbook*. Thousand Oaks, CA: Sage.

Skinner, M., Cloutier, D., & Andrews, G. (2014). 'Geographies of ageing: Progress and possibilities after two decades of change', *Progress in Human Geography*.

World Health Organization (WHO) (2017). Proposed working definition of an older person in Africa for MDS Project. Retrieved from: http://www.who.int/healthinfo/survey/ageingdefnolder/en/.

# NINETEEN

# Experiences of Southern-African Skilled Migrants in Rural and Regional NSW, Australia

*Ignatius Chida, Ndungi Mungai and Manohar Pawar*

## Abstract

This chapter aims to discuss opportunities and challenges experienced by Southern African migrants settled in rural and regional New South Wales, Australia. Drawing on in-depth interviews of seventeen migrants, it analyses the push and pull factors experienced by them. It identifies the social and economic challenges faced by migrants while settling in rural and regional places in a new country. The analysis has implications for retaining skilled labor in the countries of origin and meaningfully supporting migrants and benefiting from their knowledge and skills in destination countries.

## Introduction

There is a broad bipartisan policy agreement by the major political parties on accepting skilled migrants from overseas as a way of alleviating acute skill shortages faced by Australia's rural and regional areas. However, in July 2017, the Federal Government of Australia made some changes on the permanent and temporary programs on skilled migration including the temporary work skilled visa subclass 457. Among these changes was the abolition of the 457 visa and replacement with modifications to skilled migration visas that are employer-sponsored. The relevant occupation included general skilled migration list, visa validity and skills assessment (Department of Immigration, 2017). While it is too early to assess the impact, it is likely that these changes will affect the sector both negatively and positively. On the other hand, Australian territory and state governments have taken measures of promoting recruitment of overseas skilled migrants once the skilled vacancies fail to be filled with local people (Department of Parliamentary Services 2012).

Such regional migration measures obligate Australia to appropriately meet the economic, social and emotional wellbeing needs of those recent skilled migrants as well as others experiencing hardship. Australia introduced measures to meet culturally diverse needs of migrant populations by introducing the Multicultural policy. Principle 2 of this policy reiterates the need for government services to be appropriately responsive to the needs of populations from culturally and linguistically diverse backgrounds (The People of Australia, Australia's Multicultural Policy 2011). This study contributes to the understanding of the needs of skilled migrants in regional Australia in terms of challenges and opportunities faced by them and therefore will help inform policy and service reforms so that wellbeing of the migrants is enhanced.

## Migration and Settlement

The Dual Labour Market theory as the core theoretical framework was used to guide the study. Lee (1966) holds that the decision for people to migrate is believed to be influenced by both factors from the country of origin and destination. The Dual labor market theory suggests that international migration emanates from essential skilled labor demands of the modern industrial societies. In dual labor market, workers move from one place to another because of factors such as poor employment relations, low or poor wages, and little prospect for promotion. Other factors also include low level of skilled jobs, poor remuneration among others (Beer & Barringer, n.d). Thus the movement of skilled migrants to modern industrial societies such as Australia may be necessitated by a rise in demand for skilled labour occasioned by an ageing society and rural urban migration. Such a situation is consistent with Australia's current rural and regional migration program where demand has influenced rural and regional skilled migration policy change in order to alleviate the acute and chronic skills shortages (Department of Parliamentary Service 2012).

## Multiculturalism

There is a growing body of literature revealing myriad challenges and opportunities faced by migrants during early years of settlement in Australia. Migrants in general experience relatively similar settlement and other challenges in the initial stages of arrival in a host society.

Multicultural services provisions have created heated debates among the human services industry. This is especially so in the western world where there is currently often a push to recruit overseas skilled migrants to fill-in the needy areas experiencing shortages of qualified personnel. As stated earlier, in Australia, regional skilled migration has won bipartisan government policy support both at the federal and state levels in an effort to alleviate current acute skill shortages in those areas. In a recent Commonwealth Parliamentary inquiry, The Parliament of the Commonwealth of Australia (2012) revealed concerning, widespread systemic irregularities in services provision for culturally and linguistically diverse (CALD) populations. While migrants contribute much towards their rural and regional communities, there is evidence showing that they face many challenges during early settlement years (Mungai, 2014).

Research by Department of Parliamentary Services (2012) shows that the shortage of skilled labour can prevail concurrently with high unemployment status because the specific employers are seeking special skills and experiences. Some of the issues that precipitate such situations in rural NSW and regions of Australia include inadequate training, labour wastage, inability to cope with technological changes and requirements for fresh skills to match the changes in work demands. An enquiry into the causes of skilled labour shortages in NSW (2013) regions by the Local Government Association of NSW and the Shires Association of NSW established that an ageing workforce was partly responsible. The enquiry indicated that from 2016, NSW will have people who are older (55–64 years) than youthful population and more departures than entrants into the job market. Therefore, resulting in increased labour shortages in Australia, hence more opportunities for skilled migrants. Changes brought about by globalisation and an ageing population are the main factors contributing to rural and regional skilled labour market changes and shortages (Khoo, McDonald, Voigt-Graf & Hugo 2007).

Jupp (1992) argues that skilled migrants have high aspirations and will do everything possible to ensure that they live in a safe and clean environment. Many developing Southern African countries are characterised by poor infrastructure and lack of essential amenities and social services. This, in particular, makes many professionals aspire to move from their developing countries of birth to developed countries like Australia. In doing so they encounter issues of bureaucracy, discrimination, geographical location challenges, lack of knowledge about services available to them and rights of entitlement to certain resources which pose potential barriers to successful settlement (Doyle, 2001). Language, including accents, and cultural differences can present barriers to equitable access to services and resources.

In its endeavour to embrace other cultures into the mainstream, the Australian government has introduced the Multicultural policy (The People of Australia, Australia's Multicultural Policy 2012). In Principle 2, the policy reiterates the government's commitment to a just, inclusive and socially cohesive society for all members of society. Despite such policy, informal communication between one of the researchers (first author) and this population group, it became evident that some Southern African skilled migrants in rural and regional NSW were facing settlement and other challenges in the region that warranted closer investigation.

A study by the Department of Immigration and Citizenship (2011) revealed that due to rapid economic decline and political unrest in Zimbabwe, many skilled migrants were forced to migrate to Australia and other countries in search of secure economic sanctuaries. Building on this, the current study extends to cover other countries in the Southern Africa region. Evidence suggests that there is a dearth of literature examining the current state of the challenges and resettlement issues faced by Southern African skilled migrants in rural and regional NSW, Australia (Missingham, Dibden, & Cocklin 2006). In order to fill this knowledge gap at both scholarly and policy levels, the chapter aims to analyse the resettlement and related challenges faced by Southern African skilled migrants in regional NSW and suggest broad policy measures needed to support successful transition.

## Research Method

In this study context, the epistemology was advanced from two main factors: first, that Southern African skilled migrants have some challenges settling into the Australian work environment, whether rural or regional NSW; second, those Southern African skilled migrants have real working opportunities if they are able to overcome barriers within their personal knowledge.

By employing a qualitative research method (Jones, 2001; Hammersley, 2000), in depth interviews were conducted with 17 (black) Southern African skilled migrants from Botswana, Malawi, Mozambique, South Africa, Swaziland, Zambia and Zimbabwe. Secondary data was also collected from government reports, organisational reports, textbooks and journal articles.

Utilising the dimensional analysis model that follows logic and checks plausibility and consistency in relation to context, conditions and consequences' (Schatzman, 1991: 308), data analysis was undertaken. The analysis started with the identification of the properties or dimensions of the data via an open coding process. In this phase, the researcher conceptualised the characteristics of the situation (condition of the migrants) in an abstract manner. Then the researcher assessed the interview transcripts and used phrases, words, stories or sentences in an attempt to identify main dimensions (challenges, opportunities, or experiences) evident in the participants' responses. Specific dimensions (Kools, McCarthy, Durham & Robrecht, 1996) included the form of experience, whether regrettable, threatening, welcoming, favourable, hostile, and time of the experience such as immediately after arrival or some years after arrival to NSW. Accordingly, the findings are presented below.

# Results

## Background of Participants

About three quarters (76%) of participants from Zimbabwe, Malawi, Swaziland, South Africa, Zambia and Mozambique held temporary skilled visa (457) and the remaining had permanent residence visa (sub class 189). The participants interviewed comprised four students, three part time employed, eight full time employed, and two were unemployed. The participants comprised of eleven males and six females.

# Challenges

## Recognition of the Skilled Migrant Qualifications

The majority of skilled migrants undergo overseas education assessment and re-grading and cultural challenges before finally settling. Holders of overseas qualifications struggle to have their qualifications recognised in their areas of expertise. Mark, for example, faced this challenge and doubted that even an Australian qualification would ease his problems, and stated:

> When I got here I realised that they wouldn't recognise my qualification, and was expected to do another diploma and placement within the region; however, there was no

guarantee that after completing that diploma I would get a job. (Mark, 39)

For Mary it was adjusting to the culture and language that presented a hurdle as a skilled migrant:

The main problem I encountered was language and the culture. I found the culture of this place to be so different from that of my home country. Therefore, I had a hard time adjusting. (Mary, 37)

The findings are consistent with observations that many skilled migrants are unhappy with the level of settlement support in finding employment. They encounter barriers in gaining appropriate employment when they had believed that their skilled migration status implied their qualifications were accepted. This finding is supported by Babacan (1998) who also observes that migrants from CALD backgrounds often face challenges having their overseas qualification recognised or converted into the Australian equivalent standard while others have to repeat their overseas training in Australia. Such situations result in some skilled migrants settling for lesser jobs, with various consequences, including low self-esteem and disillusionment which impacts on integration into the Australian society.

Briskman (2012) concurs with the finding on cultural non-alignment of immigrants in pointing out that migrants in general face challenges of adjusting to a new culture in their destination country, while also attempting to retain their heritage and cultural norms. This further shows that in the settlement phase for skilled migrants, social exclusion potentially poses a threat to full community integration. Watt (2006) equally observes that skilled migrants have more control over the settlement process in comparison to refugees, but their successful settlement is affected by other external influences such as the host society's attitude towards them. Therefore, the cultural challenges for immigrants in Australia need attention if integration is to be a reality and multiculturalism realized in both theory and practice.

# Racial Discrimination

While some interviewed respondents reported not having faced major problems with their stay in the region, some reported experiencing racial discrimination both in the community and at the workplace. It was also reported that communities are reluctant in wholly accepting skilled migrants. James, one of the respondents, said he experienced racism in regards to promotion at work:

> I think there is racism in the system and one can feel it … and sometimes you see people with lesser qualifications than you moving up and you remain in the same position. (James, 55)

Ndhlovu (2013) asserts that racism against African Australians on becoming and being Australians exists, noting that research participants expressed strong reservations for having to undergo an official citizenship test. Ndhlovu concludes that participants view this as a form of discrimination since the process by itself does not improve in any way the understanding of the Australian life or the cultural and linguistic identities.

## Adjusting to a New Culture and Place

Some of the issues that cause discomfort to the migrants include adjusting to a different culture. During the interviews, many respondents reported a challenge to adapt in order to fit into the lifestyle in rural and regional NSW. Moses for instance bemoaned the individualistic and autonomous culture which contrasted with the collective culture of Botswana:

> Here we tend to be a lot more independent. In Botswana your neighbour is your friend, you know, you go out together, play soccer, and have neighbours visiting. Your social life is very active, but this is not very easy in regional towns like Bathurst. (Moses, 30)

It is clear from the statement above that rural and regional NSW can be isolating and offer limited social life and recreational opportunities for skilled migrants from Southern Africa. However, this finding differs from what was observed by Wulff and Dharmalingam (2008) who upon examination of 500 skilled migrant respondents on the role of social connectedness, including those living in regional Australia, noted that 72% of the respondents reported having strong social connectedness, while 28% reported having none. While the results of the study are encouraging, it is also concerning that there is a considerable percentage reporting having no social connectedness. There could also be individual factors. Those willing to join sporting clubs and religious congregations will be well catered for while those not inclined towards popular sports and those not identifying with Christian faiths could face isolation. Isolation is recognised as a problem in rural and remote regions of Australia and farmers are reported to be distressed, frustrated and angry with government and city residents who do not appreciate their difficult circumstances (Sartore, Kelly, Stain, Albrecht & Higginbotham, 2004). Most of the South African migrants may not be in the farms but the risk of isolation and lack of amenities is relative to metropolitan areas.

## Becoming Accepted

Many respondents in the study shared sentiments of culture shock in their early days, but, with time, they gradually adjusted well into the mainstream community. Mark explained that while the beginning was challenging due to different cultural background, mutual appreciation developed over time:

> Yes, actually I can see there's a great change because I'm sure the local people now know us and they have accepted us for who we are. But initially when we came you'd find the way people used to speak to us back then is different to now. (Mark, 39)

The findings show that despite some challenges in the migrants' settlement in the region, mutual suspicion had given way to mutual appreciation. This demonstrates that culture shock is a temporary social and acculturation process and prior education and preparation would make the experience less stressful (Zhou, Jindal-Snape, Topping & Todman, 2008). The government is in a position to ensure both migrants and the host community are well prepared for the encounter.

Chartered Accountants of New Zealand and Australia (2017) suggest that culture shock is holding many immigrants in NSW Australia from utilizing their full potential in their respective professions. This is a problem for Australian employers since employees from Africa, China, India and Japan make a significant number of the workforce. Ndhlovu (2010) postulates that the cultural differences could be explained by the variations in language competence, communication patterns and expressions between the Australian-born residents and skilled migrants and does not only lead to misunderstandings but also has an impact on the general performance by firms. This implies that the government needs to create programs to promote awareness among skilled immigrants to understand the local culture and for the host communities to understand the migrants and their cultures.

## Opportunities

### *Employment Opportunities*

From the analysis, most respondents (94%) migrated to Australia due to better employment opportunities offered by rural and regional NSW. Thus they perceived employment as the greatest opportunity and the main pulling factor for migrating to NSW. This was confirmed by one of the respondents who stated:

> When they interviewed me for the job back home that's where the job was. So yeah, I didn't know much about Australia ...

they just told me that a place called Orange is where the job was, so I just came. (Mercy, 30)

The above statement is in line with the Dayton-Johnson et al. (2009) conclusion that skilled migrants are pulled by better employment opportunities available in the host nation.

## Better Wages

Migrants view NSW as offering better-paying jobs than their original countries. Participants who considered wages as the key opportunity in NSW were mostly those in medical professions such as doctors and nurses. As one respondent stated:

We needed to make more money because our salaries were very low for the amount of time we put in the education. What we were getting out of it was just becoming more difficult [to live on] and that was the main driving force to come to Australia, but at the same time wanting to go to a place where there are better opportunities for expanding knowledge in the medical field. (Joyce, 31)

Respondents citing high wages as an opportunity in NSW implies that low wages in countries of origin are pushing them out and it is likely that should they find themselves in a similar situation they will move on.

## Better Socioeconomic and Political Conditions

Many participants noted the importance of a broader, more stable political and socio-economic environment such as that found in NSW. Some of the skilled migrants went to NSW due to political instabilities in their nations of origin, with some of them almost turned into refugees. One of the respondents stated:

NSW is very different. In Zimbabwe we went through quite a hard time trying to make ends meet, hence we decided to apply for jobs overseas and fortunately; my wife ended up getting a job in Australia. (Albert, 56)

New South Wales also offered a better social environment for skilled migrants to raise their family than in their countries of origin. Two respondents noted that they participate and are involved in various social activities like sports and organising fundraising activities for children.

## Educational Opportunities

Some respondents migrated to NSW because of educational opportunities. One of the respondents conceded:

If I want to advance in my studies really I better do something. I wanted to do my PhD through UNISA in South Africa … but looking at the funds because the funds were being eroded it was going to be difficult, wouldn't have been able to pay fees. I thought why not go to a place where I'll have the funds and then be able to pay for myself. So that's when I decided of leaving the country to come to Australia. (Margaret, 55)

The above statements show that better education facilities offered by Australia is a pull factor, especially to migrants from developing economies, to make a decision to move and settle in the region.

## Conclusion

From the preceding discussion, it is quite evident that there are various factors that are attracting Southern African skilled migrants to New South Wales. These factors have been identified as employment opportunities and better salaries. However, the challenges faced by these skilled migrants as discussed above may negatively affect the outcomes of the rural and regional skilled migration program, if not addressed in a timely fashion. It is evident that economic issues play a key role in immigration decisions. Results from this research show that migrants are influenced by a number of factors to move from developing nation to a developed nation.

The findings show critical issues on which Australian Territory and State governments need to take action in order to sustain the regional skilled migration program and obtain positive outcomes. Based on the findings and conclusions, recommendations presented for consideration include: management of information regarding the main factors affecting migrants from each country of origin to ensure that the same conditions are not replicated in the country of destination and cause further social problems. There is a need for the signing of International bilateral agreements to ensure due recognition of skilled migrants' qualifications to ease the transition. Formation of community-based initiatives aimed at facilitating seamless settlement by skilled immigrants, in order to address social integration and cultural issues needs to be promoted. The rural and regional skilled migration program should encourage more investors in NSW, to ensure that more opportunities are created so as to alleviate the lack of job opportunities that could push the migrants out of rural and regional areas thus undermining the success of the migration into the area so far. Finally, what makes the study innovative is, its focus on rural and regional areas, which are often neglected; unlike other studies, the researchers themselves had the experience of migrating and settling in such areas and their commitment to giving voice to the current migrants through this research; and its potential contribution to and impact on policy and program measures so as to enhance the wellbeing of migrants and their communities.

While the research has highlighted pertinent issues, it is a small scale qualitative research with limitations in terms of generalisation. It highlights issues that a larger quantitative research could take on and include a wider range of migrants. A larger research could even be more ambitious and cover more regional areas.

# References

Briskman, L. (2012). 'Integrating migrants and refugee in rural settings'. In J. Maidment & U. Bay (eds.), *Social work in rural Australia: Enabling practice* (pp. 146–60). Crows Nest, NSW: Allen & Uniwn.

Babacan, H. (1998). 'Out of sight out of mind: Issues facing non-English speaking communities in rural Australia'. In A. W. Anscombe & R. Doyle (eds.), *Aboriginal and ethnic communities in rural Australia: An edited collection of papers on Aboriginal and ethnic communities in rural Australia as presented at the Rural Australia–Toward 2000 Conference* (pp. 41–51). Wagga Wagga, NSW: Centre for Rural Social Research, Charles.

Chartered Accountants Australia and New Zealand (2017). Culture shock holds back Asian employees. Available from https://www.acuitymag.com/business/culture-shock-holds-back-asian-employees.

Department of Immigration and Border Protection (2011). Country Profile: South Africa retrieved 13 April 2014 from: http://www.immi.gov.au/media/statistics/country-profiles/_files/south-africa.pdf.

Doyle, R. P. (2001). 'Social work practice in an ethnically and racially diverse Australia'. In M. Alston & J. McKinnon (eds.), *Social work: Fields of practice* (pp. 58–68). Melbourne: Oxford University Press.

Department of Parliamentary Services (2012). *Skilled migration: Temporary and permanent flows to Australia*. Canberra, Australia: Prepared by Phillips, J., & Harriet, S.

Hammersley, M. (2000). *Taking sides in social research*. London: Routledge.

Jupp, J. (1992). 'Access and equity: the basic concepts'. In J. Jupp & A. McRobbie (Eds.), *Access and equity evaluation research* (pp. 1–13). Canberra: Australian Government. Publishing Service.

Jones, A. (2001). Some experiences of professional practice and beneficial changes from clinical supervision by community Macmillan nurses, *European Journal of Cancer Care,* 10(1), 21–31.

Lee, E. S. (1966). 'A theory of Migration', *Demography.* 3(1), 47–57.

Khoo, S., McDonald, P., Voigt-Graf, C., & Hugo, G. (2007). 'A Global Labour Market: Factors Motivating the Sponsorship and Temporary Migration of Skilled Workers to Australia', *Centre for Migration Studies of New York, IMR,* 41(2), 480–510.

Mungai, N. W. (2014). 'Resettling refugees in rural Areas: Africans,

Burmese, Bhutanese and Afghans in the Riverina NSW, Australia'. In A. T. Ragusa (ed.), *Rural Lifestyles, Community Well-being and Social Change* (pp. 145–205). Sharjah, UAE: Bentham Science Publishers.

Ndhlovu, F. (2013). 'Too Tall, Too Dark to be Australian: Subjective Perceptions of Post-refugee Africans', *Critical Race and Whiteness Studies e-Journal*, Vol. 9(2), 1–17.

Ndhlovu, F. (2010). 'Belonging and Attitudes towards Ethnic Languages among African migrants in Australia', *Australian Journal of Linguistics* 30(2), 283–305.

Sartore, G., Kelly, B., Stain, H.G., Albrecht, G., & Higginbotham, N. (2008). 'Control, uncertainty, and expectations for the future: a qualitative study of the impact of drought on a rural Australian community', *Rural and Remote Health*, 8: 950. Retrieved from: http://www.rrh.org.au/articles/subviewnew.asp?ArticleID=950.

Schatzman, L. (1991). 'Dimensional analysis: notes on an alternative approach to the grounding of theory in qualitative research'. In D. R. Maines (ed.), *Social organization and social process: essays in honour of Anselm Strauss.* New York: Aldine de Gruyter.

Watt, P. (2006). 'An intercultural approach to "integration"'. *Translocations: The Irish Migration, Race and Social Transformation Review,* 1 (1), 154–63.

Wulff, M., and A. D. (2008). 'Retaining Skilled Migrants'. In 'Regional Australia: The Role of Social Connectedness'. *Int. Migration & Integration,* 9 (2), 147–160.

Zhou, Y., Jindal-Snape, D., Topping, K., & Todman, J. (2008). 'Theoretical models of culture shock and adaptation in international students in higher education', *Studies in Higher Education,* 33(1), 63–75.

# TWENTY

# Cancer Can Be Fought Courageously and Successfully: Swapping the Musical Chairs

*George Rafael*

## Abstract

This chapter is a story of my experience of fighting cancer. It provides my personal and professional background, diagnosis and treatment of cancer under a crisis situation, a narration of how I approached it and insights for similar patients and carers, both family and professional.

I was born and raised in Alexandria Egypt, where I completed my degree in Social Work (BSc. of Social Work). Continuing the postgraduate course in those prevailing socioeconomic contexts of the country was difficult. I was employed as a social worker in the Education Department. I studied Law until final year where the situation in Egypt was not promising and became harder to live. I was unable to envisage any future for the children. Therefore my family and I decided to come to Australia. It was most prominent move and decision in our life, but we never regretted it.

Upon our arrival in Adelaide, we found it was a great and quiet city. I had to begin the social work bridging course followed by part-time employment at Noarlunga Health Service – mental health services, then, Royal Adelaide Hospital covering a colleague on leave. At that time I was part of team A, which included the Emergency Department. It was a great experience and learnt a lot.

During my work in the Emergency Department, I helped many people who were homeless, individuals with the suicidal attempt, people diagnosed with cancer. Likewise, other social workers who devoted themselves and never recognised by the government, I used to work longer hours to be sure that the client is safe and sound. For instance, one of the cases where I spent most of the day to help a young daughter finding accommodation because she accompanied her father who was diagnosed with cancer. Personally, I felt happy as it was mission accomplished but missed my son's birthday outing with the family.

Then gained a permanent position at Port Pirie Health Services, where I was the first mental health social worker to be appointed in the mental health team. Followed by appointment at 'The Wakefield Regional Health Services, where I worked for eleven years as a senior social worker in mental health team.

Later, I was redeployed to Noarlunga Health Services. I based at the Hospital which serviced with palliative care. Most of the cases were diagnosed with various types and different categories of cancer. I practised as a clinical social worker who provides social work care to acute patients. At that time I did not have any experiences about how deep the pain is! I utilised techniques that include a sympathetic and friendly approach, particularly to those who were at the terminal stage. The primary focus was divided into two categories, first: care to clients who were terminally ill and second: care for clients who have hope and could respond to the treatment and cure. In both conditions, the principal goal was to provide Quality Life even though for those who are experiencing a short time for clients who are in terminal condition.

The role of the social worker in the palliative care area was to liaise between the patients, their families, and the treating team. The problem-solving and client centred approaches were utilised to help clients. The care varied between grief counselling and arranging power of attorney documents and care placement (i.e. hospice).

On the personal level, the nature of the work with people who experienced terminal illness was different from the work with people who were mentally unwell. The first needed a strong persona with emotion, compassionate approach and keeping the professional boundaries. The second required an active person, providing more understanding and maintaining the professional boundaries.

Later I moved to Victoria and worked as Rehab Consultant – Social worker at CRS till the government terminated the entire department. I decided to work as a private clinical social worker. Initially, I was happy. But the mounting workload caused internal stress in me. However, I immersed my self in the private work, but I did not forget the prime goal was to provide the best service.

Due to the nature of our profession we provide service with happiness and confidence to lift up our clients out from their difficulties so that they can solve their problems. Therefore my stressors were disguised away from my clients, but I kept denying my feelings as I am a person that has no problem at all. This augmented when I had to increase the hours to cover my wife's loss of her work. We have to rely on one income and to keep the same level of living. I used to leave home at early morning and return exhausted between ten and eleven at night.

The quiet time did not last for long where the storm began. My wife had a sudden double stroke and had to be hospitalised for several months. Which, we thank God, it was detected early and ended up with aphasia (speech and other problems). This situation added more strain to my daughter and my self, as we have to practice housekeeping, cooking, washing, and trips to the hospital, in addition to our daily work. Eventually, the treating team were able to control the stroke, and they moved my wife to the rehabilitation for recovering. Late September she was discharged and return home.

As it says, 'The deep breath before the plunge'. There were four days post my wife's returning home. Those four days were like a deep breath before the plunge. It was Thursday where I worked in full energy, before the 'Friday – 2015 Grand Final'. I felt so fatigued and exhausted for no reason.

I thought it was the hayfever because it was spring. As usual, I consumed different types of antihistamine pills. Until afternoon I felt drained to the point I felt my body aching, I took Panadol and slept deeply. Later I wake up as I was dumped into a pool, from being sweat. Besides strange sweat from my head to toe. I kept consuming painkiller till I will see my GP on Monday. I visited my GP, and he advised for a blood test. He took the sample by himself. Monday afternoon he contacted me while I was driving and encouraged to go to the Emergency Department (ED) as soon as possible. He stated that the blood results were not healthy and the white cells were abnormal. Until this moment, I did not have any thought that I am sick. Then I was shocked when he told me that means he suspects – it is more likely – cancer in the blood – leukaemia! The GP contacted my daughter and advised her to take me to the ED and not to let me drive as I had a serious illness and needed to be checked in the hospital. I admitted to the ED and found that my GP was organised everything for quick admission.

It was leukaemia. This news was shocking, and I felt that the clock of my life has stopped, but felt num when presented to the ED. Somehow, I was in disbelief and denial stages, and until my meeting with the Haemotologist's Registrar and his assistant the medical intern student. In the back of my mind, it was a just investigation, and I will go home. I was worried about my clients, who will attend their appointments the following day. It was about 11 pm and no chance to cancel the bookings. The Registrar informed me that they would start a thorough investigation, but I may stay between a week to several months it depends on the results. These results signified and confirmed the preliminary outcome, which was an abnormality of white blood cells, 'leukaemia' (Acute Myeloid Leukaemia inversion +/- 16). At this stage all the negative thoughts hit me, and I found it is not a dream.

The second day of the admission, the nurse came with an introduction package and discussed with the family and to myself the treatment plan using the chemotherapy, and its side effects. I began the chemotherapy course with the induction shot (consolidation chemotherapy or intensification therapy). It was extremely aggressive chemicals to attack all the white blood cells (good and bad). The preparation for this shot was shocking as the nurses wore protective gear against the radiation, everything in the room would be treated as radioactive and segregated in a purple pin. All these magnified the pain and it was unbearable.

I felt most of the side effects include hair and appetite loss. It was a terrible experience. The only persons stood by me was my daughter, the course supervisor, the social worker (part-time), the nurse's staff, the specialist (head of the haemotologist department) and the Registrar and his assistant. Although I had all the support but felt lonely to the unknown future, where I prepared for the worst outcomes.

Initially, the death came to my mind, where I was not prepared. I was not afraid of death, but I was worried about my wife, my aged parents, and most of all, my daughter's wedding which I will miss and may be delayed. All negative thoughts came to my mind. The past experiences of supporting clients to pay the last sight on their died relative that came to my mind. The following day I was thinking of therapy that I used to provide to my clients, particularly those who had cancer. It came to my mind three cases which affected me profoundly. The first case was a young girl age 17 diagnosed with metastatic melanoma. She had an angelic, smiley face and always smiled and laughed when her parents and young brother visited her. My first impression was that she is strong and has no fear of being close to the end. The thorough assessment proved me wrong. She was camouflaging her inner feelings not to affect her parents and young brother. This made me trying hard to keep smiling and convince myself that I have to be strong for my family and friends.

The second case was a man in his forties who diagnosed with bone cancer. He had an active life and a father of four. He was attending the chemotherapy, and I received the referral before the last shot then I have seen him as an outpatient. He was a fighter because since he was diagnosed with cancer, he began to research about alternatives including Natural-path medicine besides the medical regime. He found that there is a particular plant that just grown in the USA that proved to be useful in similar cancer cases. He ordered and tried to use it. This trial gave him the strength to think positive and became stronger. He decided to take his family and drive by himself to Cairns, QLD. I invited him to be an inspiring speaker and inspired many of the cancer group members. This case gave me hope to remember what I was telling my clients always to keep the hope as may be tomorrow there would be the new curable medicine that will help them. Personally, I thought of that which gave me hope, and I kept telling myself when the time will come it will come, so not to worry now.

The third case was a young mother who was diagnosed with the late stage of breast cancer. She is a mother of five young children. She never had any previous health problem or pain, but when she did the scan and tests which proved the spread of the illness in her body. The specialist estimated six months to live. The news freaked out her husband who was unable to cope. He was depressed and did not support her. He was concerned that he will become a single father and had to look after five children in young age. He decided to sell their house and send the children to his mother living overseas. I provided counselling to the client who felt depressed because of her condition that muddled her husband and destroyed the family. However, it was good news, and miraculously she responded to the treatment and became well post the segmental mastectomy. This case was a challenging case but gave hope and profoundly positive.

I asked myself, whether is it factual to apply these positive approaches/cases to myself? To be stronger, I was fluctuating between convincing myself that I am not afraid and doubt of the therapy. During that time I have heard many stories where the patient's life ended or others who kept taking several shots of chemotherapy that reached thirty! But my feelings were severely down when I am on my own and put a smile when someone enters the room. The only thing that I kept reading is the Bible and listening to positive sermons how to keep faith in God.

The social worker was excellent in explaining the steps to sort out my affairs, and she provided comfort talk therapy (CBT), at this stage it came to my mind the experiences when I used to organise the attorney paper and guardianship applications for clients who were on the edge and end of their life. I got my family and asked my son to take over my financial affairs. At this time I experienced waves of depressive episodes. In the same day, my feelings will fluctuate between belief and disbelief. I felt the life came to an end and if it is at night, I will see my life journey as a movie – good and bad situations. The fluctuation between hope and hopelessness, being left alone and helpless. Leaving my life in the hands of the treating team not knowing whether the treatment will be effective or stop it due to the side effects. All I asked God if I could live till I could attend my daughter's wedding? However, it was too early to predict.

The chemo shots used to take place for four days morning and afternoon then have a rest for ten days, to monitor the blood levels. After that, I could be discharged from the hospital for a week. That occurred for the first three shots. Later my liver started to be affected and malfunction where the chemo shots dropped to 80% and on alternate days. The oncologist was worried about the liver's record.

A piece of good advice was to drink water as much as I could to flush the chemicals away from the body and to help the died cells to go out of the system. One of the medications that I was lucky to be under trial, a white syrup which was very expensive and not subsidised ($600) for a small bottle and once it is opened it cannot be kept for a long time. It was a new Canadian drug under trial for cancer. I think this helped the body to recover quickly. I remember that this medicine became under government subsidies before the last shot of the chemotherapy.

With the chemotherapy there were depressive waves kept until in the afternoon one day, one of the nurses enlightened me inadvertently stating that the results from the induction were positive and the body responded to the chemotherapy. I was the happiest person, but I had to wait for the specialists, the registrar, and the medical team to confirm the results.

The medical team advised that the results were positive and the next plan was to be in remission until all the bad cells are cleared. The next step was to commence chemotherapy treatment that is less aggressive than the consolidation therapy. My feelings still fluctuate between happiness as I am in remission and there is hope at the end of the tunnel and between sadness that I have to continue the chemotherapy. During that time I had to take the course of the treatment for consecutive four days twice daily. These shots are to kill all the white cells. Therefore the immune system reaches zero, and I was receptive to any virus could cause an infection, that means the end of life. The hospital kept me in isolation for many months during the treatment. Then wait for the bone marrow to manufacture the new cells. I needed many blood transfusions both white platelets and red cells. I nearly suffered from paranoia. I was monitoring the daily blood test progression including the neutrophils, which I used to write the numbers on the whiteboard on every day. I was severely depressed when the cells do not recover quickly. I experienced many episodes of severe depressive symptoms when the temperature went high, and I got infected, the treatment was to stop regular painkiller and to put on the strongest antibiotic drops where the pain was unbearable.

I tried to keep strong for my family. My research (Doctor of Social Work) supervisor provided one of the best books, *Celebration of the Cells,* written by Mr R. M. Lala, a cancer survivor (Lala, 1999). I was fortunate to spend the time reading this book that gave me hope, massive faith and how to deal with cancer. Now I can see the difference in the feelings of being professional and the feeling of being patient. I think the feeling of being professional just provided a clinical approach and sympathetic feels to the patient and their families. However, at the end of the day, we draw the professional boundaries which I would not take the problem with me home. I would believe that the patient is in safe hands in the hospital. In the second scenario where I am a patient, I feel down as Mr Lala questioned *'why me?'* But with the prayers, I thought I needed to pray not only for myself but also for all the patients around me and all patients who suffer from cancer. I can hear the agony and the pain during the night where the nurses provided extraordinary work to comfort them and ease the pain.

The book provided me with comfort as it explained step by step how to go through these situations. I felt someone being through this before and victoriously overcame cancer. Lala went through more chemotherapy, and he explained at each time to have a chemo shot, 'welcome them as a saviour' to the body. This statement made me accepted the shots easily, in addition to the encouragement of my daughter who kept counting down the number of the shots. Besides, I used the breathing technique which we advise our clients to use when severely anxious.

My daughter daily provided me pomegranate juice to help the blood to recover sooner, besides the fresh food (as Lala recommended in the book). She used to come and take me out when I was allowed to out of isolation. We used to walk on the corridors to help the blood to circulate and strengthen the muscles.

I felt depressed when I have seen the staff members going home at five o'clock. I remembered when I used to work in the hospital, but now I am like a prisoner. I cannot go out. The quite and long corridors reminded me as in prison. On many occasions, I fell in tears as I discovered that the Chemotherapy treatment causes severe depressive episodes that come in waves. Thus the head of nurses referred me to a psychologist who was very passionate, and I used the metaphors to explain my feelings. It was challenging as inside me I know the therapeutic approach, and I did not want to be resistive. I described my feelings were like

> In the beginning, I am in a small boat in the ocean, and all of sudden a big wave hit me and turned my life upside down. The storm was strong, and I lost everything. Till I heard that I am in the remission phase, that was like the little boat has seen the light tower from a far distance. I remembered the song 'The Fight Song' for Rachel Platten which gave another expression of the feelings fighting with hope. (Platten, 2015)

As Mr Lala stated that prayers are essential to provide hope. I felt that the prayers of people I know that was heard and I recovered. I remember our parish priest used to visit me weekly and pray for me.

Since my knowledge increased about the leukaemia, I began to argue with the treating team to reduce the sessions of the chemotherapy shots, because every time it causes severe depression. I argued to be reduced from six to four. Some specialists from contemporary school agreed to cut it to four shots and keep monitoring, but the old school haematologists insisted that the least shots should be not less than six. My daughter kept encouraging me to keep going and agreed with the specialists. I remember one day I asked my specialist in tears whether I will be able to attend my daughter's wedding? She was very confident and answered with yes, which happened, and I have made it and was a happy ending.

I kept asking most – if not all – of the haematologists whether the leukaemia was a result of the stress? The majority answer was no, and some stated it is a contributing factor and very few said yes. However, I am convinced that it is a major contributing factor that drops the immune system to be open to attack itself. Like the old Egyptian say – 'my blood has been poisoned,' when stressed. However, I learnt to use self-actualisation approach to fulfil the ability for self-confidence.

Discharge and rehabilitation phase was planned for six months. It mainly included regular full blood tests and bone marrow biopsy every month then every three months until now (2017) to make sure the progress is on track. Following healthy diet including vegetarian food and fresh fruit juice, light physical exercise as much as possible without getting tired and rest and relax. Post the last chemo shot; I was happy as it is over. I was able to attend my daughter's wedding. I am still alive. I am able to help my clients in more understanding when they go through that pain. I would do my best to go through with them the journey of their pain and difficulties.

## Conclusion

By providing my personal and professional background in brief, I have presented in this chapter my experience of cancer diagnosis under difficult family circumstances and how I have faced it courageously and successfully. Swapping the roles of social work services provider to receiver helps to generate empathy from one's own wounds, though it is important to empathise without such experience. Everyone's experience is unique and different and so is my own and in that sense, it has some elements of innovativeness. Drawing strength from my positive client experiences, genuine and warm care provided by my daughter, my supervisor and significant others, supportive medical team, my own faith and positive outlook, all have contributed to the successful fight against cancer. Based on this experience and reflections on them, I would like to offer the following notes to clients/people affected by cancer and similar health issues.

A note to the patients: I love the fact that I can help my clients/people saying, 'I know exactly what you've been through as I have been through it as well.' This might ease their pain knowing that there is hope.

A note for future carers: I understand, using therapy only is not enough as it needs from the social worker to show that we share more with them and respect their feelings.

A note for professional practitioners – nurses, medical, and allied health professionals: I have all respect for your profession, but you need to be aware that, social workers also are part of the treating team. It is not that just we organise the patients' affairs, but we provide support that would comfort the patients, their families and their carers thus we complement each other as a team.

## References

Lala, R. (1999). *Celebration of the Cells – Letters from a cancer survivor*. New Delhi: Viking, Penguin India.

Platten, R. B., D. & Levine, J. (Producer) (2015). Fight Song. [Multimedia], Retrieved 10 January 2015 from https://www.youtube.com/watch?v=FNEYY-DT0T0 & https://www.youtube.com/watch?v=e8qDOGLCSFo.

# TWENTY ONE

# Challenges in Social Work and the Need for Innovation

*Manohar Pawar, Wendy Bowles and Karen Bell.*

This chapter concludes the book by posing some of the main challenges and need for further innovation, broadly for the whole social work as a discipline beyond CSU. It reflects on the chapters covered in the book and its limitations. By briefly discussing some of the challenges relating to social work education, practice and research such as further reaching out to disadvantaged communities, social work pedagogy and teaching content, social work research and knowledge building, poverty and inequality, political and economic ideologies, digital technology and robotics, universal basic income policy and the professional bodies, it argues for the necessity to innovate.

As stated in the first chapter, the main objective of this edited book is to critically reflect on our education, practice and research; and to share our insights and innovations to the larger benefit of society. Has the book achieved this objective? We believe, partly it has. Originally, when we considered this idea, our intention was to critically reflect on 25 years of CSU's social work education, practice and research, and analyse and write. We did have a series of discipline meetings to systematically translate these objectives. Although such opportunity was created, ultimately it was left to individual authors to undertake this exercise and write on their reflective analysis about whatever they think is appropriate to achieve the objectives of the book. The authors have chosen topics based on their own interest, submitted drafts, which were reviewed by editors and further improved by authors. Despite these efforts, we leave with a sense that it is difficult to capture 25 years of work of several colleagues in this volume. Thus it is only a glimpse of what has been achieved through the CSU social work program. The compilation of these chapters as you have seen has been organised under three themes of social work conceptualisation, education and practice, and research. As the topics covered under three parts are interconnected, it is possible that others may reorganise differently with a different logic.

Innovations in learning and teaching included an integrated social work model, which is comprehensive and open ended, and forms a fundamental basis of the CSU social work program. Provocative thoughts on post-conventional social work and ecosocial work, focus on virtue-led practice, teaching of social work with ecological, gender and human rights perspectives demonstrate the innovative minds of social work educators at CSU.

In the practice arena, CSU social work educators have demonstrated ethical approaches to international study programs, transformative ways of working with students' prior learning, working in partnership with students to evaluate educative groups for families at risk, keeping children safe in the school environment, creative use of non-violence approaches in field education, achieving mental wellbeing and recognising disability and ways of supporting students as they study by distance. Innovations in social work research included practitioner-led and practice focused research relating to understanding the lived experience of acute mental health inpatient care through hermeneutic phenomenology, ways of using cooperative enquiry to bring together educators, practitioners and research participants, exploring informal learning through auto-ethnography, understanding migrants' needs and issues in rural and remote areas, particularly relating to ageing and employment, and sharing a successful story of a cancer survivor. At any reckoning, these innovative efforts are modest, but they do offer certain insights about fundamental challenges social work confronted with and the need for further innovation to better work with people and better serve them.

How we further create social work knowledge and share it with people across the globe is a critical challenge. Through distance and now online education, to some extent, it has been possible to reach out to certain communities and people, to share social work knowledge to better prepare them to serve people locally, nationally and globally. Is this adequate in terms of quality and quantity? We believe that we need to extend our reach to disadvantaged communities and individuals in rural and remote areas (as well as urban areas) and create opportunities for them to acquire knowledge and to work as partners and colleagues with more powerful groups. As traditional ways of doing things may not be the way forward, there is a need for further innovation to learn to work more collaboratively.

Meeting the challenge of engaging in further research relating to social work pedagogy and teaching content is a crucial one. It may call for reaffirming existing practices, despite several external threats, for example, digital technology, and/or adopting and adapting new teaching modalities such as mass open online courses (MOOC, for example, see EDX, 2012–18). Although each one has its own advantages and disadvantages, innovative approaches are needed to combine the best elements of both. Given the growing number of specific issues and contexts of practice, social work education is faced with the classic dilemma of generic versus specialised education. As a rural and regional focused program, CSU social work focuses on developing generic knowledge and skills so that social workers are able to competently work with any issues presented to them. It is difficult to find qualified social workers for each specialist area of professional practice, particularly in rural and remote areas. Thus generalist social work education makes sense in the CSU context, and some graduates do later complete a specialised qualification or engage in specialised practice. In the field, there is a need for skilled approaches to: working with Aboriginal Australians, ageing, child welfare and protection, disability, domestic violence, ecology, gender, gender diverse communities, mental health, social and community development. There is pressure on the social work curriculum to include all these issues in terms of knowledge, skills and practice, but there is limited space in the curriculum to accommodate all these specialisations. Any society that causes and reproduces inequalities with such magnitude must find innovative ways to address them. It is important to engage in transformative social work and to proactively practise rather than responding reactively.

This is where social work research and theoretical developments are needed, but very much lacking to date. As the profession is based on interdisciplinary knowledge, it draws from various social sciences, such as psychology, sociology, politics, economics, and law. After over 100 years of its existence, it should be in a position to articulate its own distinctive knowledge-base and theories. To some extent it has occurred (see Payne, 2014; Thompson, 2006; Pawar and Anscombe, 2015), but it appears much less in comparison to similar social sciences and there is great potential to accomplish this. The challenge is to bring together social work educators and practitioners on a larger scale, allocate adequate resources and undertake research to contribute to practice-based knowledge building and solutions to emerging – as well as existing – issues.

Although poverty is reducing globally, it is persistent and perhaps increasing in some pockets (Pawar, 2017). When one thinks of poverty, it is easy to shift the focus externally to developing countries, but it is also important to recognise poverty in our own neighbourhood, whether it relates to Aboriginal Australian communities and the deprived situation of detained asylum seekers offshore and onshore, and to recently resettled refugees and migrants. In addition, there are specific disadvantaged groups such as women, children and young people and those affected by domestic violence. Older Australians, people living with disabilities and people living homeless can easily fall into poverty (ACOSS and SPRC, 2016). Many charitable organisations often report that their queues for food and material distribution are increasing every year. These patterns of disadvantage occur in a context of growing inequality and social injustice, despite a relative rise in income levels for the upper echelons of society. Poverty and inequality have been serious subjects of social work concern since its inception. It is important to actively challenge poverty and inequality and to critically examine the extent to which it is covered in social work courses and addressed in the field. Poverty and patterns of privilege and inequality have become naturalised parts of our lives. As social workers, we need to rethink how we address this great challenge in innovative ways. Sustainable Development Goals with 169 targets (United Nations, 2015; Pawar, 2017) and social work and social development agenda (IFSW/IASSW/ICSW, 2010) provide great opportunities for addressing poverty and related issues by employing global practice approaches (Cox and Pawar, 2013; Pawar and Weil, 2016).

The prevailing political and economic ideology – liberalism, free markets, privatisation, and managerialism on the one hand, and emerging conservative nationalistic politics on the other hand – are undoing years of hard work on race, class, gender and any other sectionalism, and human rights-based and social and environmental justice approaches. This poses significant challenges to the social work profession and the people they work with. The fundamental ethos of social work is contrary to these dominant ideologies which seem to be sustaining poverty levels, patterns of privilege and resultant inequalities. The role social work plays to resist and or oppose these ideologies and yet work with or within these structures may appear confusing, contradictory and like a difficult balancing act. There is a need to discover innovative ways to sustain social work values and principles despite these challenging political and economic ideologies.

The digital revolution brings with it advancements in information and communication technology (ICT) and robotics. As new technology is applied in production systems and in our day-to-day lives, there is likely to be a period of unemployment and structural adjustment (Pawar and Midgley, 2017). What are the impacts of these kinds of unemployment and what should be the response of social work education, practice and research? Will social workers' employment also be affected by the digital revolution? These are challenging questions. Unemployed people will be no longer uneducated and unskilled. What impact it will have on their mental and social health and that of their families and children? What roles do social workers need to play in the context of such fundamental change? Do we have enough social workers to deal with such scenarios?

Perhaps in work roles or professions where empathy and physical proximity are required, such technological developments will not have such a direct impact on their employment. This is heartening for social work and similar professions.

In view of this fast-approaching reality, universal basic income (UBI) as universal policy and strategy has been suggested and isolated experiments on UBI are underway in different countries. There is a range of views on such a radical policy (Ito, 2018). One of the important means of production was labour (and the others were land and capital) and if such labour is replaced by technology on a massive scale, then we cannot simply blame individuals. People and their institutions have an ethical responsibility for providing resources to people to engage them constructively in communities. This is a fertile ground for social workers to contribute in the area of UBI policy-making and to meaningfully engaging with unemployed people. It is important to think and act innovatively to engage with this critical issue.

Another challenging area is the role of professional bodies. Do they exist for self-fulfilment and self-promotion or for serving others? Is there a suitable balance between the two? In Australia helping professions have been categorised into social workers, welfare workers, youth workers, community workers and human services workers (Healy and Lonne, 2010), and there is often a sense of invisible hierarchy among them. It has been a challenge to bring social welfare professions together and to work together with mutual respect. There is a need to innovatively overcome this divide so that the profession has a large workforce to work in unity for social justice and human rights.

During the first 25 years of social work education at CSU, the university has achieved a lot and this should be sustained in the coming years. As per the student numbers, it is the largest social work school in Australia. If these trends continue, we hope it will be the largest social work school in all respects. We wonder, what the next 25 years will bring and what will the challenges be when we are celebrating the golden jubilee of CSU social work. As demonstrated in this volume, we hope social work educators, practitioners and researchers will continue to undertake ground-breaking work in the future. Whether the issues of poverty and inequality become things of the past or whether they continue to persist social work may find its presence in a big way in all CSU campuses. They may also need to get ready to prepare social workers to work with migrants and their communities as climate change continues to impact on our planet. Social work is a people-oriented profession and we hope, despite many challenges that social work continues to prioritise social justice, sustainability and human rights in all that we do to make a positive difference in the world.

While the social work discipline has demonstrated great potential for innovation and leadership in its first 25 years, much more is required if social work is to address the challenges it faces locally, nationally and globally. The current growth in student numbers itself poses a significant challenge about how to maintain and improve quality education and the kinds of research and practice partnerships with students that have been one of the hallmarks of CSU social work. This is a challenge shared by all universities as social work student numbers soar across Australia.

On the other hand, with the increasing reach of large, international higher education providers, will there be the opportunity for the kinds of local and international innovations from relatively small, regionally-based providers such as CSU that have been showcased in this book?

Whatever the challenges social work at CSU has had 25 years of achievements of which we are very proud. The contributions by our students, practitioners and academics to our local, regional, national and international communities speak for themselves. We look forward to embracing the next 25 years, at a time when the increasing pace of change is the only certainty.

## References

ACOSS (Australian Council of Social Service) and SPRC (Social Policy Research Centre) (2016). *Poverty in Australia 2016*. Strawberry Hills, Sydney: Australian Council of Social Service.

Cox, D. & Pawar, M. (2013). *International social work: Issues, strategies, and programs,* (2nd edn.). Los Angeles: Sage.

EDX (2012–18). EDX courses, accessed 30 March 2018 https://www.edx. org/course?course=all.

Healy, K. and Lonne, B. (2010). The social work and human services workforce: Report from a National Study of Education, Training and Workforce Needs. Strawberry Hills, NSW: Australian Learning and Teaching Council.

International Federation of Social Workers, International Association of Schools of Social Work, and International Council on Social Welfare. *The Global Agenda 2010*. Accessed 1 March 2015, http://ifsw.org/the-global-agenda/.

Ito, J. (2018). The paradox of Universal basic income. Accessed 30 March 2018 https://www.wired.com/story/the-paradox-of-universal-basic-income/.

Pawar, M. (2017). 'Social development: Progress so far'. In Midgley, J. and Pawar, M., *Future directions in social development*, Basingstoke: Palgrave Macmillan.

Pawar, M. and Anscombe, A. W. (2015). *Reflective social work practice: Thinking, doing and being*. Melbourne: Cambridge University Press.

Pawar, M. and Midgley, J. (2017). 'Beyond goals and targets: Future of social development'. In Midgley, J. and Pawar, M., *Future directions in social development*, Basingstoke: Palgrave Macmillan.

Pawar, M. and Weil, M. (2016). 'Global community practice for the global agenda'. In *Encyclopaedia of Social Work*, New York: NASW and Oxford University Press.

Payne, M. (2014). *Modern social work theory* (4th edn.). Oxford: Oxford University Press.

Thompson, N. (2006). *Anti-discriminatory practice* (2nd edn.). Basingstoke: Palgrave Macmillan.

United Nations (2015). Resolution adopted by the General Assembly on 25 September 2015.

70/1. Transforming our world: the 2030 Agenda for Sustainable Development. Accessed 31 March 2018 http://www.un.org/ga/search/view_doc.asp?symbol=A/RES/70/1&Lang=E.

# Contributors

**Andrew Alexandra** is an Honorary Fellow in Philosophy at the University of Melbourne. Among his many publication in the areas of political philosophy and professional and applied ethics are his co-authored books, *Reasons, Values and Institutions* (2002), *Police Ethics* (2006), *Ethics in Practice* (2009), *Media, Morals and Markets* (2011), *Integrity Systems for Occupations* (Routledge, 2016), and *Empowering Social Workers: Virtuous Practitioners* (Springer, 2017).

**Bill Anscombe** is currently an Adjunct Associate Professor and in his 20 years with the Charles Sturt University Social Work disciple held positions from Lecturer to Course Director. He has a wide ranging research background including areas of Corrections, Child Protection, the Rural Church, Aboriginal and multi-cultural practice and governance and housing.

**Heather Barton** has been associated with CSU since 1983 as a student, lecturer, course director and currently an adjunct lecturer. She has extensive industry experience in government and nongovernment organisations and the UK in child protection. Her current employment is with NSW Family and Community Services as a Casework Specialist.

**Karen Bell**'s connection with CSU commenced in 1992 when she supervised a placement at Wagga Base Hospital with Wendy Bowles. In 1993 she facilitated her first residential school group. She is Associate Professor of Social Work and her research interests include the philosophy of social work, post-conventional theory and ecosocial work.

**Heather Boetto** began teaching at CSU in 2003, initially as a casual lecturer, and since 2008 as a permanent staff member. Heather is now a Senior Lecturer in Social Work and Human Services, and her research interests include environmental or ecosocial work, gender and international social work.

**Wendy Bowles** moved from Sydney to rural NSW when she joined CSU for the start of the social work program in 1991. Currently she is Professor of Social Work. Her research interests include social work practice, research, education, ethics and supervision, field education, rural social work, disability, and ecosocial work.

**John Burns** completed a SW Degree at UNSW in 1974 and MSW at CSU in 2009. During his career John supervised CSU social work students and is still connected to CSU in retirement through student supervision. He maintains a research interest in parenting education in the field of child protection.

**Ignatius Chida** joined CSU Dubbo campus in 2013, and is Lecturer in Social Work and Human Services. Ignatius' research interests include migration and settlement issues; ageing population in rural and regional Australia; and emerging issues on African Diasporas.

**Karen Dempsey** has extensive experience in community health, trained in non-violent communication skills and has a passion for environmental social work and Deep Ecology. Karen has coordinated landcare projects which included indigenous contributions in Story and art, and currently coordinates a peace group. Karen applies nonviolence widely in Field Education.

**Rohena Duncombe** worked for many years as a Community Health Social Worker in Albury and Byron Bay NSW and has been with CSU since 2000. Her research interests include supporting online/distance education students, anxiety management in the group setting, teaching case management and service delivery to people living with disadvantage.

**John Healy** has been a lecturer at CSU since 2008. John's research interests include, the sociology of religion, qualitative methods, aging and adult learning. As well as teaching at CSU John studies Old-time American fiddle music and has performed at folk festivals around Australia and Internationally.

**Bronwyn Hyde** holds the position as Local Health District Project Manager of a statewide program transitioning people with enduring mental illness from longstay hospital care to community. She completed Doctor of Social Work degree in 2017 through CSU researching the lived experience of acute mental health inpatient care, publishing three articles on this topic.

**Richard Hugman** is Professor of Social Work at UNSW. A key area of Richard's work is in the field of professional ethics. Richard has a long association with the Social Work program at Charles Sturt University, having been an external member of the Board of Studies since 2003; since 2014 he has also been a joint leader of the ARC funded project 'Virtuous Practitioners', with Manohar Pawar and Bill Anscombe.

**Susan Mlcek** is Associate Professor in Social Work and Human Services at CSU, where she started teaching in 2004. Her teaching and research pedagogies are informed by a Māori-Indigenous worldview, as well as principles of *Andragogy – the science of helping adults to learn*. Current research interests include: decolonising methodologies, auto-ethnography, and critical reflection on Whiteness behaviours.

**Ndungi Wa Mungai** moved from Melbourne to join CSU in 2010, after working with the homeless, asylum seekers and refugees, and on a PhD focusing on young Sudanese men. He is currently a senior lecturer and his areas of interest include human rights, ageing, food security, refugee studies and social and ecological sustainability.

**Manohar Pawar** joined CSU 1998 and is currently Professor of Social Work. His areas of interest and publications include: Empowering social workers: virtuous practitioners (Springer, 2017); international social work

(Sage, 2013); Social and community development practice (Sage, 2014); Future directions in social development (Palgrave Macmillan, 2017); and water/food policy.

**George Rafael** is a Doctor of Social Work scholar at CSU. He has a long experience as clinical social worker – mental health. George works with people who suffer from depression, self-harm, PTSD as a result of workplace bullying, which is his doctoral research area. He is also specialised in life-skills therapy.

**Monica Short** joined CSU in 2011 as a lecturer. Previously she worked for large government organisations in generic social work positions to management. Monica's research focuses on the intersections between disciplines – for example, social work, sociology and theology. She has published in the following areas: co-operative inquiry, community engagement, (dis)ability, field education and religion.

**Cate Thomas** first worked at CSU 1988–92, and then returned in 2012 as a senior lecturer in social work after many years in the field. Cate has worked as a private social policy consultant, delivered keynote addresses, worked in senior leadership positions, and is now an Associate Dean Academic at CSU.

Prior to joining CSU **Bruce Valentine** spent 38 years in the NSW Public Service in health and welfare roles. At CSU his career spans teaching, research and supervision, including developing CSU's unique approach to RPL. Other areas include out-of-home-care, legislation, Indigenous self-management and social justice, his PhD topic.

**Fredrik Velander** joined CSU in 2010. He is a Doctor in International Health and lectures in social work, his research interests include mental health, mindfulness, organisational and community development and recent publications include *Vulnerabilities and Abuse* (Oxford University

Press, 2017), *Culturally Secure Community Development* (Niruta Publications, 2014), Velander, F., Schineanu, A., Liang W. and Midford, R. (2010), 'Digging for gold and coming up blue: a health survey in the mining industry', *Journal of Health, Safety and Environment*, 26(5): 389–401.

**Sabine Wardle** joined CSU in 2014 after her extensive work in social work field education and vocational education. Sabine is a lecturer in Social Work and her research interests include end of life and palliative care, ageing, grief and loss, environment and sustainability and field education.